BRIAN HERBERT • KEVIN J. ANDERSON
DEV PRAMANIK • ALEX GUIMARÃES

DUNE

HOUSE ATREIDES

VOLUME ONE

Published by

Designer	Editor	Senior Editor
Marie Krupina	**Jonathan Manning**	**Dafna Pleban**

Ross Richie CEO & Founder
Joy Huffman CFO
Matt Gagnon Editor-in-Chief
Filip Sablik President, Publishing & Marketing
Stephen Christy President, Development
Lance Kreiter Vice President, Licensing & Merchandising
Bryce Carlson Vice President, Editorial & Creative Strategy
Kate Henning Director, Operations
Spencer Simpson Director, Sales
Scott Newman Manager, Production Design
Elyse Strandberg Manager, Finance
Sierra Hahn Executive Editor
Jeanine Schaefer Executive Editor
Dafna Pleban Senior Editor
Shannon Watters Senior Editor
Eric Harburn Senior Editor
Sophie Philips-Roberts Associate Editor
Amanda LaFranco Associate Editor
Jonathan Manning Associate Editor
Gavin Gronenthal Assistant Editor
Gwen Waller Assistant Editor
Allyson Gronowitz Assistant Editor

Ramiro Portnoy Assistant Editor
Kenzie Rzonca Assistant Editor
Shelby Netschke Editorial Assistant
Michelle Ankley Design Lead
Marie Krupina Production Designer
Grace Park Production Designer
Chelsea Roberts Production Designer
Samantha Knapp Production Design Assistant
José Meza Live Events Lead
Stephanie Hocutt Digital Marketing Lead
Esther Kim Marketing Lead
Breanna Sarpy Live Events Coordinator
Amanda Lawson Marketing Assistant
Morgan Perry Retail Sales Lead
Holly Aitchison Digital Sales Coordinator
Megan Christopher Operations Coordinator
Rodrigo Hernandez Operations Coordinator
Zipporah Smith Operations Coordinator
Jason Lee Senior Accountant
Sabrina Lesin Accounting Assistant
Lauren Alexander Administrative Assistant

DUNE: HOUSE ATREIDES Volume 1, June 2021. Published by BOOM! Studios, a division of Boom Entertainment, Inc. Dune: House Atreides is © 2021 Herbert Properties LLC. All rights reserved. Originally published in single magazine form as DUNE: HOUSE ATREIDES No. 1-4. © 2020, 2021 Herbert Properties LLC. BOOM! Studios™ and the BOOM! Studios logo are trademarks of Boom Entertainment, Inc., registered in various countries and categories. All characters, events, and institutions depicted herein are fictional. Any similarity between any of the names, characters, persons, events, and/or institutions in this publication to actual names, characters, and persons, whether living or dead, events, and/or institutions is unintended and purely coincidental. BOOM! Studios does not read or accept unsolicited submissions of ideas, stories, or artwork.

BOOM! Studios, 5670 Wilshire Boulevard, Suite 400, Los Angeles, CA, 90036-5679. Printed in China. First Printing.

ISBN: 978-1-68415-689-4, eISBN: 978-1-64668-233-1

Limited Edition:
ISBN: 978-1-68415-690-0, eISBN: 978-1-64668-234-8

DUNE™

HOUSE ATREIDES

Written by
Brian Herbert & **Kevin J. Anderson**

Illustrated by
Dev Pramanik

Lettered by
Ed Dukeshire

Colored by
Alex Guimarães

Cover by
Jae Lee & June Chung

Special Thanks to **Frank Herbert, Byron Merritt, Kim Herbert, John Silbersack, Mary-Alice Kier, Marcy Morris, Anne Groell, Patrick Lobrutto, Janet Herbert, Nita Taublib, Charles Kochman, Charlotte Greenbaum**, and **Rebecca Moesta**.

CHAPTER
ONE

Cover by
Jae Lee & **June Chung**

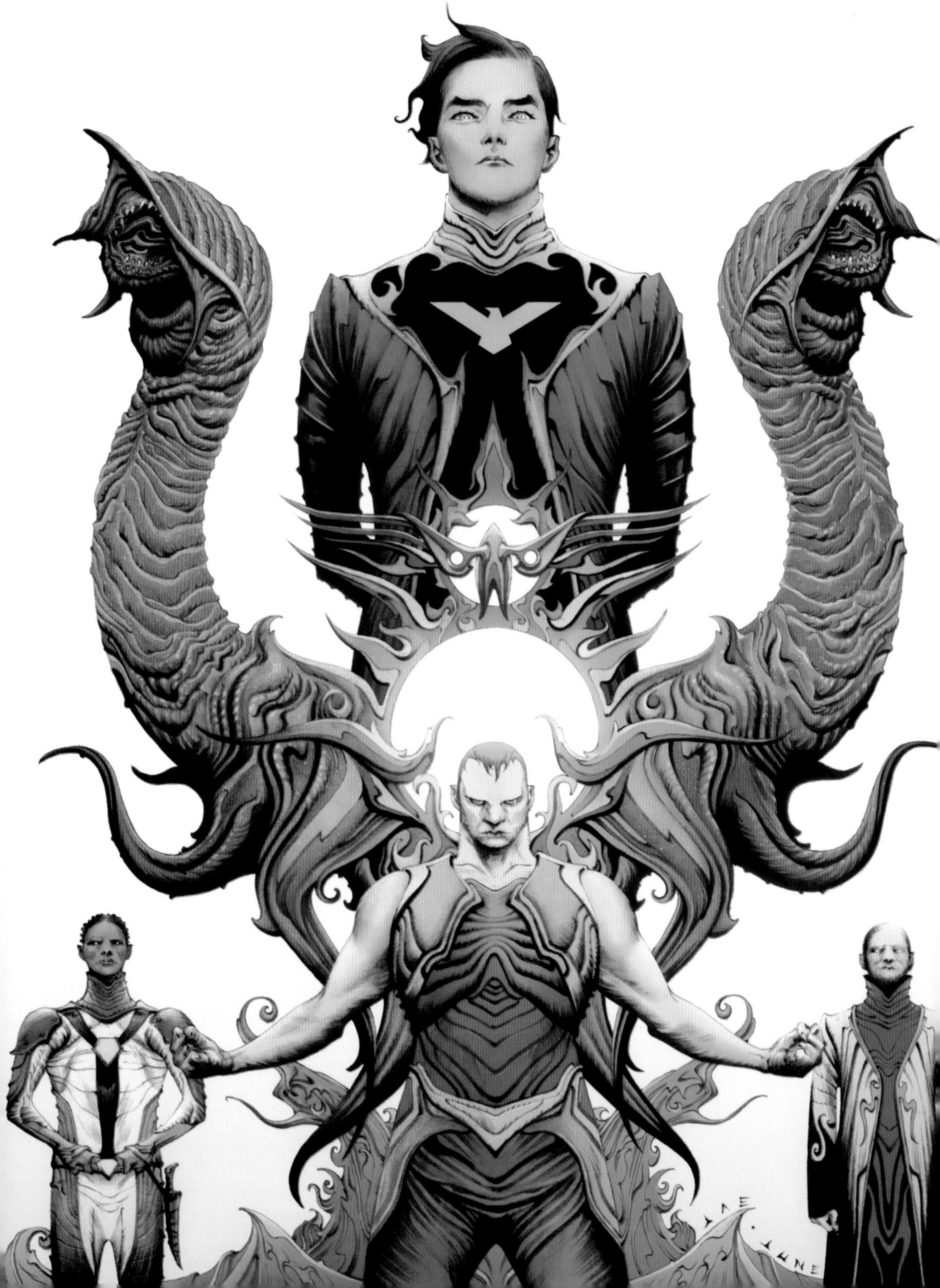

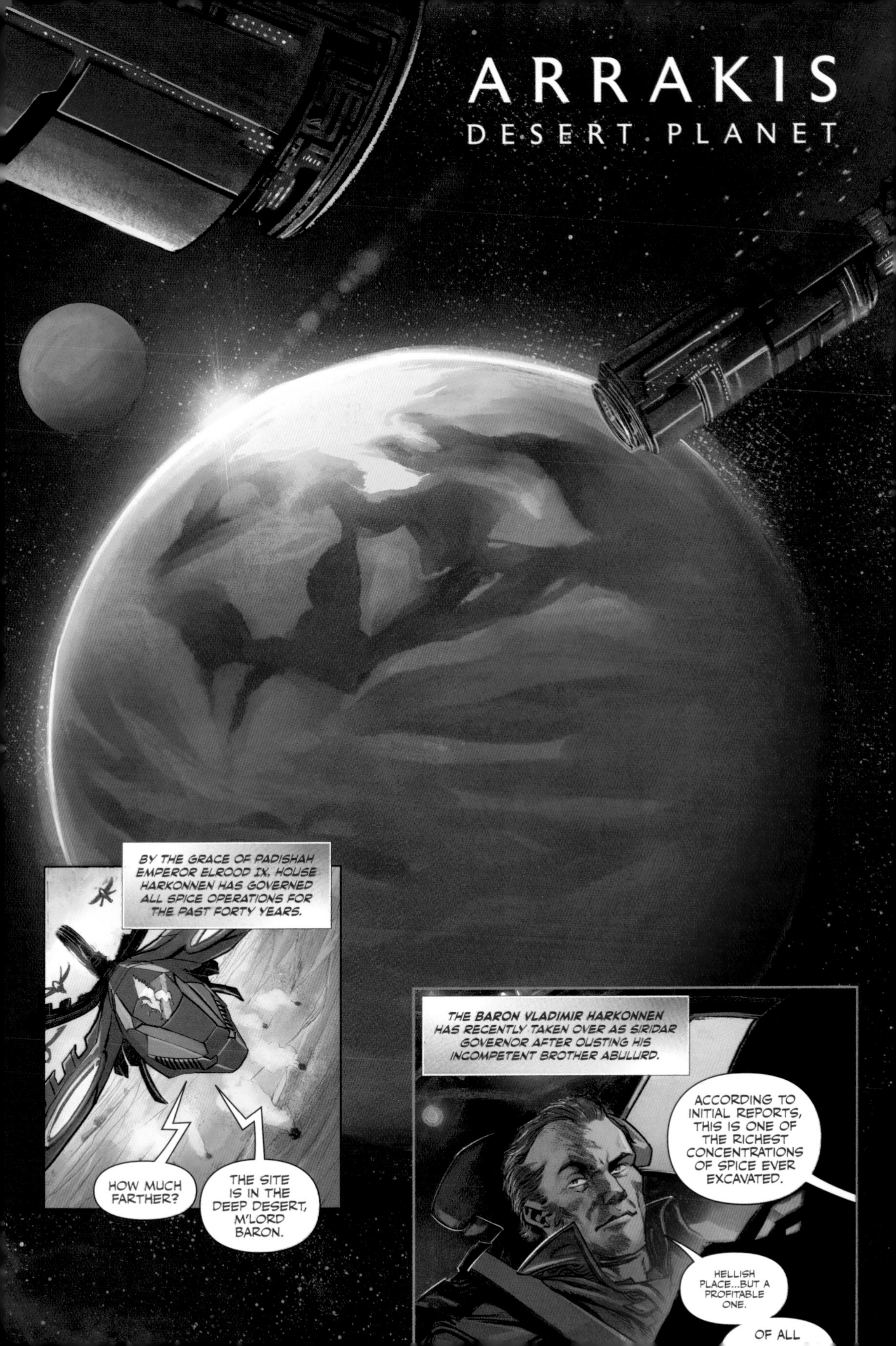
ARRAKIS
DESERT PLANET
BY THE GRACE OF PADISHAH EMPEROR ELROOD IX, HOUSE HARKONNEN HAS GOVERNED ALL SPICE OPERATIONS FOR THE PAST FORTY YEARS.
HOW MUCH FARTHER?
THE SITE IS IN THE DEEP DESERT, M'LORD BARON.
THE BARON VLADIMIR HARKONNEN HAS RECENTLY TAKEN OVER AS SIRIDAR GOVERNOR AFTER OUSTING HIS INCOMPETENT BROTHER ABULURD.
ACCORDING TO INITIAL REPORTS, THIS IS ONE OF THE RICHEST CONCENTRATIONS OF SPICE EVER EXCAVATED.
HELLISH PLACE...BUT A PROFITABLE ONE.
OF ALL

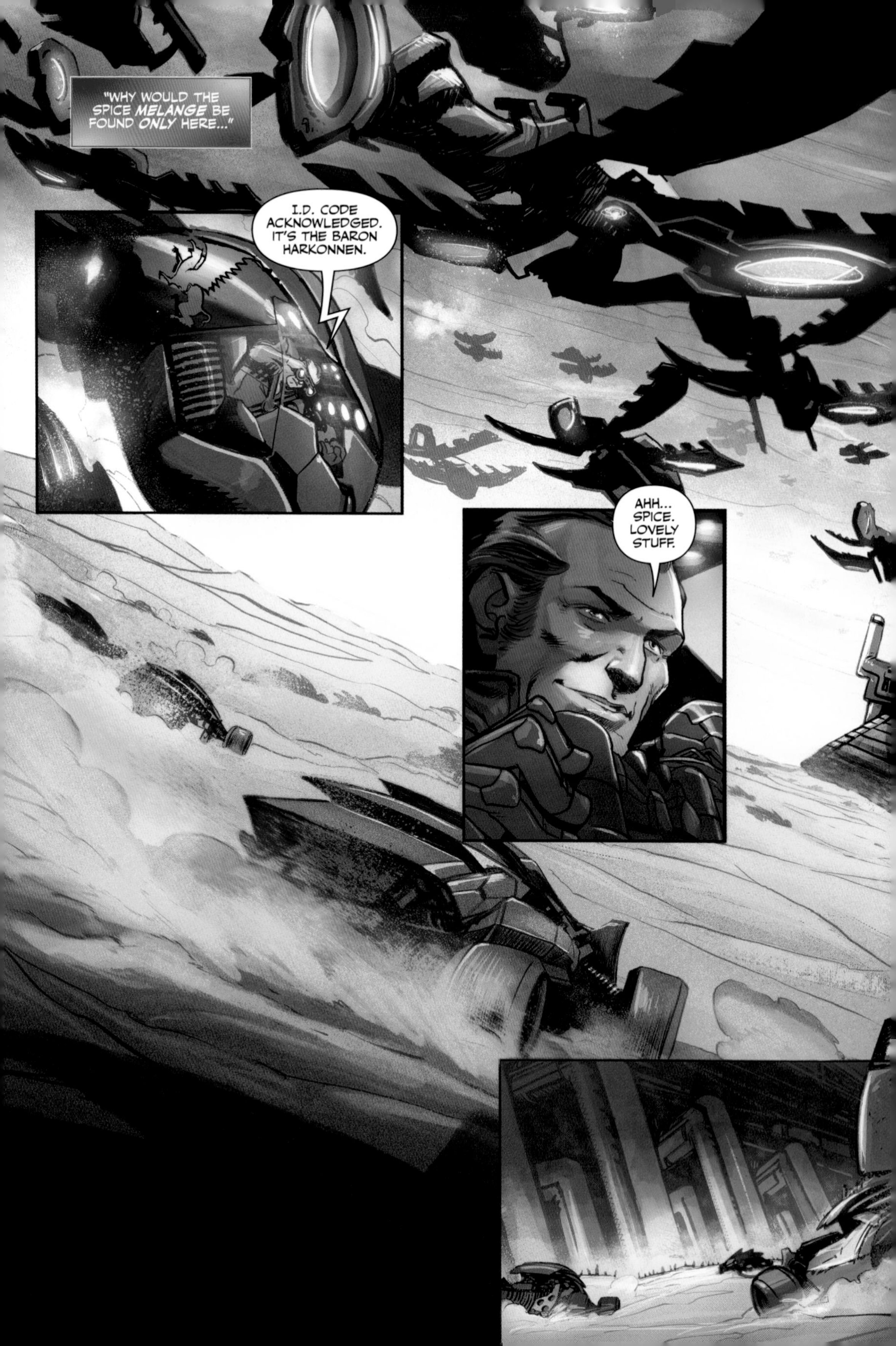
"WHY WOULD THE SPICE *MELANGE* BE FOUND *ONLY* HERE..."
I.D. CODE ACKNOWLEDGED. IT'S THE BARON HARKONNEN.
AHH... SPICE. LOVELY STUFF.

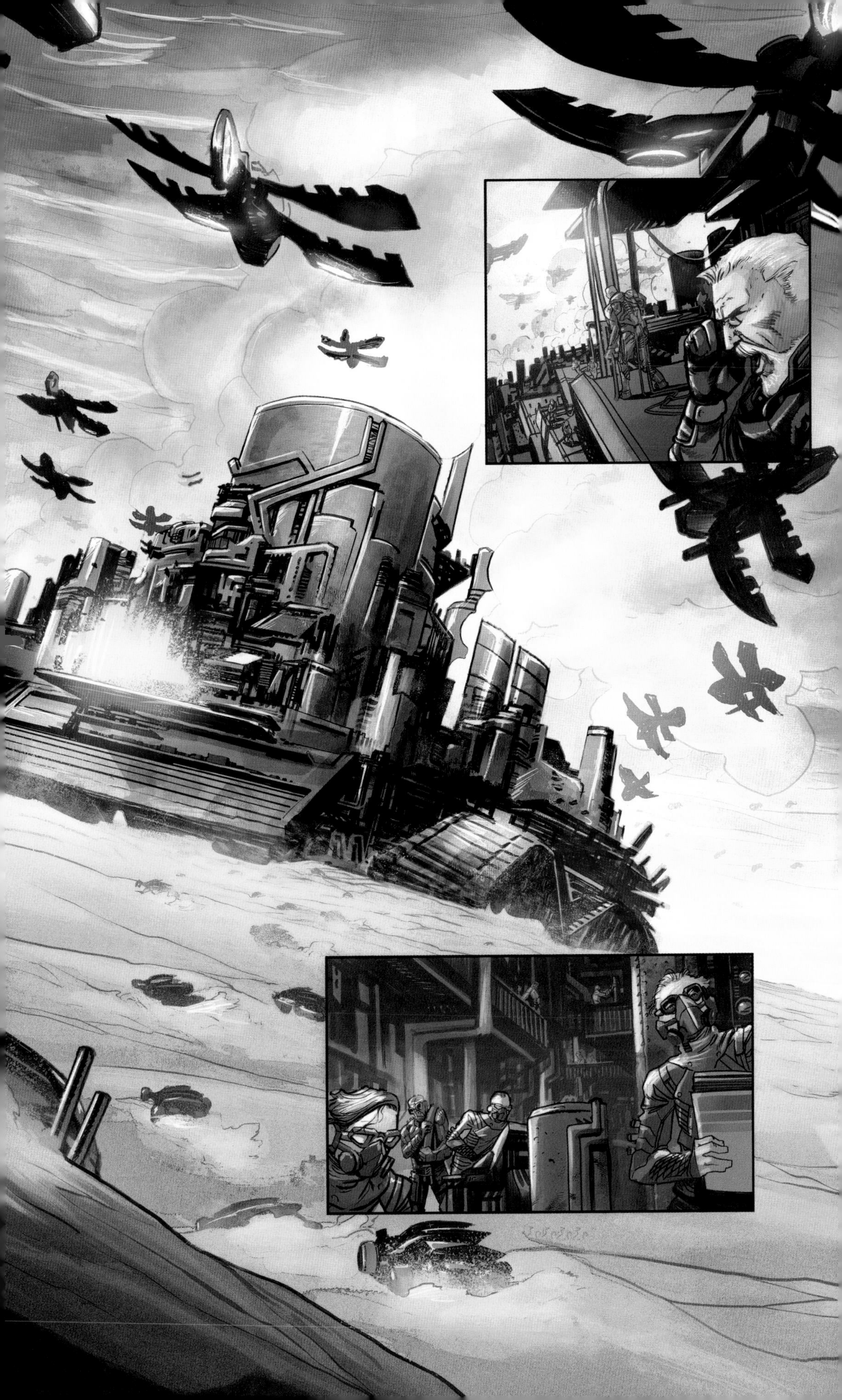

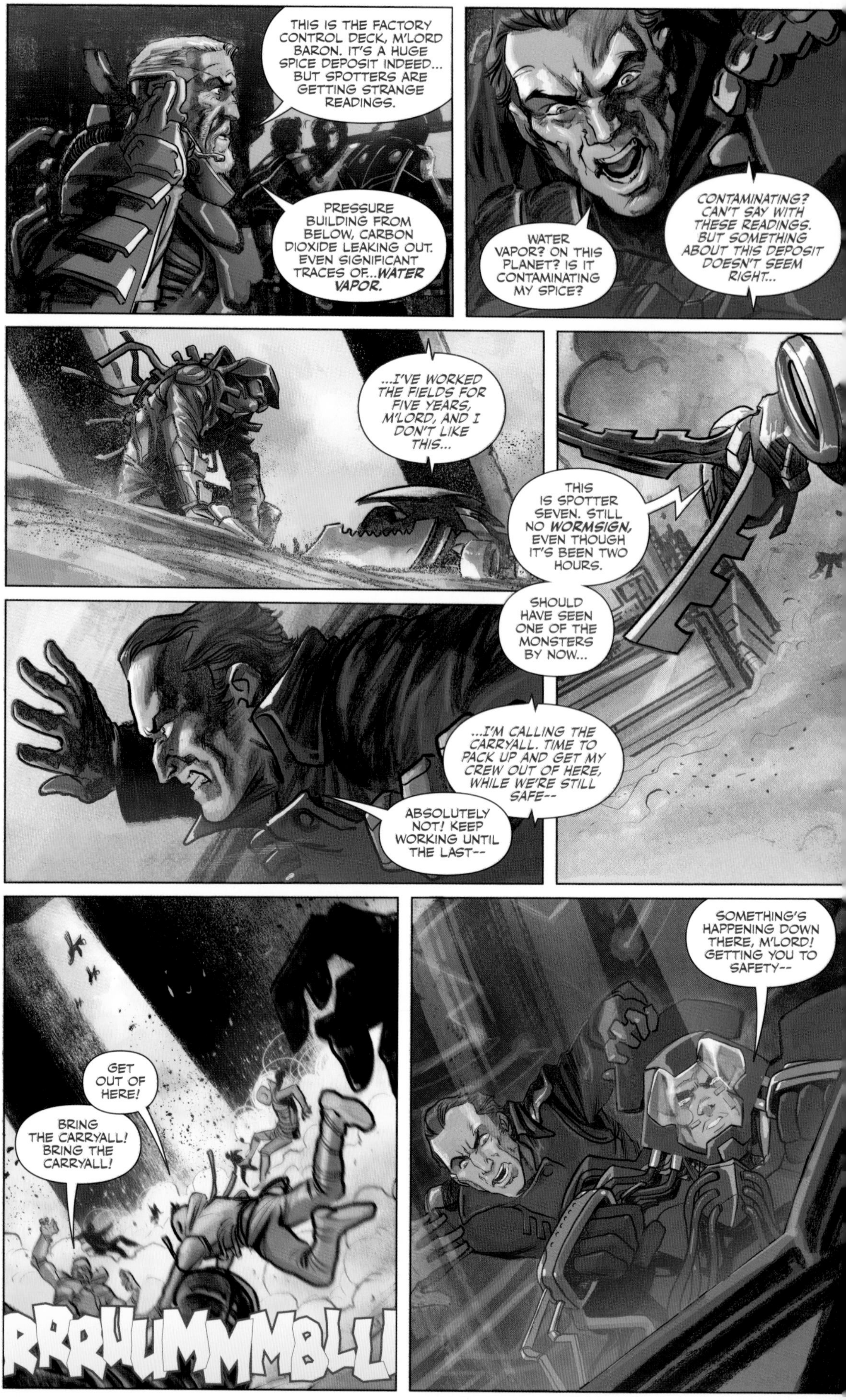
THIS IS THE FACTORY CONTROL DECK, M'LORD BARON. IT'S A HUGE SPICE DEPOSIT INDEED... BUT SPOTTERS ARE GETTING STRANGE READINGS.
PRESSURE BUILDING FROM BELOW, CARBON DIOXIDE LEAKING OUT. EVEN SIGNIFICANT TRACES OF...*WATER VAPOR.*
WATER VAPOR? ON THIS PLANET? IS IT CONTAMINATING MY SPICE?
CONTAMINATING? CAN'T SAY WITH THESE READINGS. BUT SOMETHING ABOUT THIS DEPOSIT DOESN'T SEEM RIGHT...
...I'VE WORKED THE FIELDS FOR FIVE YEARS, M'LORD, AND I DON'T LIKE THIS...
THIS IS SPOTTER SEVEN. STILL NO *WORMSIGN,* EVEN THOUGH IT'S BEEN TWO HOURS.
SHOULD HAVE SEEN ONE OF THE MONSTERS BY NOW...
...I'M CALLING THE CARRYALL. TIME TO PACK UP AND GET MY CREW OUT OF HERE, WHILE WE'RE STILL SAFE--
ABSOLUTELY NOT! KEEP WORKING UNTIL THE LAST--
GET OUT OF HERE!
BRING THE CARRYALL! BRING THE CARRYALL!
RRRUUMMMBLL
SOMETHING'S HAPPENING DOWN THERE, M'LORD! GETTING YOU TO SAFETY--

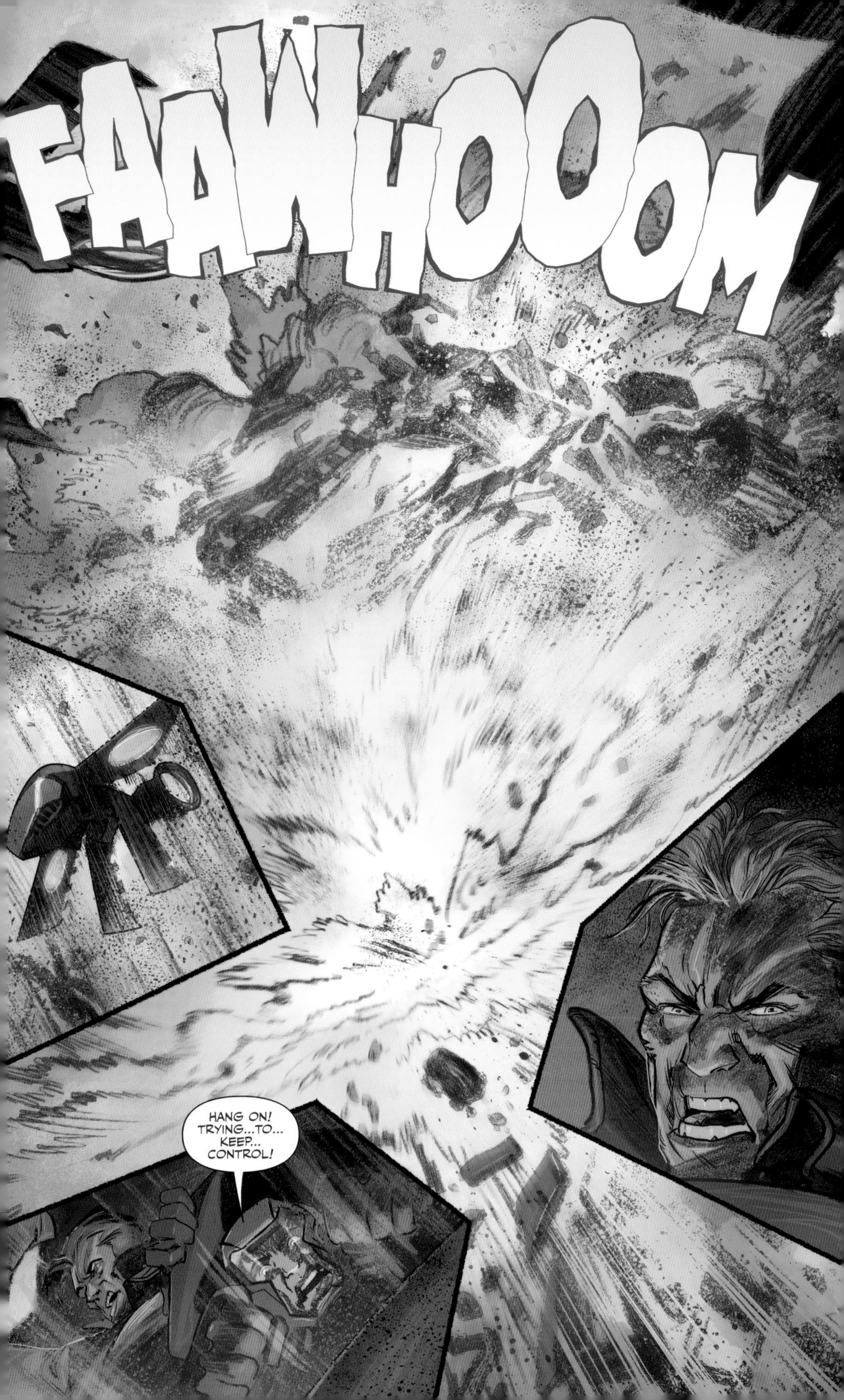
FAAWHOOOOM
HANG ON! TRYING...TO... KEEP... CONTROL!

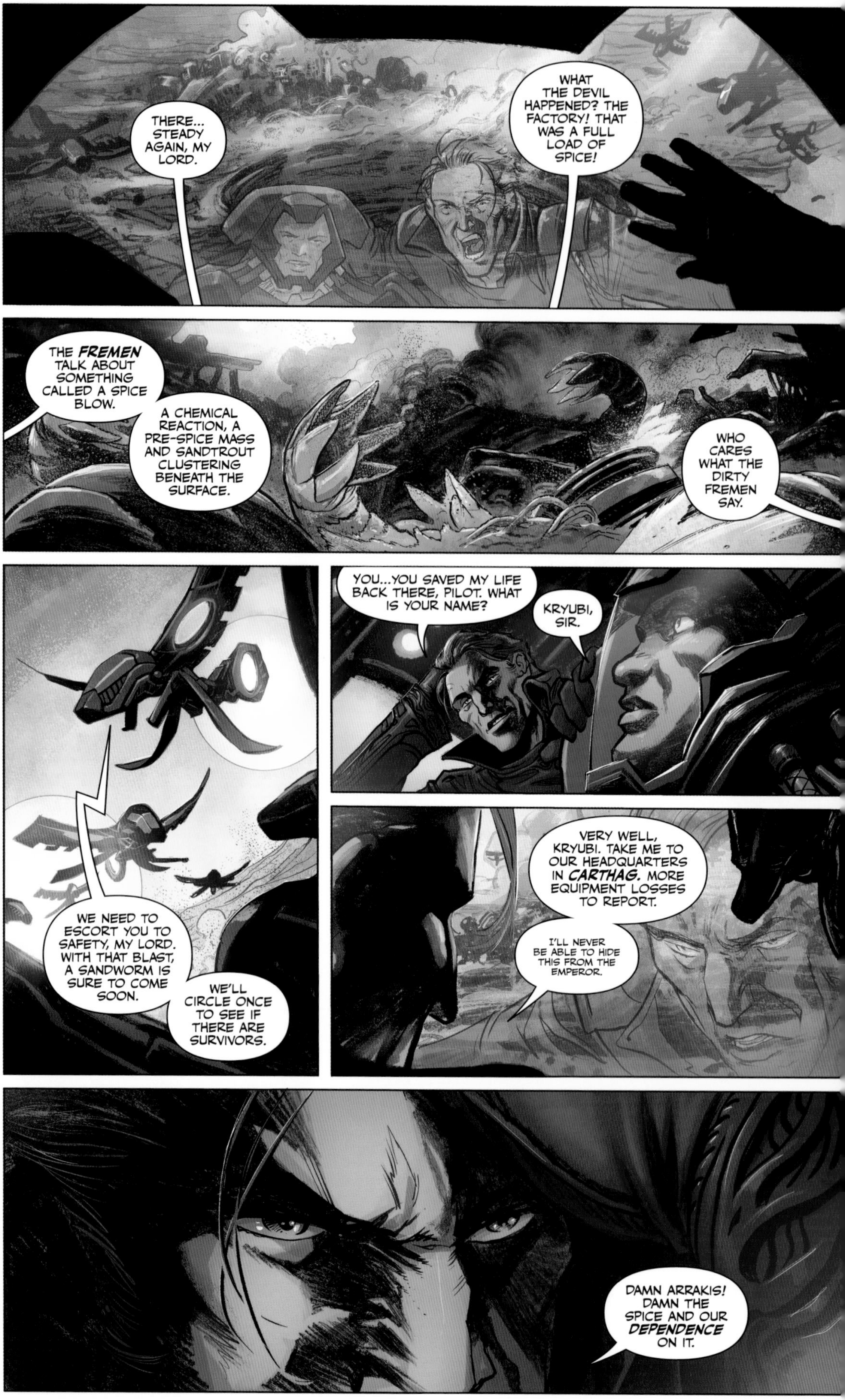
THERE... STEADY AGAIN, MY LORD.
WHAT THE DEVIL HAPPENED? THE FACTORY! THAT WAS A FULL LOAD OF SPICE!
THE FREMEN TALK ABOUT SOMETHING CALLED A SPICE BLOW.
A CHEMICAL REACTION, A PRE-SPICE MASS AND SANDTROUT CLUSTERING BENEATH THE SURFACE.
WHO CARES WHAT THE DIRTY FREMEN SAY.
WE NEED TO ESCORT YOU TO SAFETY, MY LORD. WITH THAT BLAST, A SANDWORM IS SURE TO COME SOON.
WE'LL CIRCLE ONCE TO SEE IF THERE ARE SURVIVORS.
YOU...YOU SAVED MY LIFE BACK THERE, PILOT. WHAT IS YOUR NAME?
KRYUBI, SIR.
VERY WELL, KRYUBI. TAKE ME TO OUR HEADQUARTERS IN CARTHAG. MORE EQUIPMENT LOSSES TO REPORT.
I'LL NEVER BE ABLE TO HIDE THIS FROM THE EMPEROR.
DAMN ARRAKIS! DAMN THE SPICE AND OUR DEPENDENCE ON IT.

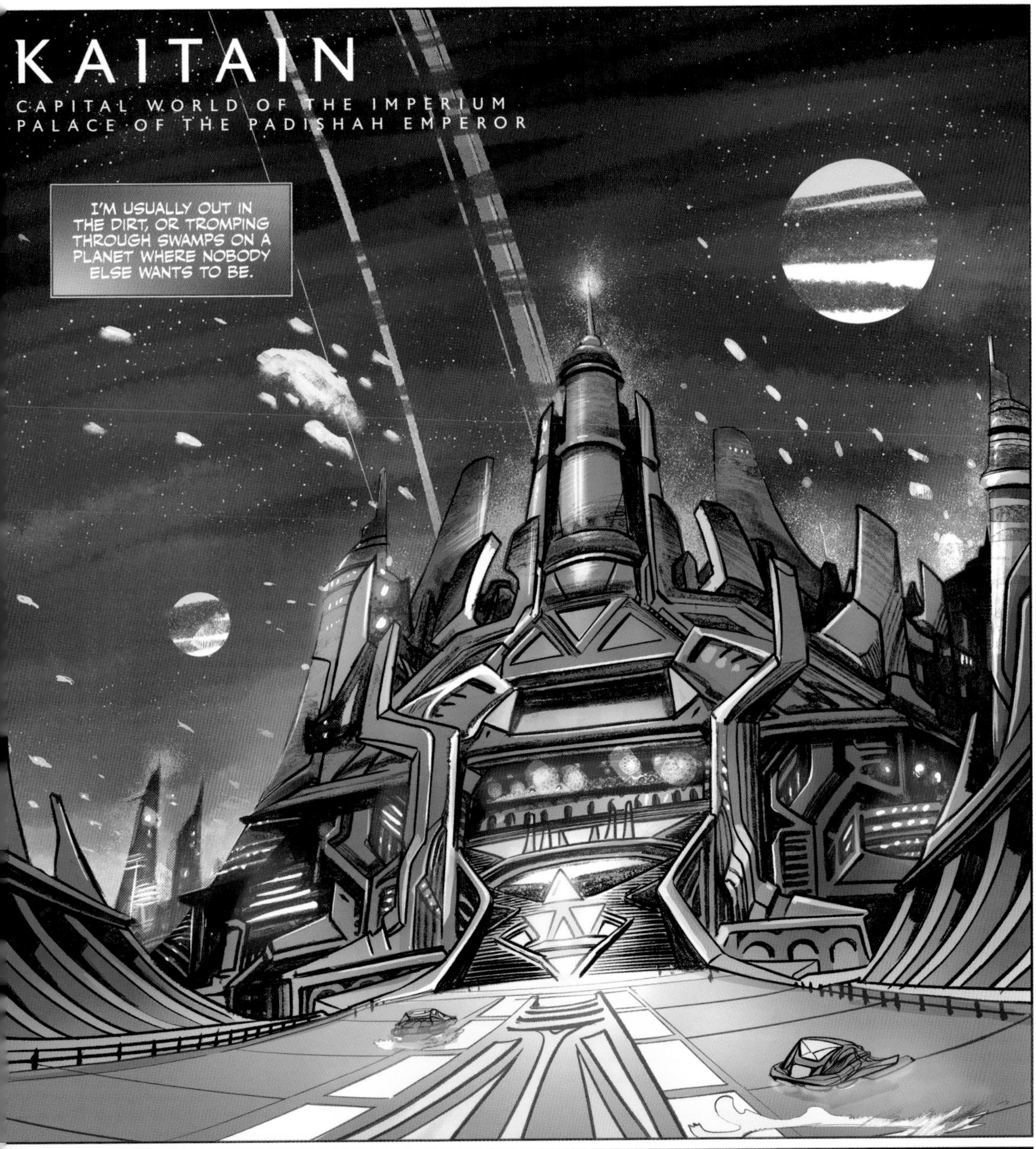
KAITAIN
CAPITAL WORLD OF THE IMPERIUM
PALACE OF THE PADISHAH EMPEROR
I'M USUALLY OUT IN THE DIRT, OR TROMPING THROUGH SWAMPS ON A PLANET WHERE NOBODY ELSE WANTS TO BE.

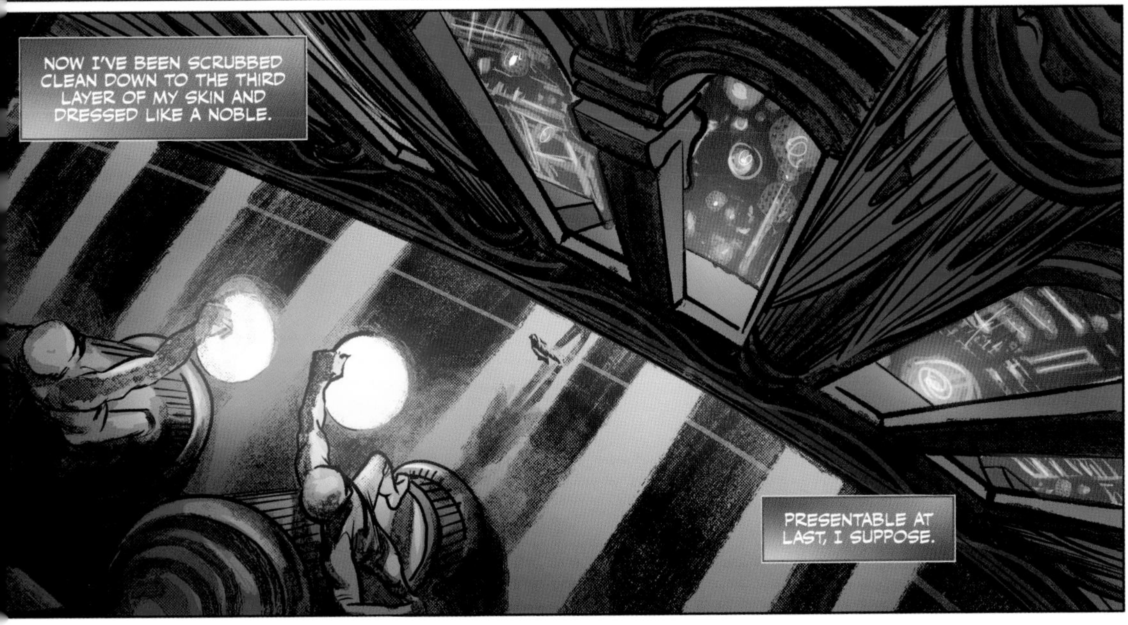
NOW I'VE BEEN SCRUBBED CLEAN DOWN TO THE THIRD LAYER OF MY SKIN AND DRESSED LIKE A NOBLE.
PRESENTABLE AT LAST, I SUPPOSE.

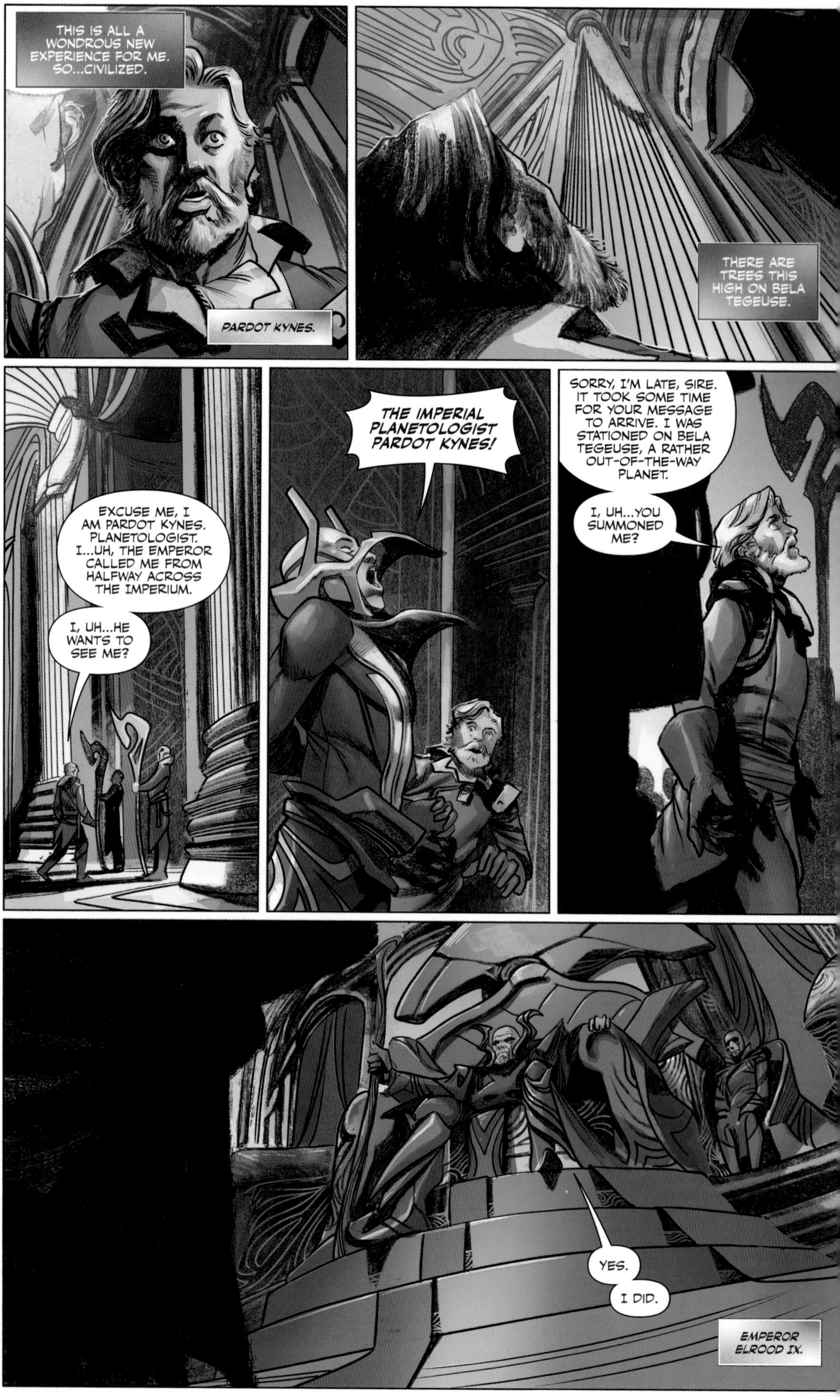
THIS IS ALL A WONDROUS NEW EXPERIENCE FOR ME. SO...CIVILIZED.
PARDOT KYNES.
THERE ARE TREES THIS HIGH ON BELA TEGEUSE.
EXCUSE ME, I AM PARDOT KYNES. PLANETOLOGIST. I...UH, THE EMPEROR CALLED ME FROM HALFWAY ACROSS THE IMPERIUM.
I, UH...HE WANTS TO SEE ME?
THE IMPERIAL PLANETOLOGIST PARDOT KYNES!
SORRY, I'M LATE, SIRE. IT TOOK SOME TIME FOR YOUR MESSAGE TO ARRIVE. I WAS STATIONED ON BELA TEGEUSE, A RATHER OUT-OF-THE-WAY PLANET.
I, UH...YOU SUMMONED ME?
YES.
I DID.
EMPEROR ELROOD IX.

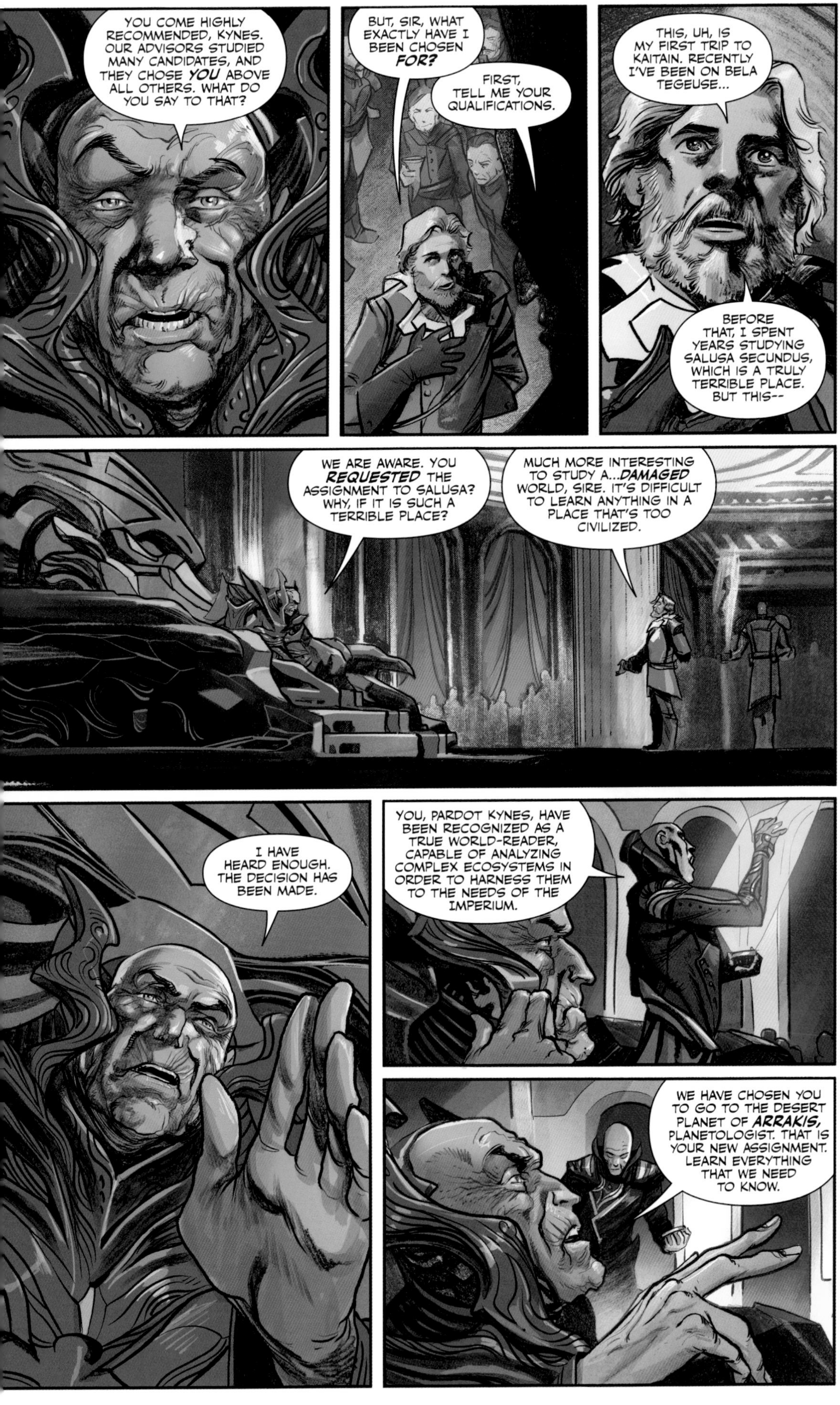
YOU COME HIGHLY RECOMMENDED, KYNES. OUR ADVISORS STUDIED MANY CANDIDATES, AND THEY CHOSE YOU ABOVE ALL OTHERS. WHAT DO YOU SAY TO THAT?
BUT, SIR, WHAT EXACTLY HAVE I BEEN CHOSEN FOR?
FIRST, TELL ME YOUR QUALIFICATIONS.
THIS, UH, IS MY FIRST TRIP TO KAITAIN. RECENTLY I'VE BEEN ON BELA TEGEUSE...
BEFORE THAT, I SPENT YEARS STUDYING SALUSA SECUNDUS, WHICH IS A TRULY TERRIBLE PLACE. BUT THIS--
WE ARE AWARE. YOU REQUESTED THE ASSIGNMENT TO SALUSA? WHY, IF IT IS SUCH A TERRIBLE PLACE?
MUCH MORE INTERESTING TO STUDY A...DAMAGED WORLD, SIRE. IT'S DIFFICULT TO LEARN ANYTHING IN A PLACE THAT'S TOO CIVILIZED.
I HAVE HEARD ENOUGH. THE DECISION HAS BEEN MADE.
YOU, PARDOT KYNES, HAVE BEEN RECOGNIZED AS A TRUE WORLD-READER, CAPABLE OF ANALYZING COMPLEX ECOSYSTEMS IN ORDER TO HARNESS THEM TO THE NEEDS OF THE IMPERIUM.
WE HAVE CHOSEN YOU TO GO TO THE DESERT PLANET OF ARRAKIS, PLANETOLOGIST. THAT IS YOUR NEW ASSIGNMENT. LEARN EVERYTHING THAT WE NEED TO KNOW.

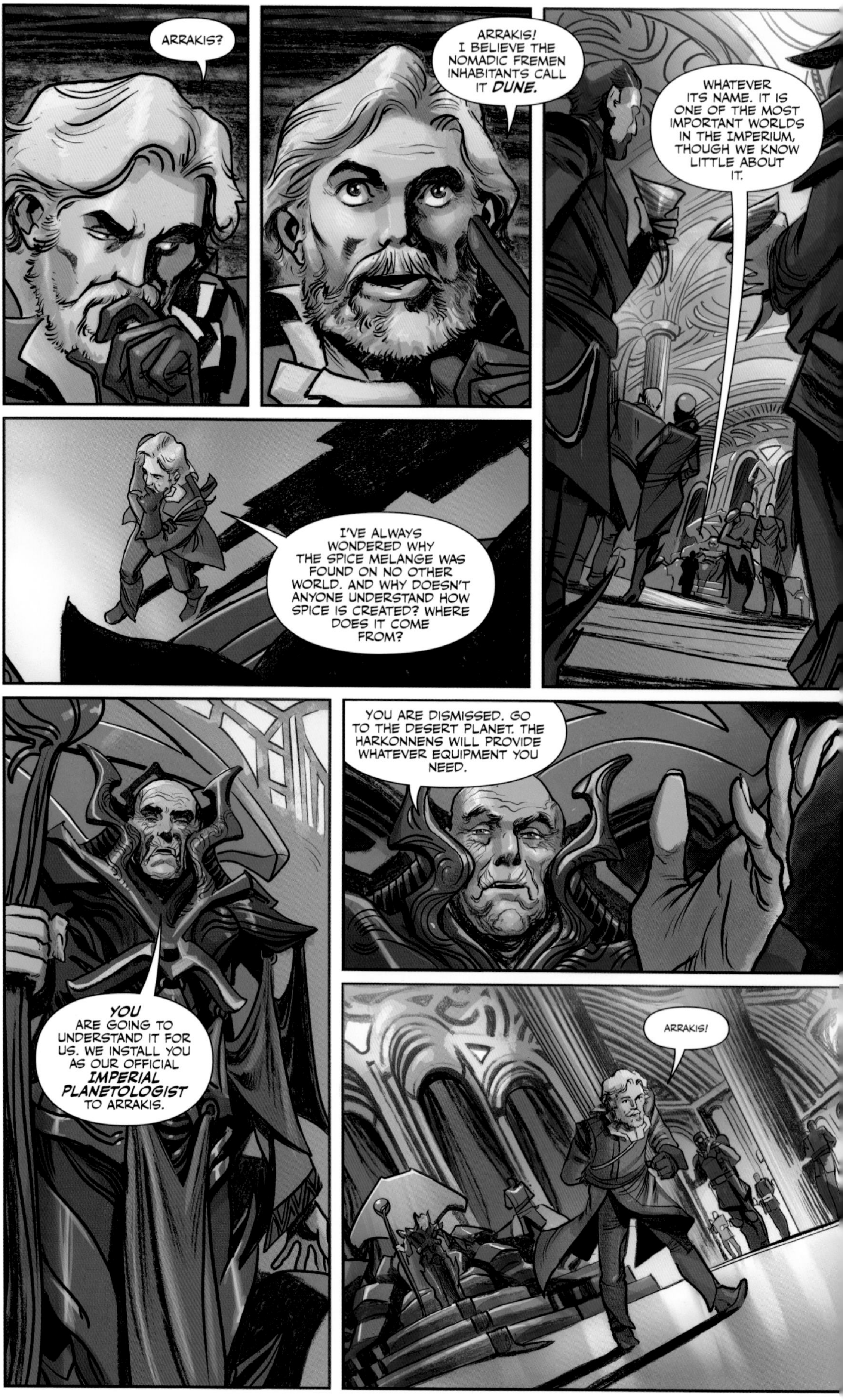
ARRAKIS?
ARRAKIS! I BELIEVE THE NOMADIC FREMEN INHABITANTS CALL IT *DUNE.*
WHATEVER ITS NAME. IT IS ONE OF THE MOST IMPORTANT WORLDS IN THE IMPERIUM, THOUGH WE KNOW LITTLE ABOUT IT.
I'VE ALWAYS WONDERED WHY THE SPICE MELANGE WAS FOUND ON NO OTHER WORLD. AND WHY DOESN'T ANYONE UNDERSTAND HOW SPICE IS CREATED? WHERE DOES IT COME FROM?
YOU ARE GOING TO UNDERSTAND IT FOR US. WE INSTALL YOU AS OUR OFFICIAL *IMPERIAL PLANETOLOGIST* TO ARRAKIS.
YOU ARE DISMISSED. GO TO THE DESERT PLANET. THE HARKONNENS WILL PROVIDE WHATEVER EQUIPMENT YOU NEED.
ARRAKIS!

SOMEONE MORE CONCERNED WITH HIS OWN CURIOSITY THAN WITH PANDERING TO THESE STUPID CLINGERS AND BUFFOONS. HOW REFRESHING.

WHO IS NEXT, CHAMBERLAIN? WHAT REMAINS ON THE SCHEDULE?

THE EARL DOMINIC--

I CAN INTRODUCE MYSELF. ELROOD AND I ARE OLD FRIENDS.

EARL DOMINIC VERNIUS OF IX, SIRE! HERE AT YOUR REQUEST.

VERNIUS! HE HELPED ME PUT DOWN THE ECAZI REVOLT YEARS AGO, AND HE STILL STRUTS LIKE A WAR HERO!

AND...HE STOLE LADY SHANDO FROM ME.

SIR! REMOVE YOUR FOOT FROM THE DAIS!

YOU HEARD MY GOOD NEWS FROM IX, SIRE?

OUR ENGINEERS HAVE UNVEILED A NEW GUILD HEIGHLINER DESIGN WITH CARGO CAPACITY INCREASED BY SIXTEEN PERCENT!

THAT IS WHY I COMMANDED YOU TO COME HERE! MY SPIES REPORTED EVERYTHING.

YOUR DESIGN STEALS MONEY FROM THE IMPERIAL TREASURY...

...FROM ME!

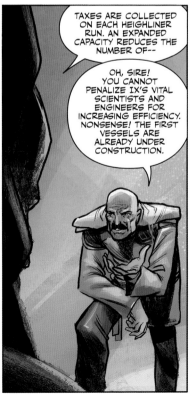

TAXES ARE COLLECTED ON EACH HEIGHLINER RUN. AN EXPANDED CAPACITY REDUCES THE NUMBER OF--

OH, SIRE! YOU CANNOT PENALIZE IX'S VITAL SCIENTISTS AND ENGINEERS FOR INCREASING EFFICIENCY. NONSENSE! THE FIRST VESSELS ARE ALREADY UNDER CONSTRUCTION.

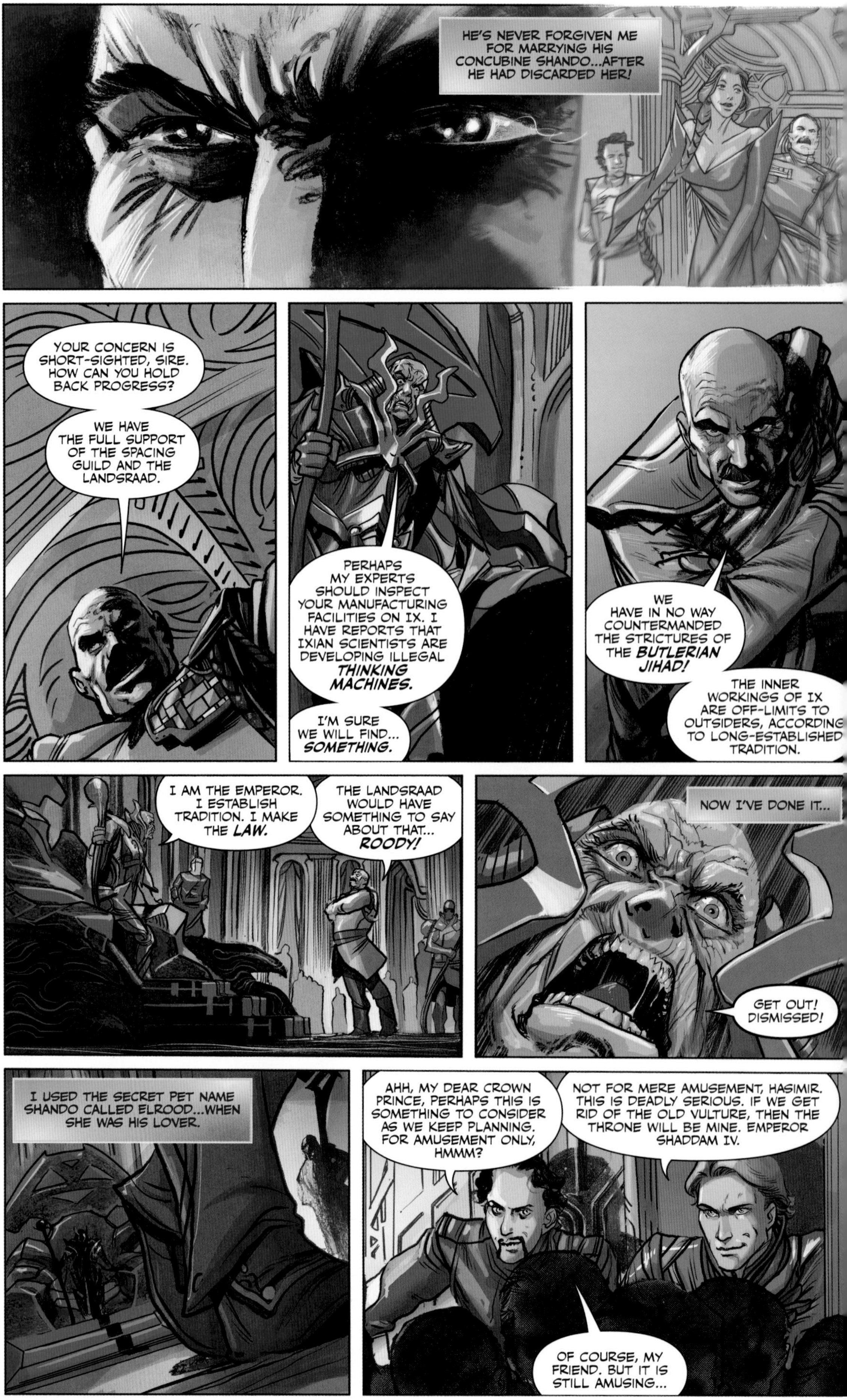
HE'S NEVER FORGIVEN ME FOR MARRYING HIS CONCUBINE SHANDO...AFTER HE HAD DISCARDED HER!
YOUR CONCERN IS SHORT-SIGHTED, SIRE. HOW CAN YOU HOLD BACK PROGRESS?
WE HAVE THE FULL SUPPORT OF THE SPACING GUILD AND THE LANDSRAAD.
PERHAPS MY EXPERTS SHOULD INSPECT YOUR MANUFACTURING FACILITIES ON IX. I HAVE REPORTS THAT IXIAN SCIENTISTS ARE DEVELOPING ILLEGAL THINKING MACHINES.
I'M SURE WE WILL FIND... SOMETHING.
WE HAVE IN NO WAY COUNTERMANDED THE STRICTURES OF THE BUTLERIAN JIHAD!
THE INNER WORKINGS OF IX ARE OFF-LIMITS TO OUTSIDERS, ACCORDING TO LONG-ESTABLISHED TRADITION.
I AM THE EMPEROR. I ESTABLISH TRADITION. I MAKE THE LAW.
THE LANDSRAAD WOULD HAVE SOMETHING TO SAY ABOUT THAT... ROODY!
NOW I'VE DONE IT...
GET OUT! DISMISSED!
I USED THE SECRET PET NAME SHANDO CALLED ELROOD...WHEN SHE WAS HIS LOVER.
AHH, MY DEAR CROWN PRINCE, PERHAPS THIS IS SOMETHING TO CONSIDER AS WE KEEP PLANNING. FOR AMUSEMENT ONLY, HMMM?
NOT FOR MERE AMUSEMENT, HASIMIR. THIS IS DEADLY SERIOUS. IF WE GET RID OF THE OLD VULTURE, THEN THE THRONE WILL BE MINE. EMPEROR SHADDAM IV.
OF COURSE, MY FRIEND. BUT IT IS STILL AMUSING...

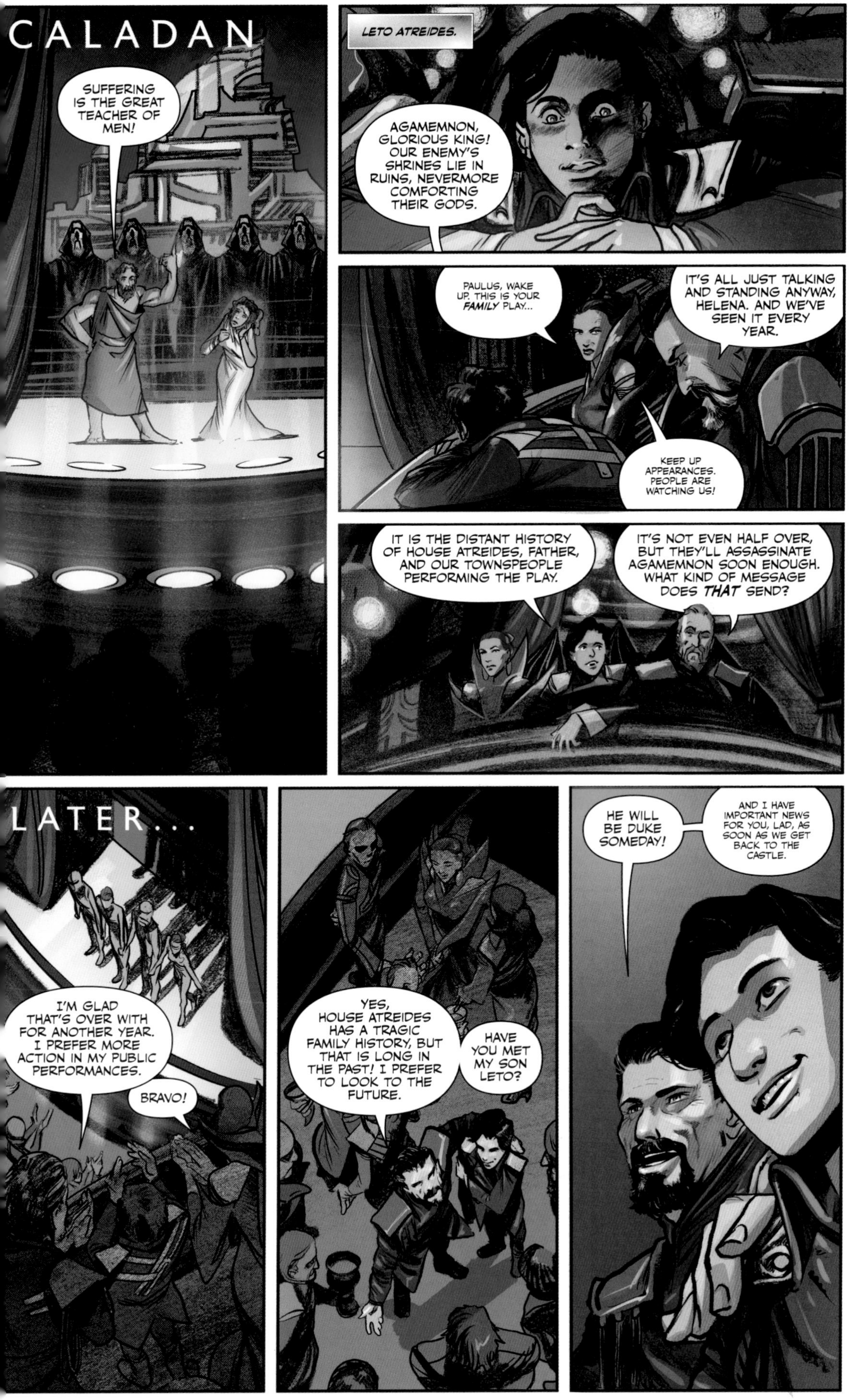
CALADAN
SUFFERING IS THE GREAT TEACHER OF MEN!
LETO ATREIDES.
AGAMEMNON, GLORIOUS KING! OUR ENEMY'S SHRINES LIE IN RUINS, NEVERMORE COMFORTING THEIR GODS.
PAULUS, WAKE UP. THIS IS YOUR FAMILY PLAY...
IT'S ALL JUST TALKING AND STANDING ANYWAY, HELENA. AND WE'VE SEEN IT EVERY YEAR.
KEEP UP APPEARANCES. PEOPLE ARE WATCHING US!
IT IS THE DISTANT HISTORY OF HOUSE ATREIDES, FATHER, AND OUR TOWNSPEOPLE PERFORMING THE PLAY.
IT'S NOT EVEN HALF OVER, BUT THEY'LL ASSASSINATE AGAMEMNON SOON ENOUGH. WHAT KIND OF MESSAGE DOES THAT SEND?
LATER...
I'M GLAD THAT'S OVER WITH FOR ANOTHER YEAR. I PREFER MORE ACTION IN MY PUBLIC PERFORMANCES.
BRAVO!
YES, HOUSE ATREIDES HAS A TRAGIC FAMILY HISTORY, BUT THAT IS LONG IN THE PAST! I PREFER TO LOOK TO THE FUTURE.
HAVE YOU MET MY SON LETO?
HE WILL BE DUKE SOMEDAY!
AND I HAVE IMPORTANT NEWS FOR YOU, LAD, AS SOON AS WE GET BACK TO THE CASTLE.

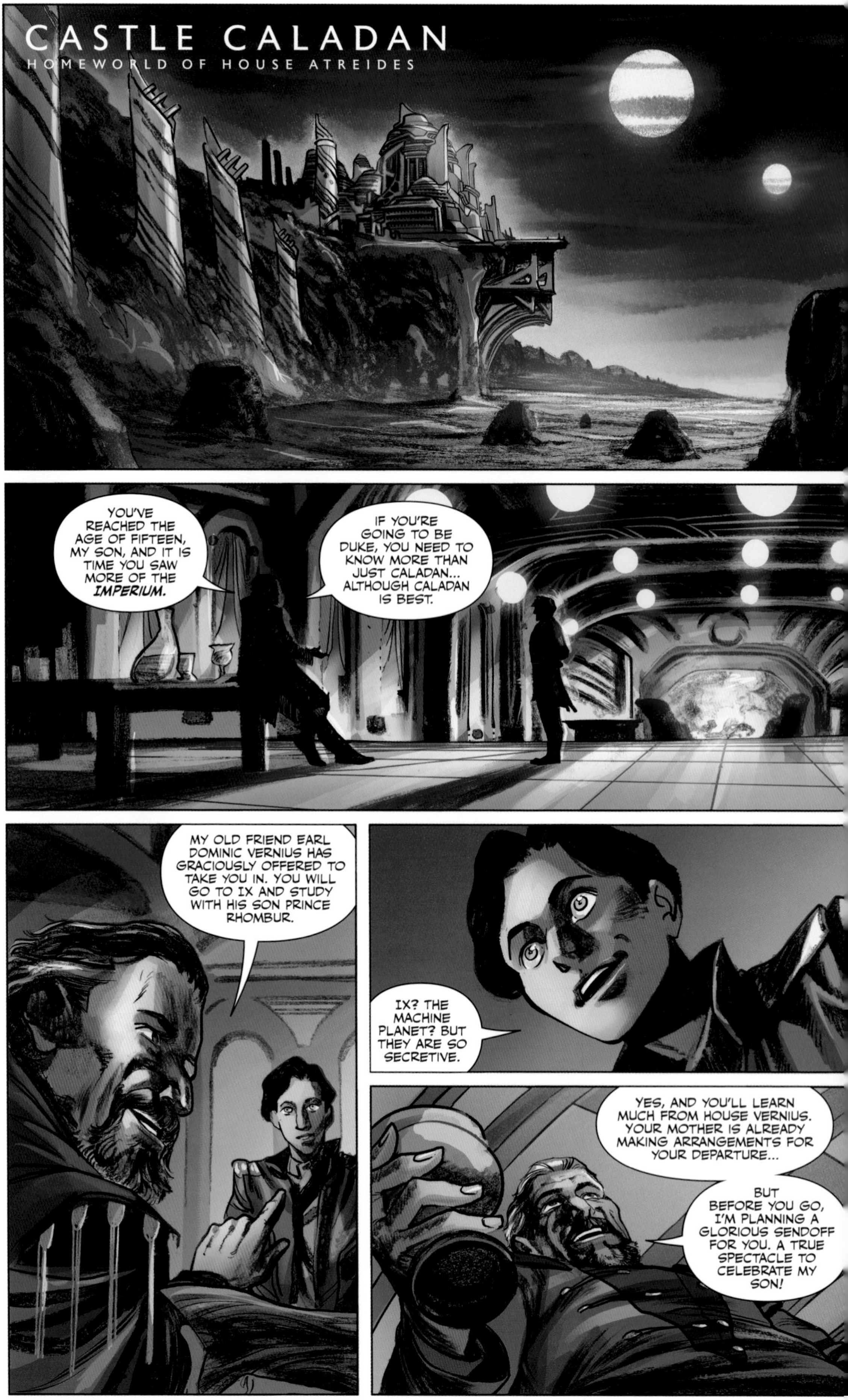
CASTLE CALADAN
HOMEWORLD OF HOUSE ATREIDES
YOU'VE REACHED THE AGE OF FIFTEEN, MY SON, AND IT IS TIME YOU SAW MORE OF THE *IMPERIUM.*
IF YOU'RE GOING TO BE DUKE, YOU NEED TO KNOW MORE THAN JUST CALADAN... ALTHOUGH CALADAN IS BEST.
MY OLD FRIEND EARL DOMINIC VERNIUS HAS GRACIOUSLY OFFERED TO TAKE YOU IN. YOU WILL GO TO IX AND STUDY WITH HIS SON PRINCE RHOMBUR.
IX? THE MACHINE PLANET? BUT THEY ARE SO SECRETIVE.
YES, AND YOU'LL LEARN MUCH FROM HOUSE VERNIUS. YOUR MOTHER IS ALREADY MAKING ARRANGEMENTS FOR YOUR DEPARTURE...
BUT BEFORE YOU GO, I'M PLANNING A GLORIOUS SENDOFF FOR YOU. A TRUE SPECTACLE TO CELEBRATE MY SON!

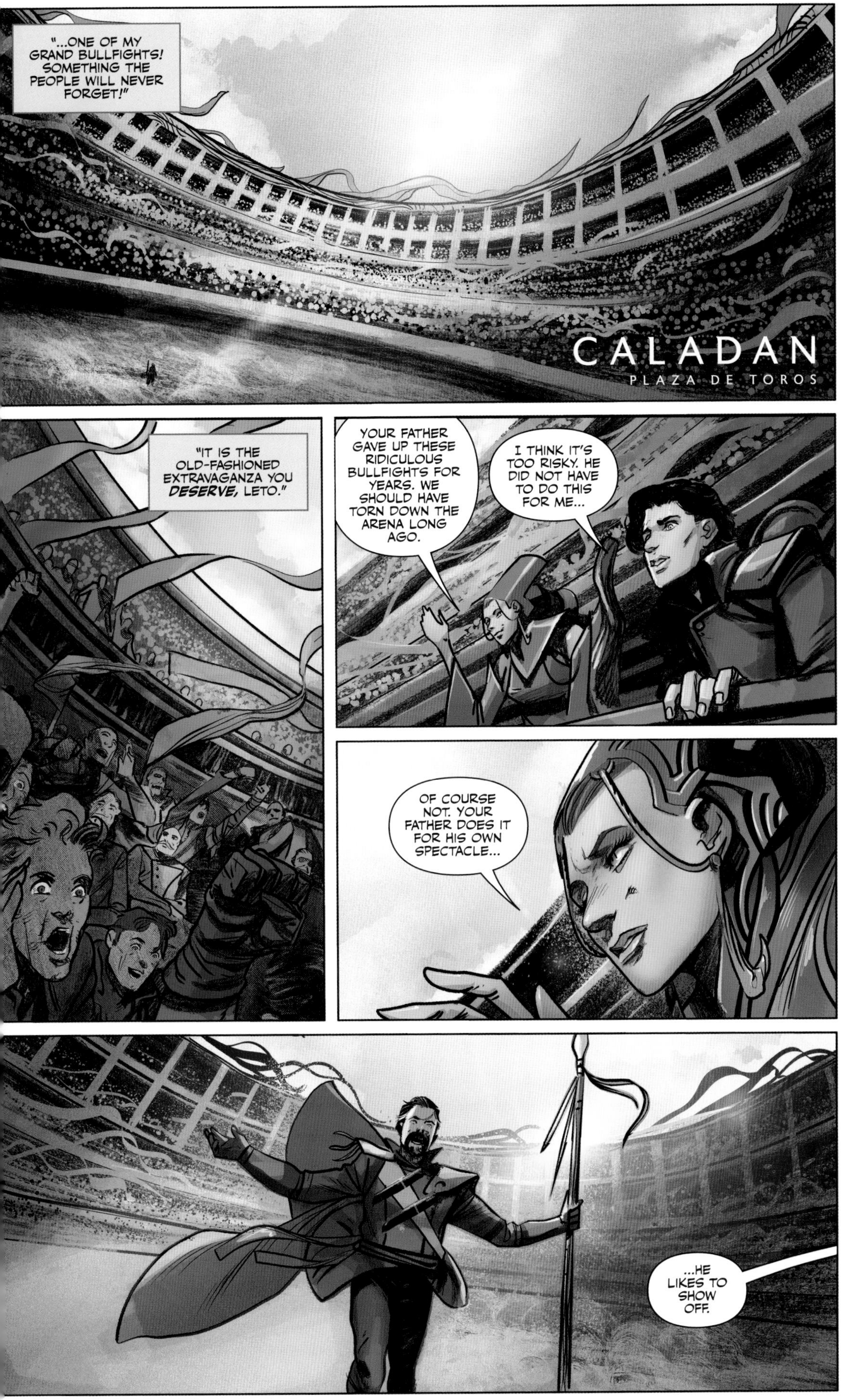
"...ONE OF MY GRAND BULLFIGHTS! SOMETHING THE PEOPLE WILL NEVER FORGET!"
CALADAN
PLAZA DE TOROS
"IT IS THE OLD-FASHIONED EXTRAVAGANZA YOU *DESERVE,* LETO."
YOUR FATHER GAVE UP THESE RIDICULOUS BULLFIGHTS FOR YEARS. WE SHOULD HAVE TORN DOWN THE ARENA LONG AGO.
I THINK IT'S TOO RISKY. HE DID NOT HAVE TO DO THIS FOR ME...
OF COURSE NOT. YOUR FATHER DOES IT FOR HIS OWN SPECTACLE...
...HE LIKES TO SHOW OFF.

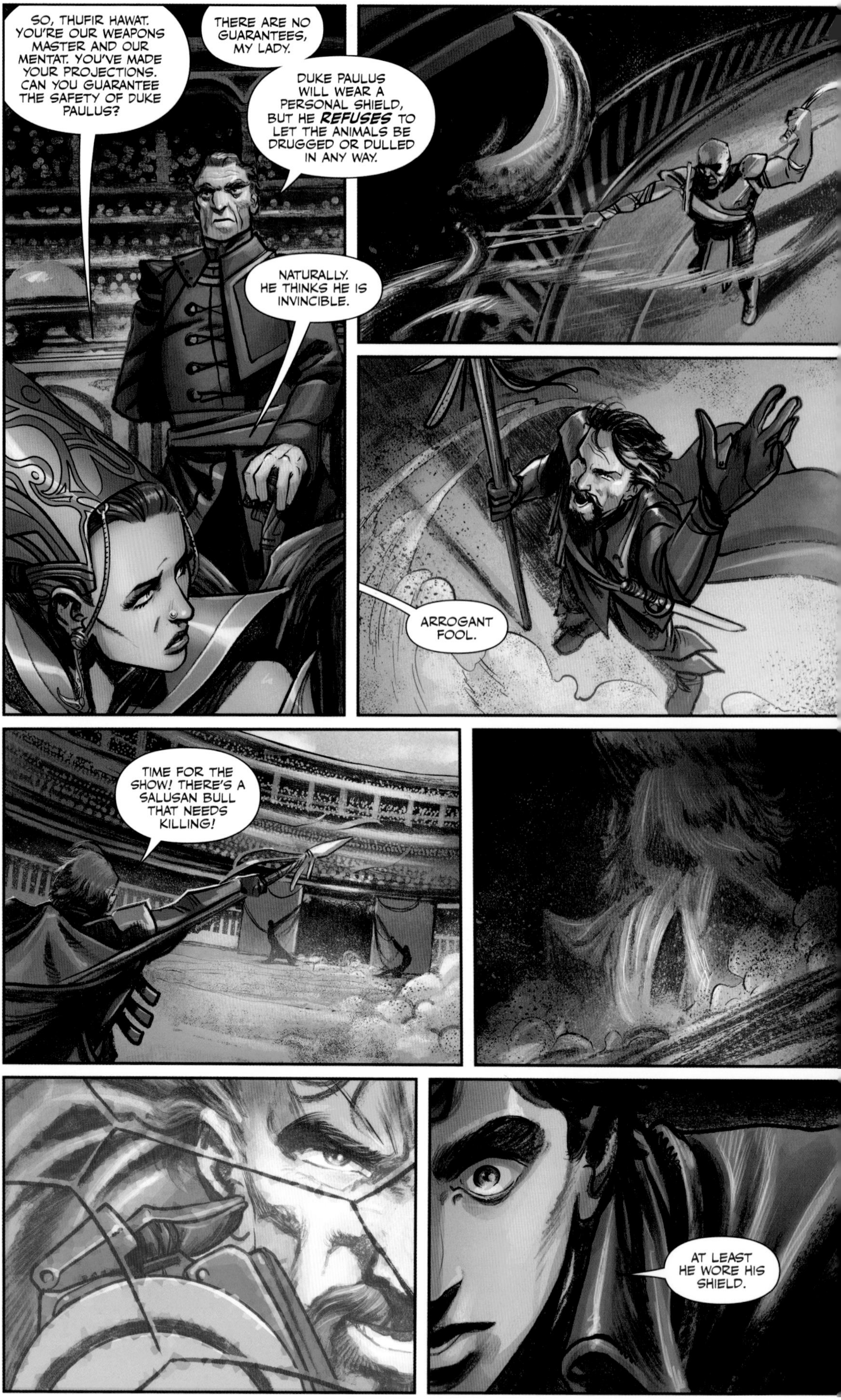
SO, THUFIR HAWAT. YOU'RE OUR WEAPONS MASTER AND OUR MENTAT. YOU'VE MADE YOUR PROJECTIONS. CAN YOU GUARANTEE THE SAFETY OF DUKE PAULUS?
THERE ARE NO GUARANTEES, MY LADY.
DUKE PAULUS WILL WEAR A PERSONAL SHIELD, BUT HE ***REFUSES*** TO LET THE ANIMALS BE DRUGGED OR DULLED IN ANY WAY.
NATURALLY. HE THINKS HE IS INVINCIBLE.
ARROGANT FOOL.
TIME FOR THE SHOW! THERE'S A SALUSAN BULL THAT NEEDS KILLING!
AT LEAST HE WORE HIS SHIELD.

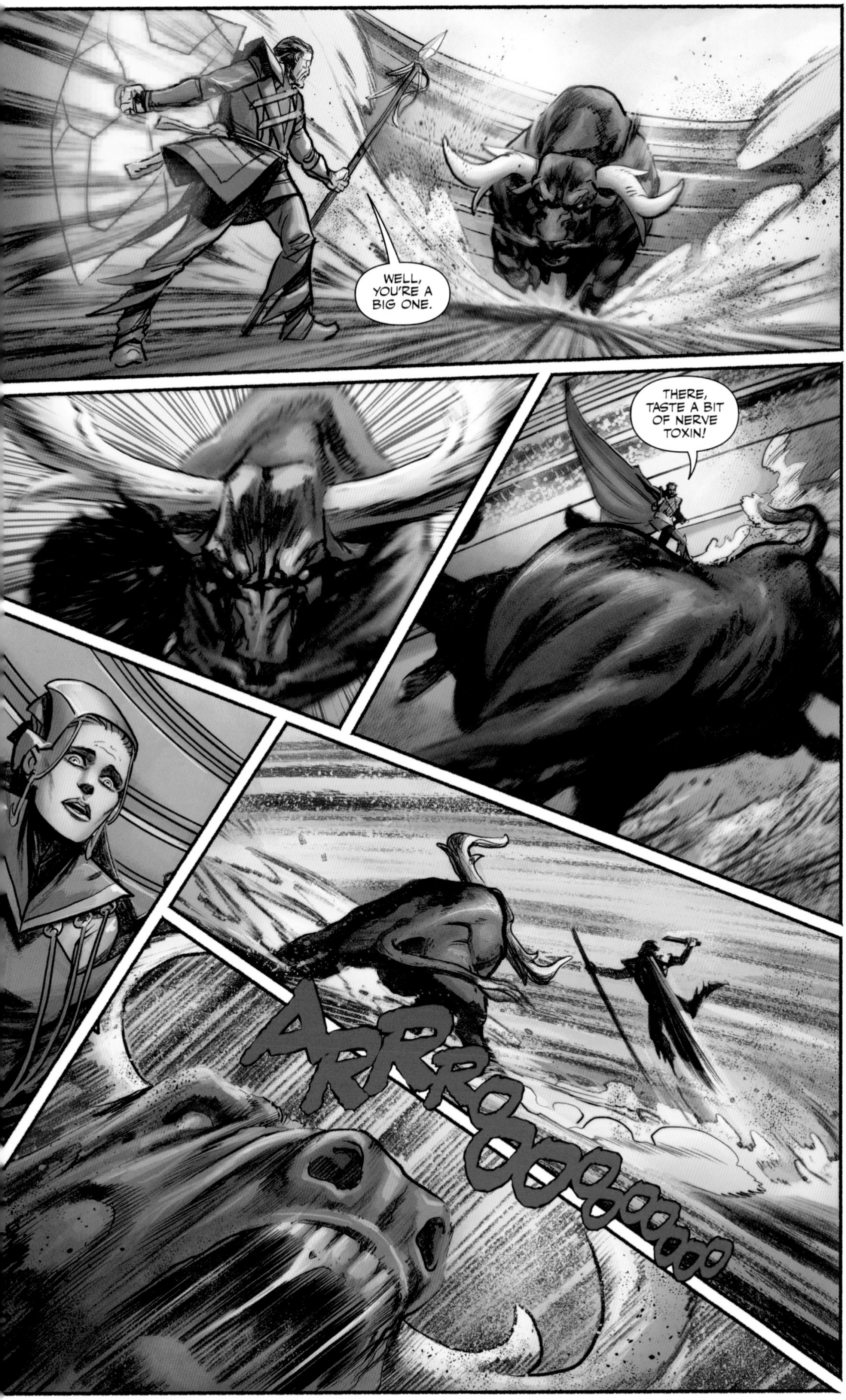
WELL, YOU'RE A BIG ONE.
THERE, TASTE A BIT OF NERVE TOXIN!
ARRROOOOOOOOO

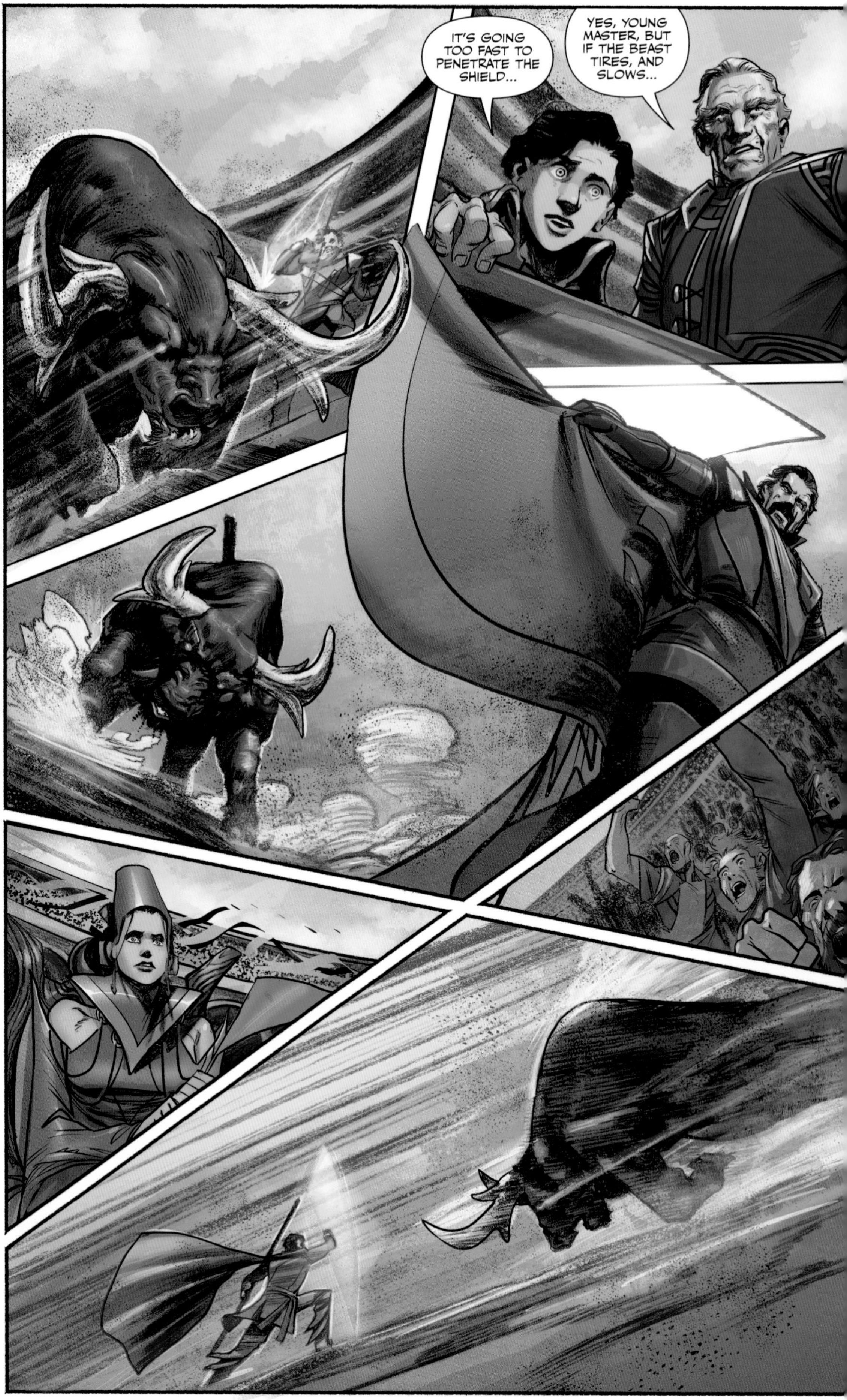
IT'S GOING TOO FAST TO PENETRATE THE SHIELD...
YES, YOUNG MASTER, BUT IF THE BEAST TIRES, AND SLOWS...

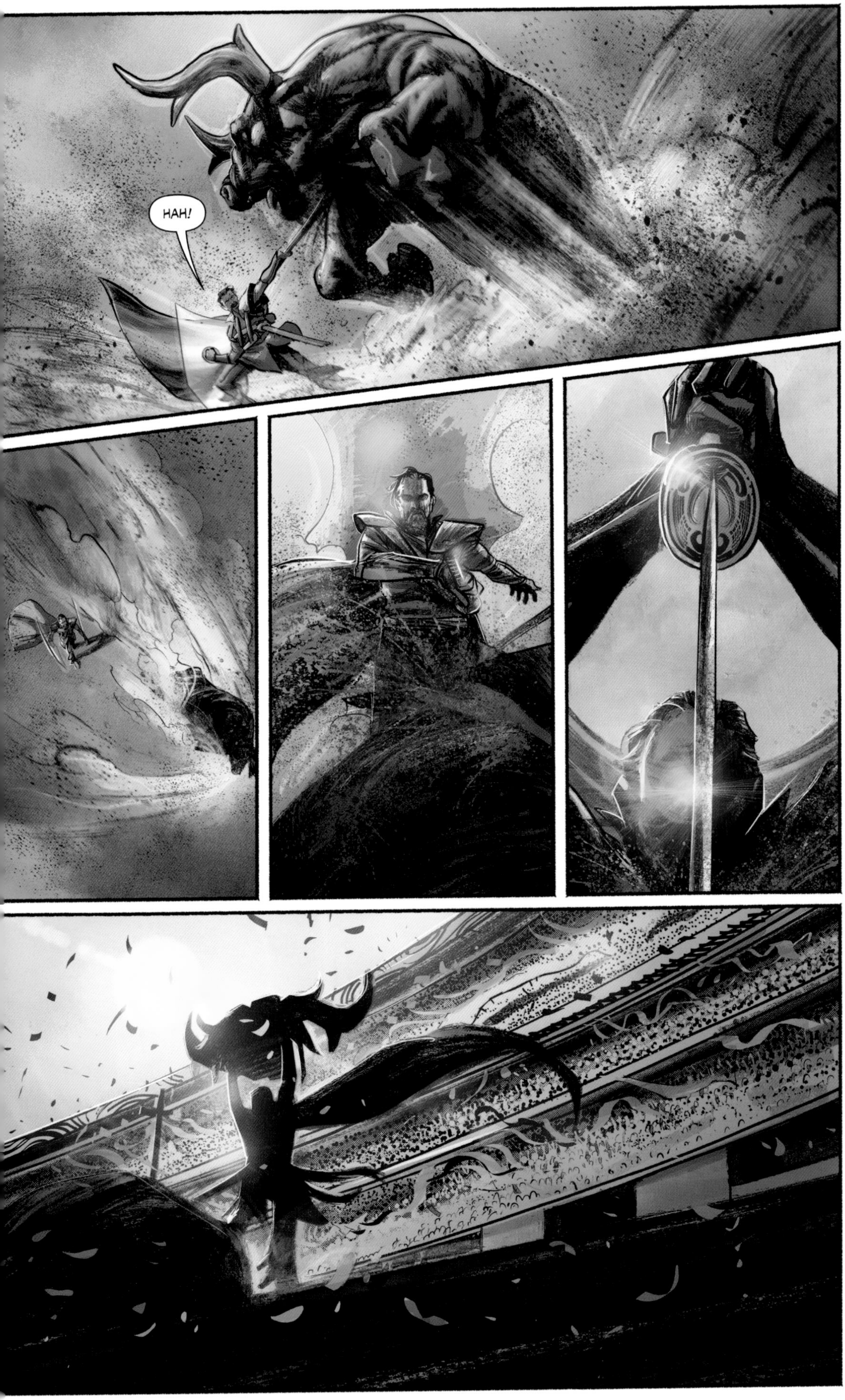
HAH!

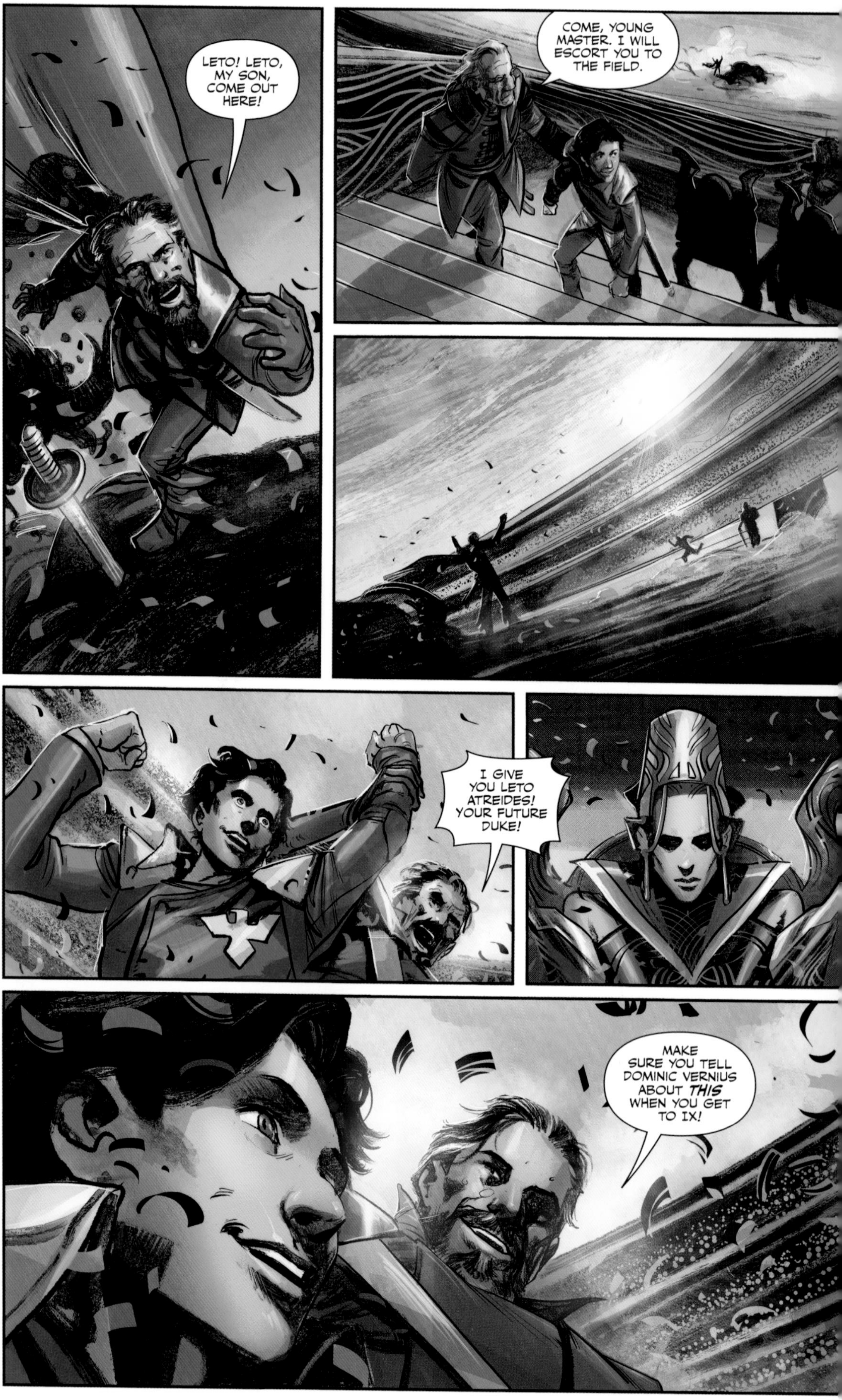
LETO! LETO, MY SON, COME OUT HERE!
COME, YOUNG MASTER. I WILL ESCORT YOU TO THE FIELD.
I GIVE YOU LETO ATREIDES! YOUR FUTURE DUKE!
MAKE SURE YOU TELL DOMINIC VERNIUS ABOUT *THIS* WHEN YOU GET TO IX!

KAITAIN
IMPERIAL PALACE
PRIVATE WING OF CROWN PRINCE SHADDAM

MMMM, THE EMPEROR WILL NEVER *DIE* ON HIS OWN, YOU KNOW, SHADDAM.

...UNLESS WE HELP SPEED IT ALONG SOMEHOW.

HE HAS ALREADY RULED FOR 155 YEARS... AND HIS FATHER RULED FOR A CENTURY HIMSELF. I DON'T THINK HE'LL EVER DIE.

CONCENTRATE ON THE SHIELD-BALL, HASIMIR. YOU'LL LOSE THE GAME.

THAT DEPENDS ON WHICH GAME WE ARE TRULY PLAYING, HMMM?

I HAVE AN IDEA...

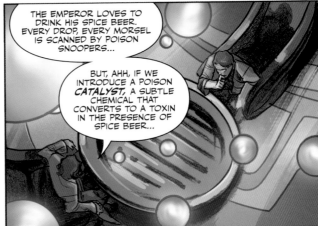

THE EMPEROR LOVES TO DRINK HIS SPICE BEER. EVERY DROP, EVERY MORSEL IS SCANNED BY POISON SNOOPERS...

BUT, AHH, IF WE INTRODUCE A POISON *CATALYST,* A SUBTLE CHEMICAL THAT CONVERTS TO A TOXIN IN THE PRESENCE OF SPICE BEER...

IT WOULD NEED TO BE SLOW IN ORDER TO REMAIN UNDETECTED... BUT A LETHAL DOSE COULD BUILD UP IN A YEAR OR TWO...

AND HOW WILL YOU DO IT? I AM TIRED OF WAITING FOR THE GOLDEN LION THRONE!

THERE, I HAVE WON THE GAME. TIME FOR A DIFFERENT SORT OF GAME.

LEAVE THE DETAILS TO ME, MY FRIEND...

I HAVE BEEN LOOKING FORWARD TO THIS A LONG TIME...

AS MUCH TO TEST MY SKILLS AS TO ACHIEVE OUR GREATEST GOAL...

HE HOLDS THE WEIGHT OF THE IMPERIUM, BUT NOT A CARE IN THE WORLD, THIS ONE...

DODDERING OLD FOOL. HE WON'T EVEN FEEL THE NEEDLE.

A LITTLE ANESTHETIC MIST, A SOPORIFIC...

UP THE NOSTRIL, THROUGH THE SINUS...TOUCH THE BRAIN...IMPLANT THE CATALYST.

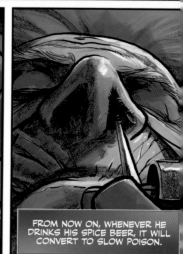

FROM NOW ON, WHENEVER HE DRINKS HIS SPICE BEER, IT WILL CONVERT TO SLOW POISON.

AND NO ONE THE WISER...

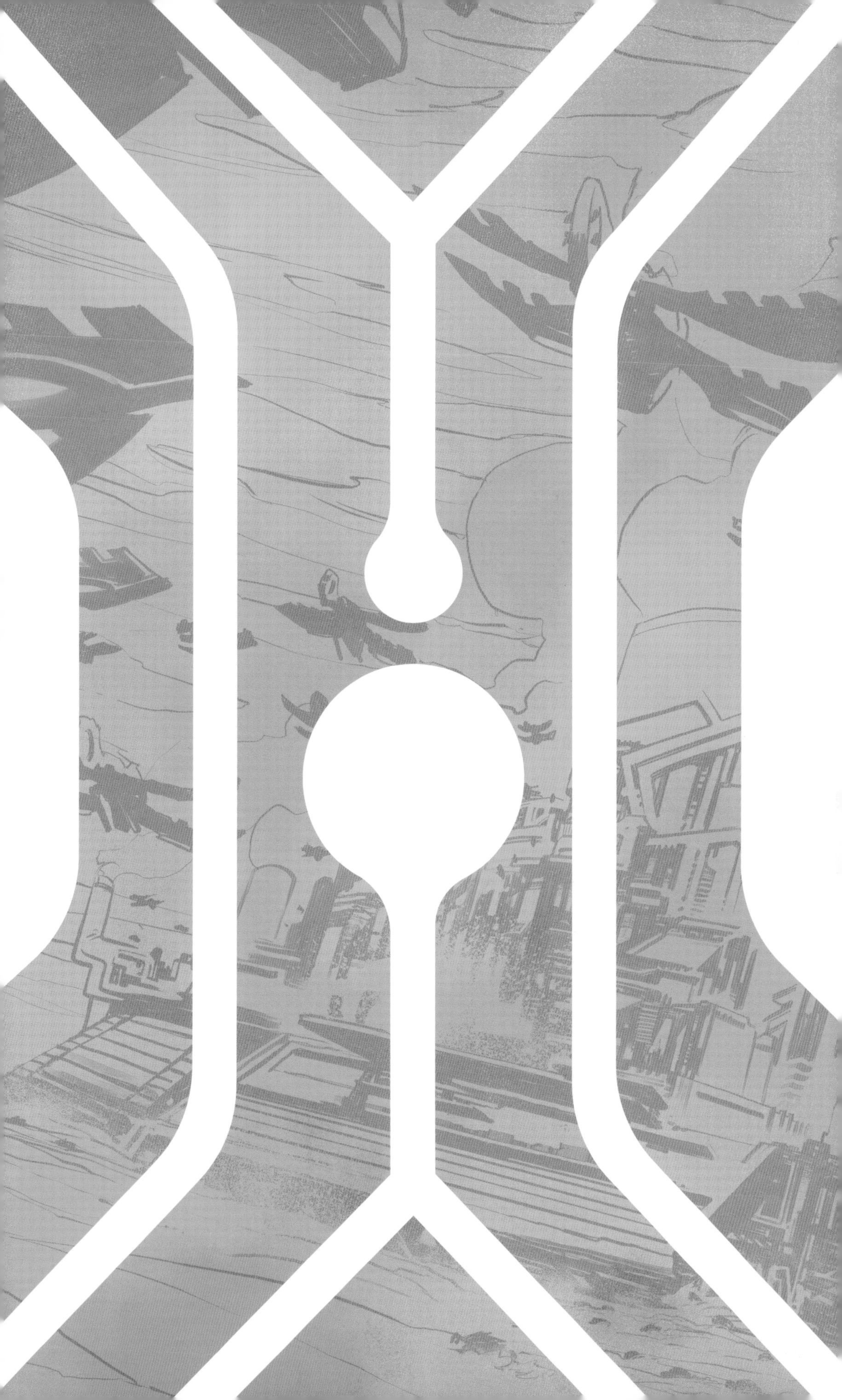

CHAPTER
TWO

Cover by
Jae Lee & **June Chung**

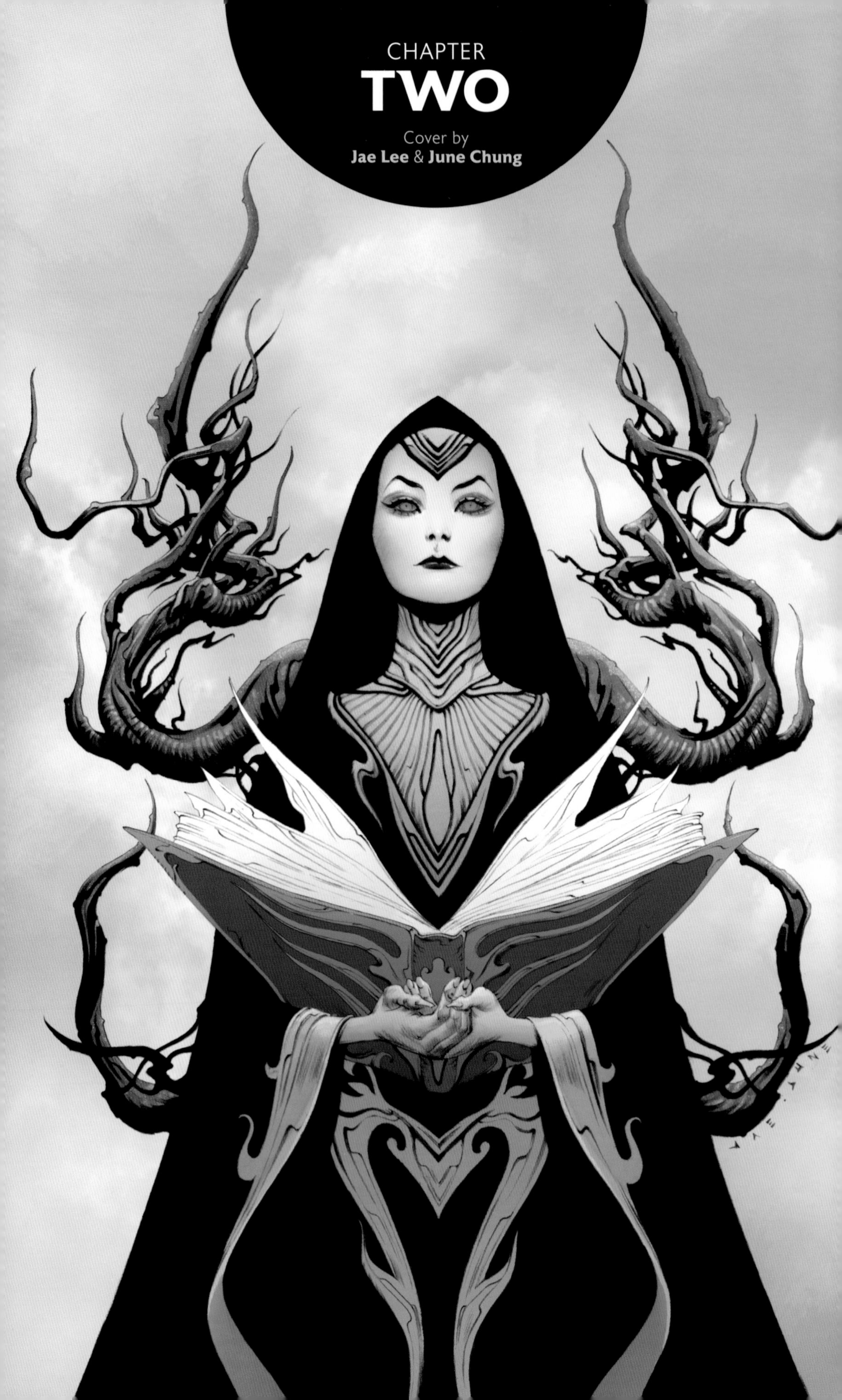

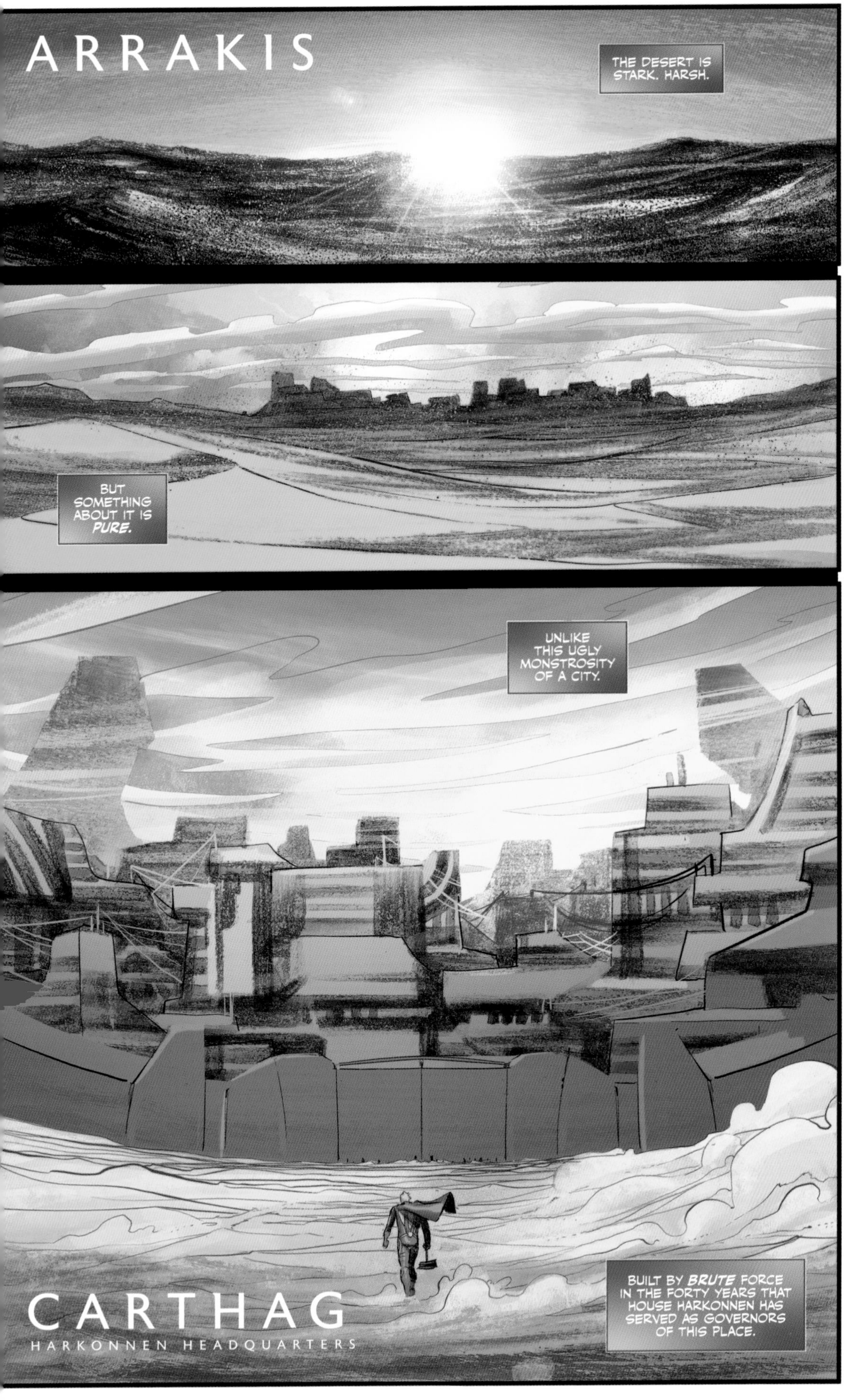
ARRAKIS
THE DESERT IS STARK. HARSH.
BUT SOMETHING ABOUT IT IS *PURE.*
UNLIKE THIS UGLY MONSTROSITY OF A CITY.
BUILT BY *BRUTE* FORCE IN THE FORTY YEARS THAT HOUSE HARKONNEN HAS SERVED AS GOVERNORS OF THIS PLACE.
CARTHAG
HARKONNEN HEADQUARTERS

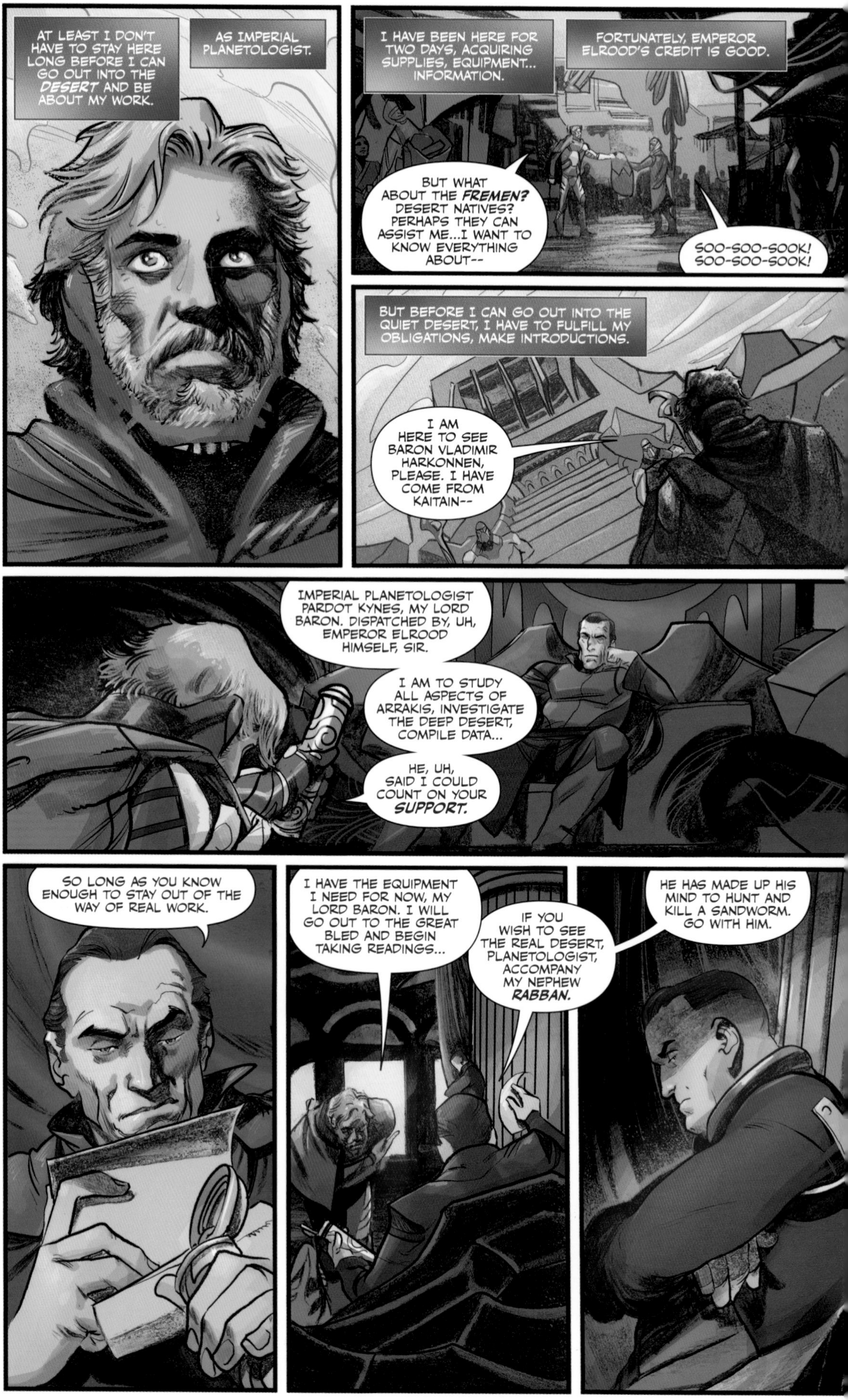
AT LEAST I DON'T HAVE TO STAY HERE LONG BEFORE I CAN GO OUT INTO THE DESERT AND BE ABOUT MY WORK.
AS IMPERIAL PLANETOLOGIST.
I HAVE BEEN HERE FOR TWO DAYS, ACQUIRING SUPPLIES, EQUIPMENT... INFORMATION.
FORTUNATELY, EMPEROR ELROOD'S CREDIT IS GOOD.
BUT WHAT ABOUT THE FREMEN? DESERT NATIVES? PERHAPS THEY CAN ASSIST ME...I WANT TO KNOW EVERYTHING ABOUT--
SOO-SOO-SOOK! SOO-SOO-SOOK!
BUT BEFORE I CAN GO OUT INTO THE QUIET DESERT, I HAVE TO FULFILL MY OBLIGATIONS, MAKE INTRODUCTIONS.
I AM HERE TO SEE BARON VLADIMIR HARKONNEN, PLEASE. I HAVE COME FROM KAITAIN--
IMPERIAL PLANETOLOGIST PARDOT KYNES, MY LORD BARON. DISPATCHED BY, UH, EMPEROR ELROOD HIMSELF, SIR.
I AM TO STUDY ALL ASPECTS OF ARRAKIS, INVESTIGATE THE DEEP DESERT, COMPILE DATA...
HE, UH, SAID I COULD COUNT ON YOUR SUPPORT.
SO LONG AS YOU KNOW ENOUGH TO STAY OUT OF THE WAY OF REAL WORK.
I HAVE THE EQUIPMENT I NEED FOR NOW, MY LORD BARON. I WILL GO OUT TO THE GREAT BLED AND BEGIN TAKING READINGS...
IF YOU WISH TO SEE THE REAL DESERT, PLANETOLOGIST, ACCOMPANY MY NEPHEW RABBAN.
HE HAS MADE UP HIS MIND TO HUNT AND KILL A SANDWORM. GO WITH HIM.

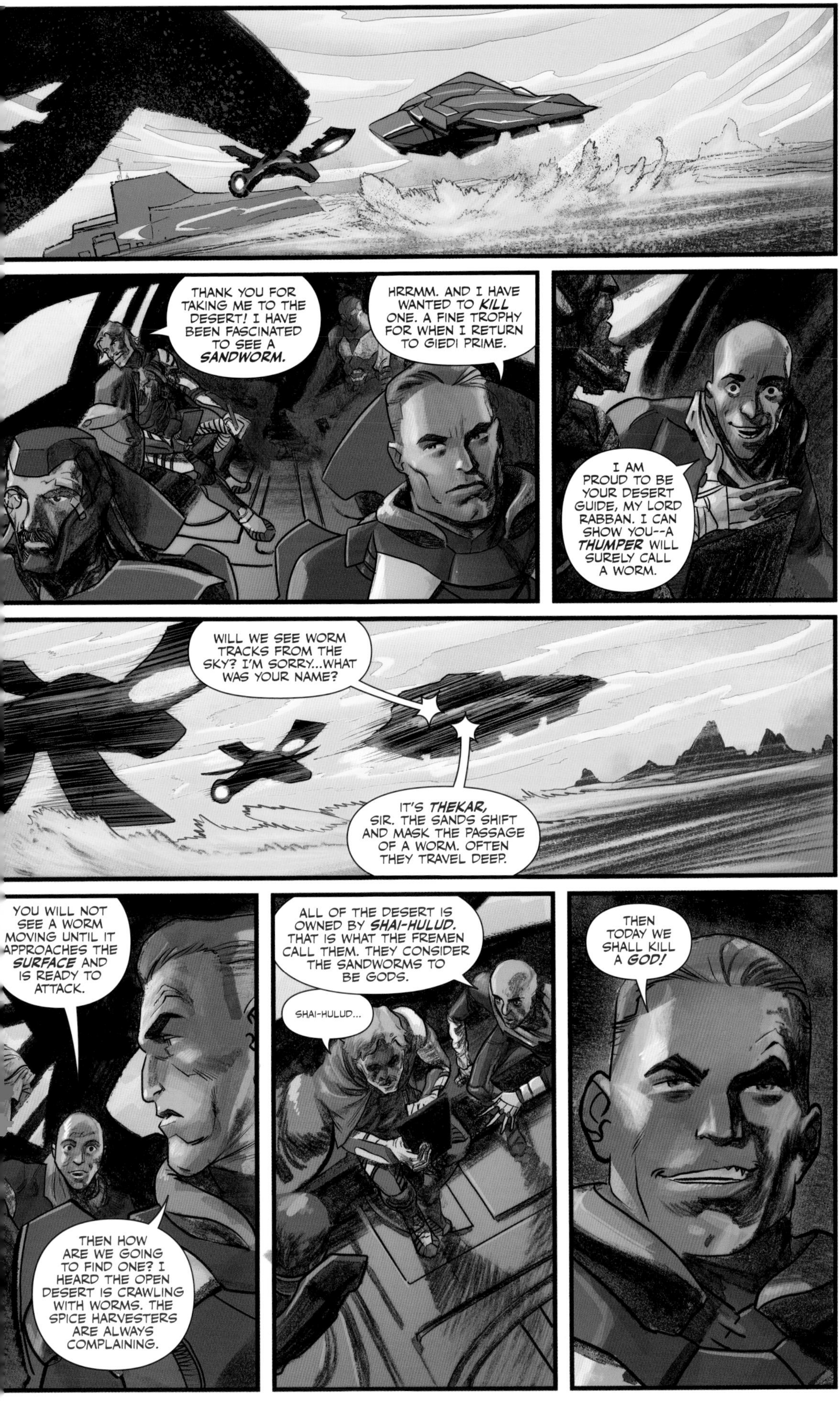
THANK YOU FOR TAKING ME TO THE DESERT! I HAVE BEEN FASCINATED TO SEE A SANDWORM.
HRRMM. AND I HAVE WANTED TO KILL ONE. A FINE TROPHY FOR WHEN I RETURN TO GIEDI PRIME.
I AM PROUD TO BE YOUR DESERT GUIDE, MY LORD RABBAN. I CAN SHOW YOU--A THUMPER WILL SURELY CALL A WORM.
WILL WE SEE WORM TRACKS FROM THE SKY? I'M SORRY...WHAT WAS YOUR NAME?
IT'S THEKAR, SIR. THE SANDS SHIFT AND MASK THE PASSAGE OF A WORM. OFTEN THEY TRAVEL DEEP.
YOU WILL NOT SEE A WORM MOVING UNTIL IT APPROACHES THE SURFACE AND IS READY TO ATTACK.
THEN HOW ARE WE GOING TO FIND ONE? I HEARD THE OPEN DESERT IS CRAWLING WITH WORMS. THE SPICE HARVESTERS ARE ALWAYS COMPLAINING.
ALL OF THE DESERT IS OWNED BY SHAI-HULUD. THAT IS WHAT THE FREMEN CALL THEM. THEY CONSIDER THE SANDWORMS TO BE GODS.
SHAI-HULUD...
THEN TODAY WE SHALL KILL A GOD!

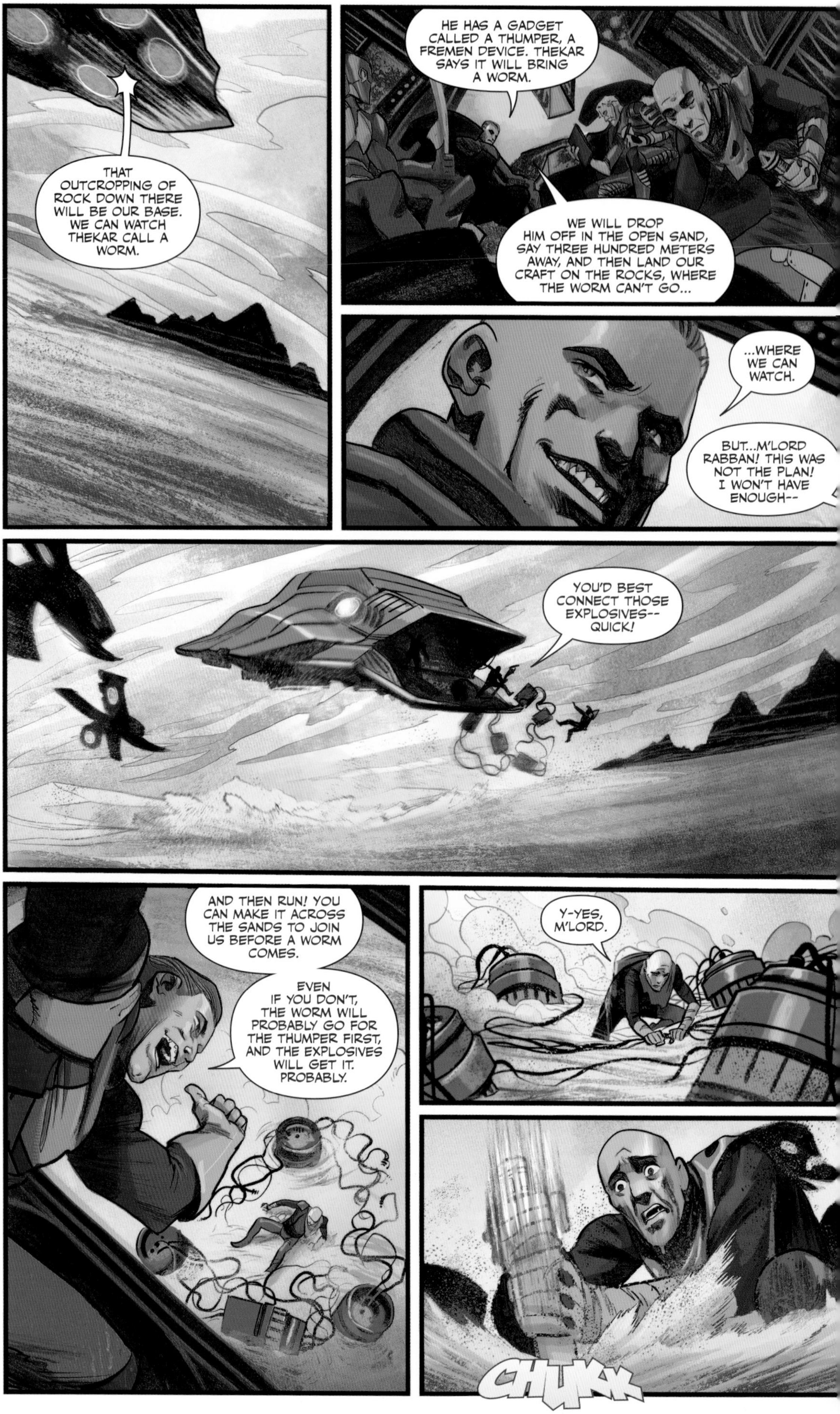
THAT OUTCROPPING OF ROCK DOWN THERE WILL BE OUR BASE. WE CAN WATCH THEKAR CALL A WORM.
HE HAS A GADGET CALLED A THUMPER, A FREMEN DEVICE. THEKAR SAYS IT WILL BRING A WORM.
WE WILL DROP HIM OFF IN THE OPEN SAND, SAY THREE HUNDRED METERS AWAY, AND THEN LAND OUR CRAFT ON THE ROCKS, WHERE THE WORM CAN'T GO...
...WHERE WE CAN WATCH.
BUT...M'LORD RABBAN! THIS WAS NOT THE PLAN! I WON'T HAVE ENOUGH--
YOU'D BEST CONNECT THOSE EXPLOSIVES-- QUICK!
AND THEN RUN! YOU CAN MAKE IT ACROSS THE SANDS TO JOIN US BEFORE A WORM COMES.
EVEN IF YOU DON'T, THE WORM WILL PROBABLY GO FOR THE THUMPER FIRST, AND THE EXPLOSIVES WILL GET IT. PROBABLY.
Y-YES, M'LORD.
CHUKK

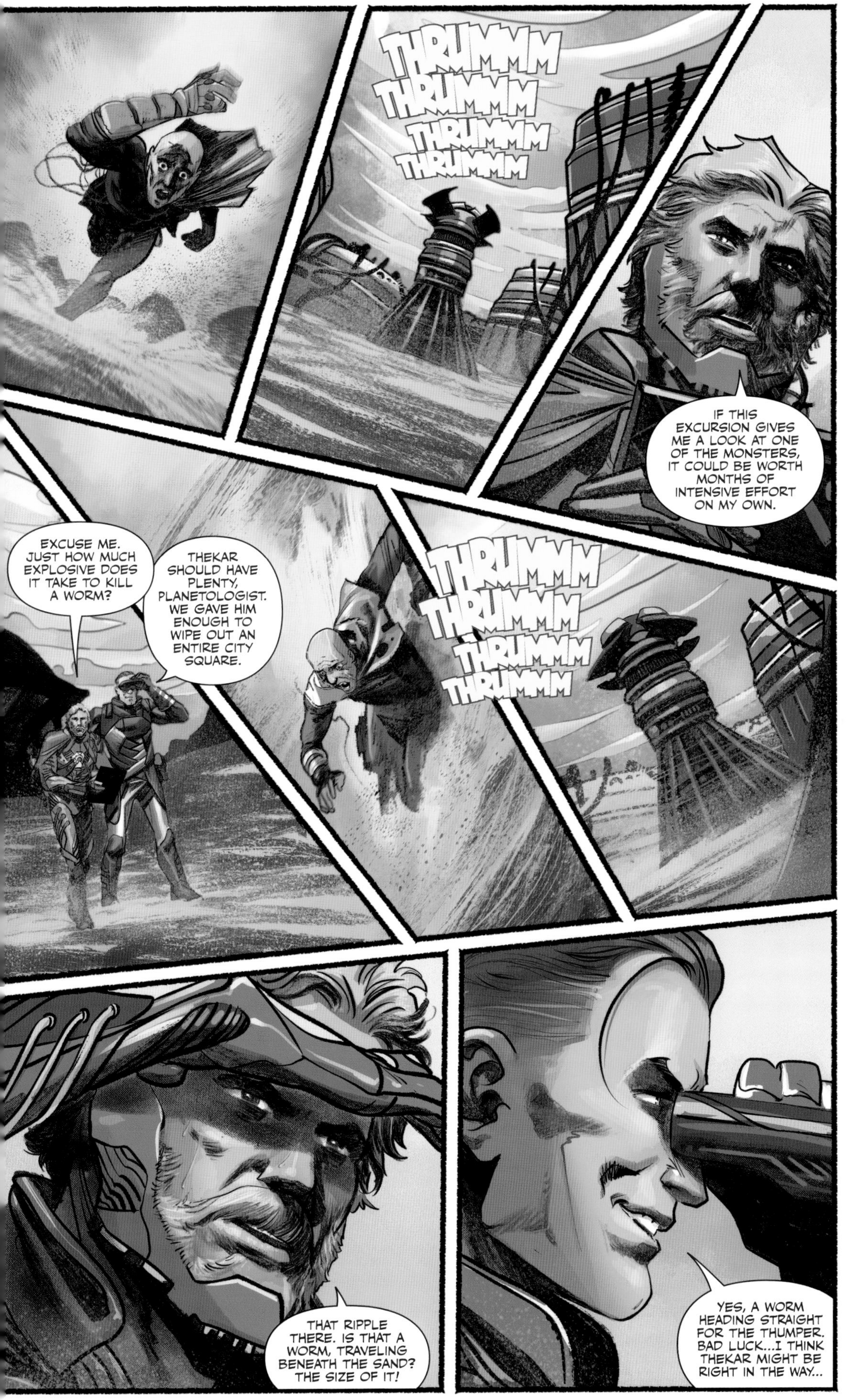
THRUMMM
THRUMMM
THRUMMM
THRUMMM
IF THIS EXCURSION GIVES ME A LOOK AT ONE OF THE MONSTERS, IT COULD BE WORTH MONTHS OF INTENSIVE EFFORT ON MY OWN.
EXCUSE ME. JUST HOW MUCH EXPLOSIVE DOES IT TAKE TO KILL A WORM?
THEKAR SHOULD HAVE PLENTY, PLANETOLOGIST. WE GAVE HIM ENOUGH TO WIPE OUT AN ENTIRE CITY SQUARE.
THRUMMM
THRUMMM
THRUMMM
THRUMMM
THAT RIPPLE THERE. IS THAT A WORM, TRAVELING BENEATH THE SAND? THE SIZE OF IT!
YES, A WORM HEADING STRAIGHT FOR THE THUMPER. BAD LUCK...I THINK THEKAR MIGHT BE RIGHT IN THE WAY...

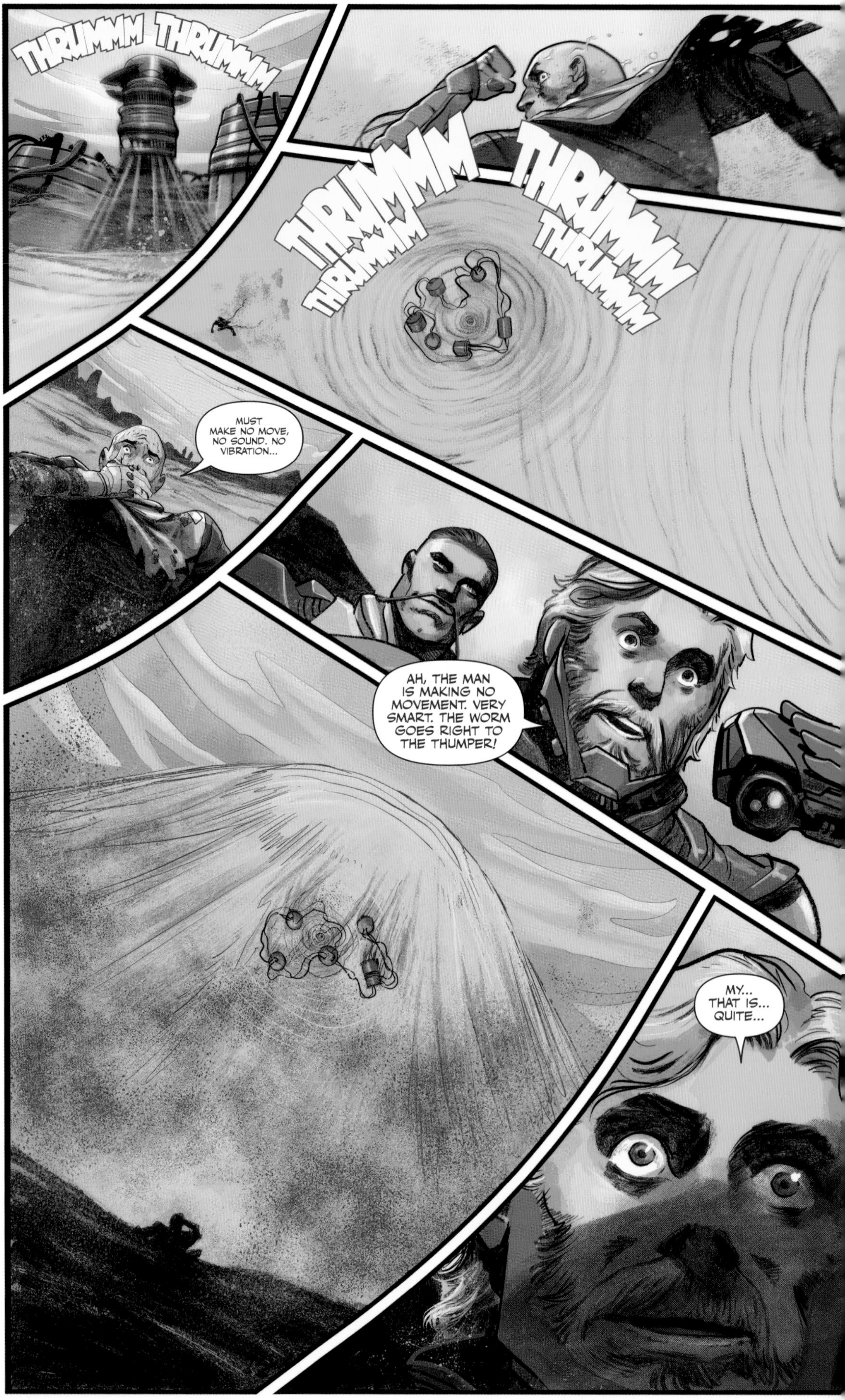
THRUMMM THRUMMM
THRUMMM THRUMMM
THRUMMM THRUMMM
MUST MAKE NO MOVE, NO SOUND. NO VIBRATION...
AH, THE MAN IS MAKING NO MOVEMENT. VERY SMART. THE WORM GOES RIGHT TO THE THUMPER!
MY... THAT IS... QUITE...

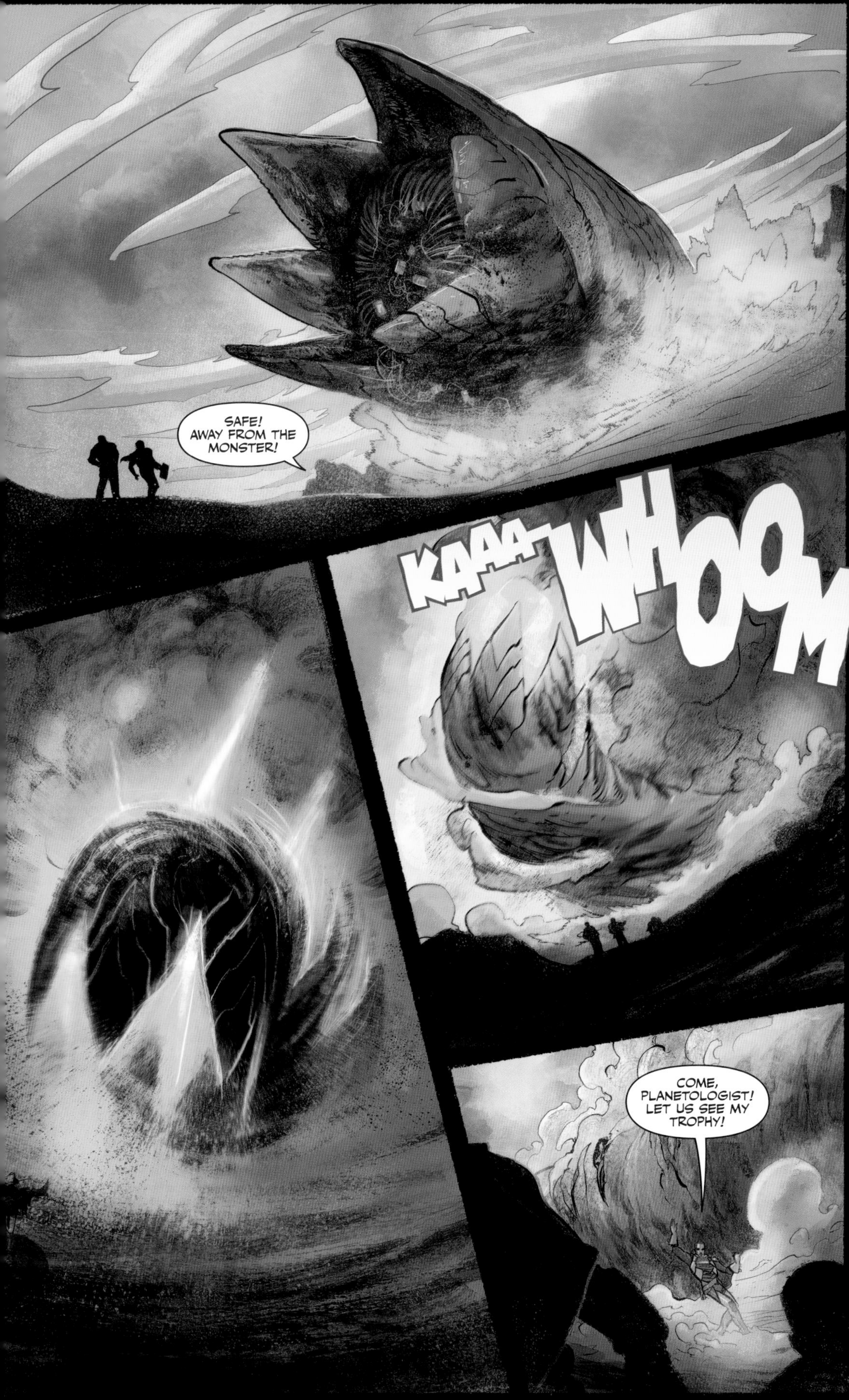
SAFE! AWAY FROM THE MONSTER!
KAAA-WHOOM
COME, PLANETOLOGIST! LET US SEE MY TROPHY!

NOW THERE'S A TROPHY, PLANETOLOGIST! MORE THAN TWO HUNDRED METERS LONG! I'LL TAKE IT WITH ME WHEN I RETURN TO GIEDI PRIME.

THIS IS AN ANCIENT ONE, M'LORD RABBAN. SHAI-HULUD.

A FASCINATING SPECIMEN. NEVER EXPECTED TO HAVE A CHANCE TO SEE A SANDWORM SO CLOSE.

BUT... IT APPEARS TO BE DISASSOCIATING, SOMEHOW.

WHAT?!

ACCELERATED DECAY...OR, NO--BREAKING INTO COMPONENT ORGANISMS?

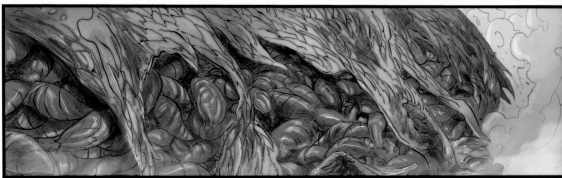

NOOOOOO! MY TROPHY!

LIKE LARGE CELLULAR STRUCTURES... OR SOME LARVAL PHASE...

WHEN I RETURN TO GIEDI PRIME, I'LL HUNT SOMETHING MUCH MORE SATISFYING.

THWOK

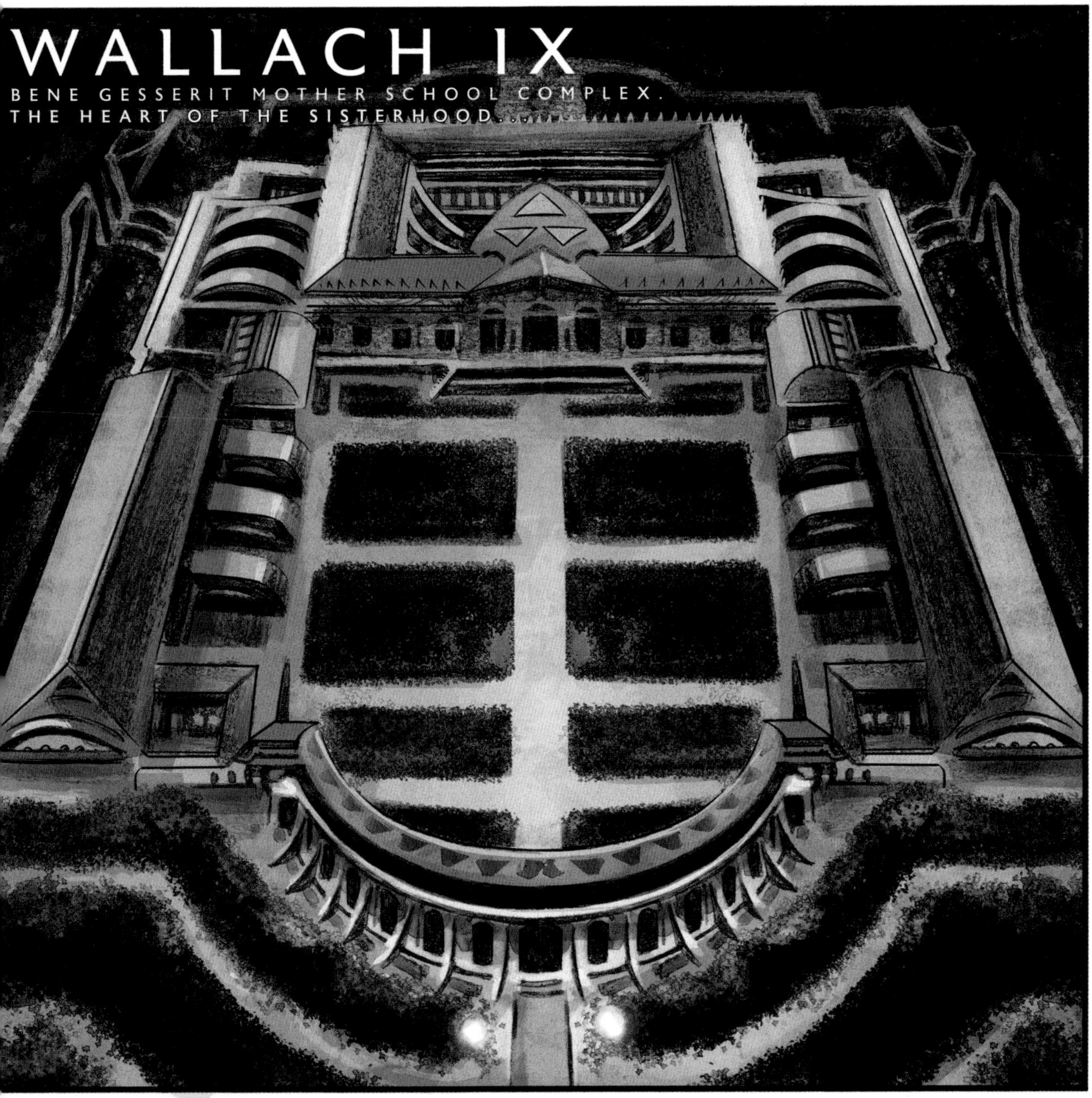
WALLACH IX
BENE GESSERIT MOTHER SCHOOL COMPLEX.
THE HEART OF THE SISTERHOOD...

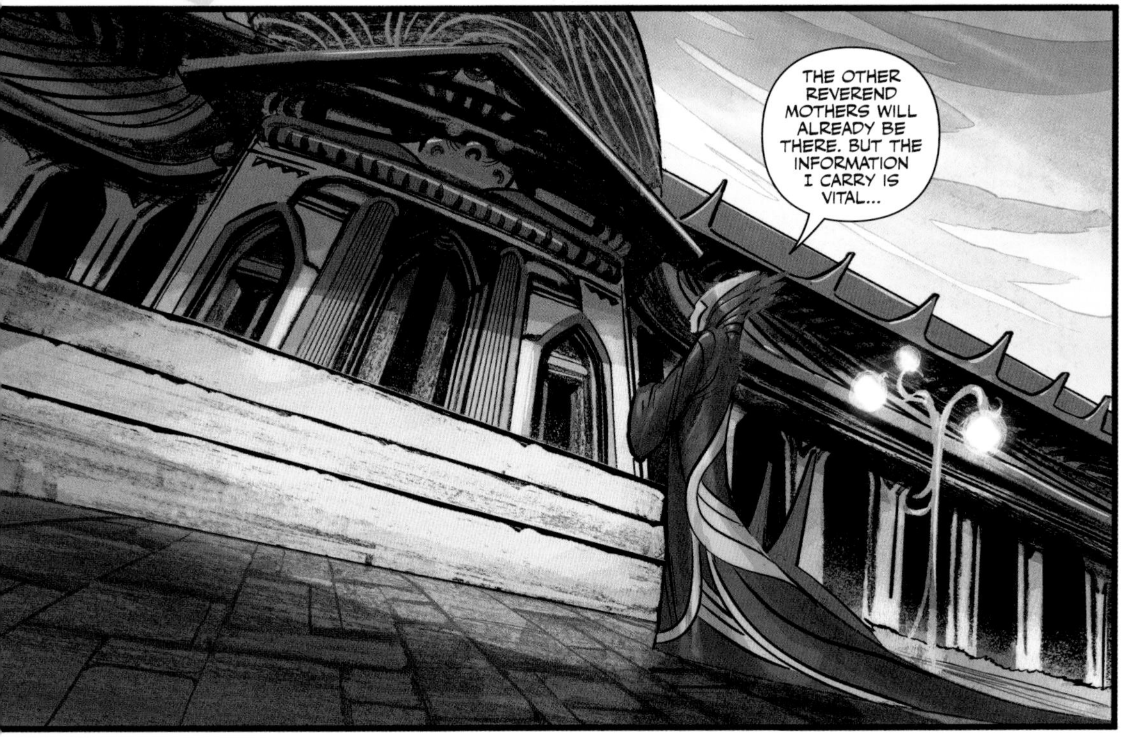
THE OTHER REVEREND MOTHERS WILL ALREADY BE THERE. BUT THE INFORMATION I CARRY IS VITAL...

NO ONE KNOWS THE PROJECTIONS YET.

THOUSANDS OF YEARS OF GENETIC CALCULATIONS, PLANNING, WAITING...DEAD ENDS.

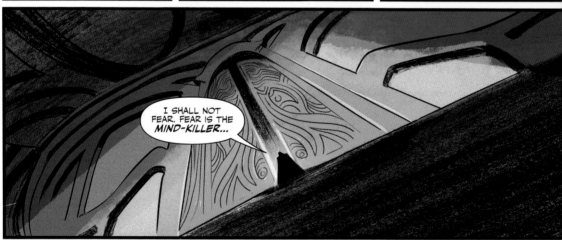

I SHALL NOT FEAR. FEAR IS THE *MIND-KILLER*...

I AM HERE. I HAVE BROUGHT THE PROJECTIONS YOU REQUESTED, MOTHER SUPERIOR HARISHKA.

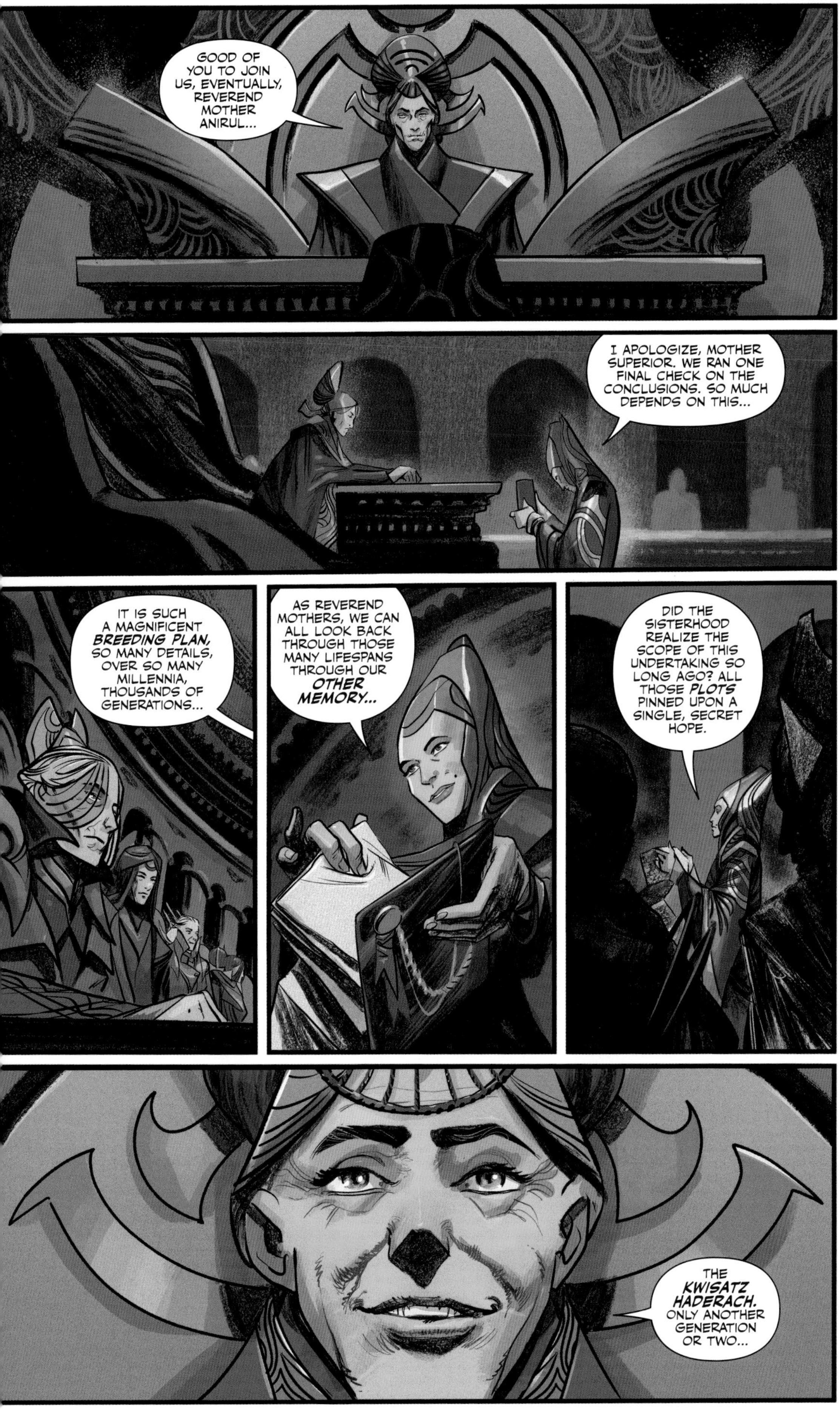
GOOD OF YOU TO JOIN US, EVENTUALLY, REVEREND MOTHER ANIRUL...
I APOLOGIZE, MOTHER SUPERIOR. WE RAN ONE FINAL CHECK ON THE CONCLUSIONS. SO MUCH DEPENDS ON THIS...
IT IS SUCH A MAGNIFICENT *BREEDING PLAN,* SO MANY DETAILS, OVER SO MANY MILLENNIA, THOUSANDS OF GENERATIONS...
AS REVEREND MOTHERS, WE CAN ALL LOOK BACK THROUGH THOSE MANY LIFESPANS THROUGH OUR *OTHER MEMORY...*
DID THE SISTERHOOD REALIZE THE SCOPE OF THIS UNDERTAKING SO LONG AGO? ALL THOSE *PLOTS* PINNED UPON A SINGLE, SECRET HOPE.
THE *KWISATZ HADERACH.* ONLY ANOTHER GENERATION OR TWO...

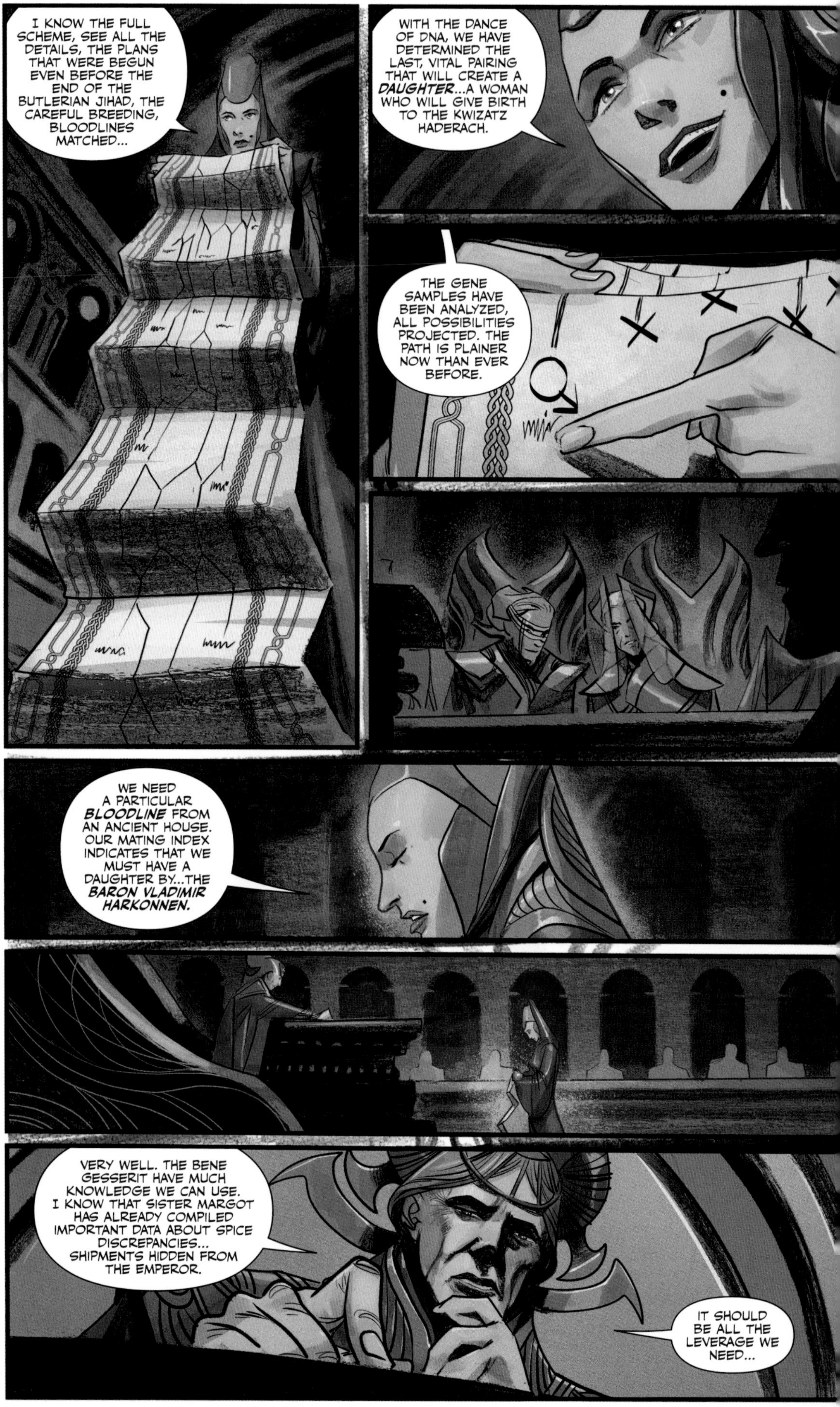
I KNOW THE FULL SCHEME, SEE ALL THE DETAILS, THE PLANS THAT WERE BEGUN EVEN BEFORE THE END OF THE BUTLERIAN JIHAD, THE CAREFUL BREEDING, BLOODLINES MATCHED...
WITH THE DANCE OF DNA, WE HAVE DETERMINED THE LAST, VITAL PAIRING THAT WILL CREATE A DAUGHTER...A WOMAN WHO WILL GIVE BIRTH TO THE KWIZATZ HADERACH.
THE GENE SAMPLES HAVE BEEN ANALYZED, ALL POSSIBILITIES PROJECTED. THE PATH IS PLAINER NOW THAN EVER BEFORE.
WE NEED A PARTICULAR BLOODLINE FROM AN ANCIENT HOUSE. OUR MATING INDEX INDICATES THAT WE MUST HAVE A DAUGHTER BY...THE BARON VLADIMIR HARKONNEN.
VERY WELL. THE BENE GESSERIT HAVE MUCH KNOWLEDGE WE CAN USE. I KNOW THAT SISTER MARGOT HAS ALREADY COMPILED IMPORTANT DATA ABOUT SPICE DISCREPANCIES... SHIPMENTS HIDDEN FROM THE EMPEROR.
IT SHOULD BE ALL THE LEVERAGE WE NEED...

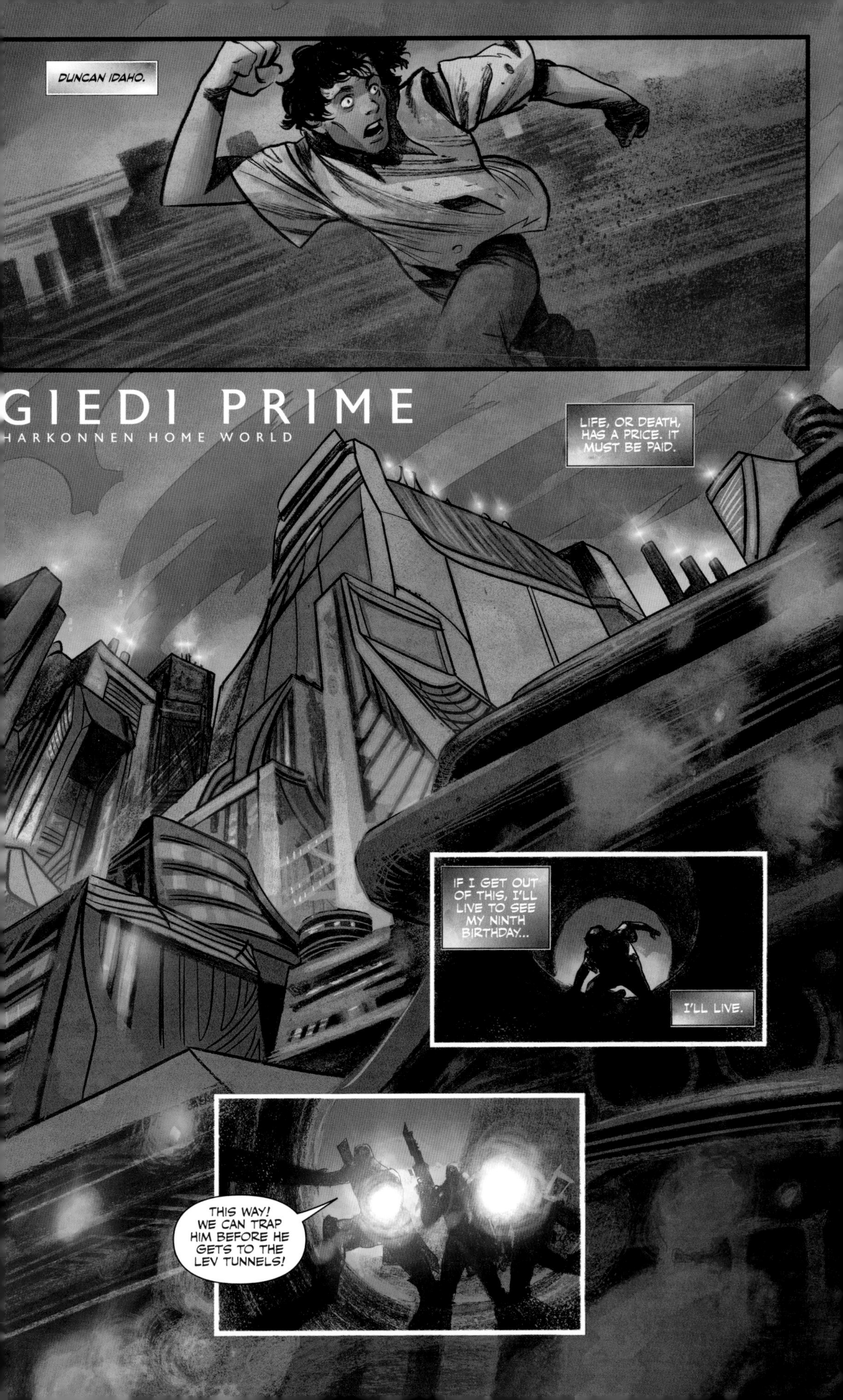
DUNCAN IDAHO.
GIEDI PRIME
HARKONNEN HOME WORLD
LIFE, OR DEATH, HAS A PRICE. IT MUST BE PAID.
IF I GET OUT OF THIS, I'LL LIVE TO SEE MY NINTH BIRTHDAY...
I'LL LIVE.
THIS WAY! WE CAN TRAP HIM BEFORE HE GETS TO THE LEV TUNNELS!

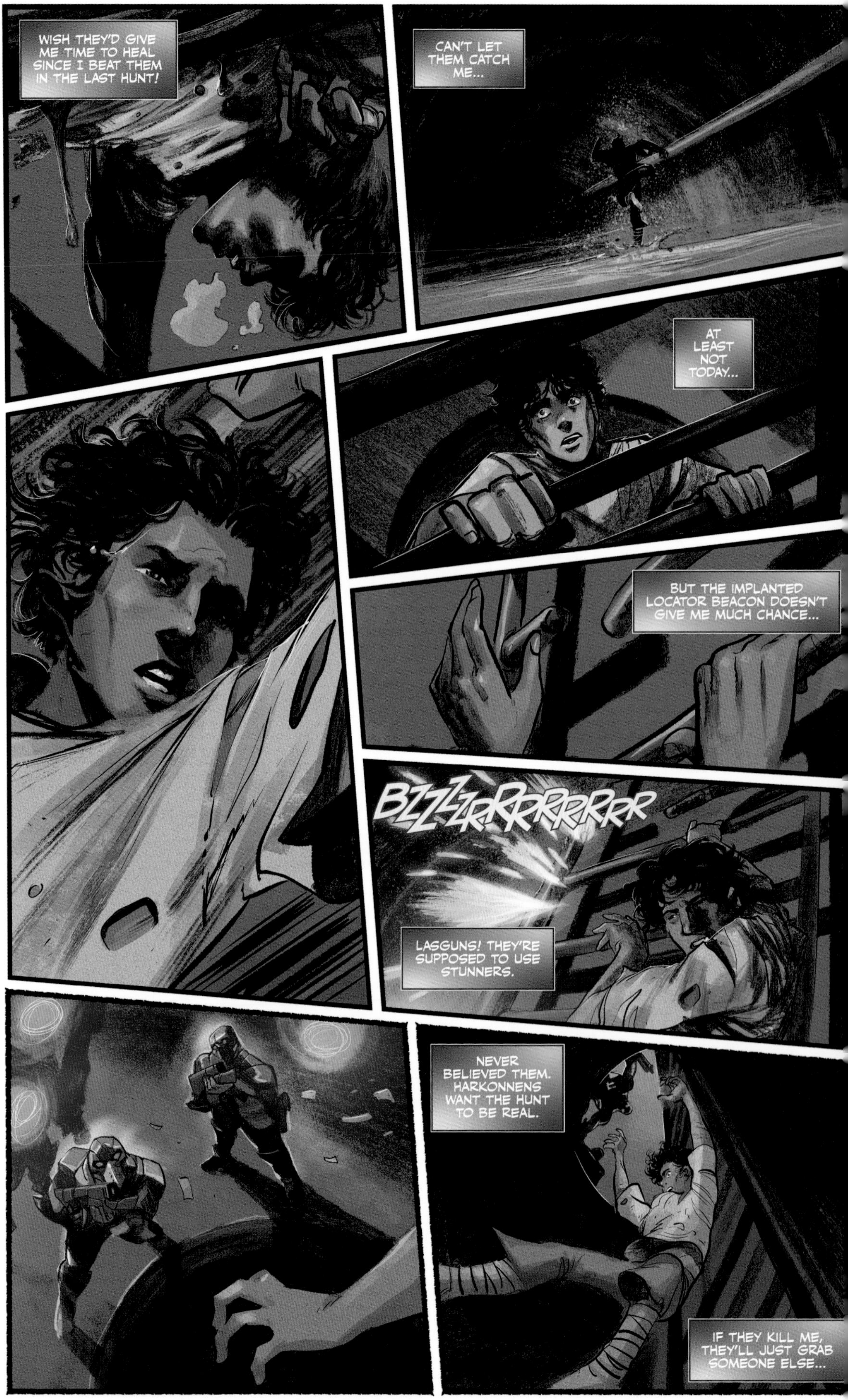
WISH THEY'D GIVE ME TIME TO HEAL SINCE I BEAT THEM IN THE LAST HUNT!
CAN'T LET THEM CATCH ME...
AT LEAST NOT TODAY...
BUT THE IMPLANTED LOCATOR BEACON DOESN'T GIVE ME MUCH CHANCE...
BZZZZRRRRRRRRR
LASGUNS! THEY'RE SUPPOSED TO USE STUNNERS.
NEVER BELIEVED THEM. HARKONNENS WANT THE HUNT TO BE REAL.
IF THEY KILL ME, THEY'LL JUST GRAB SOMEONE ELSE...

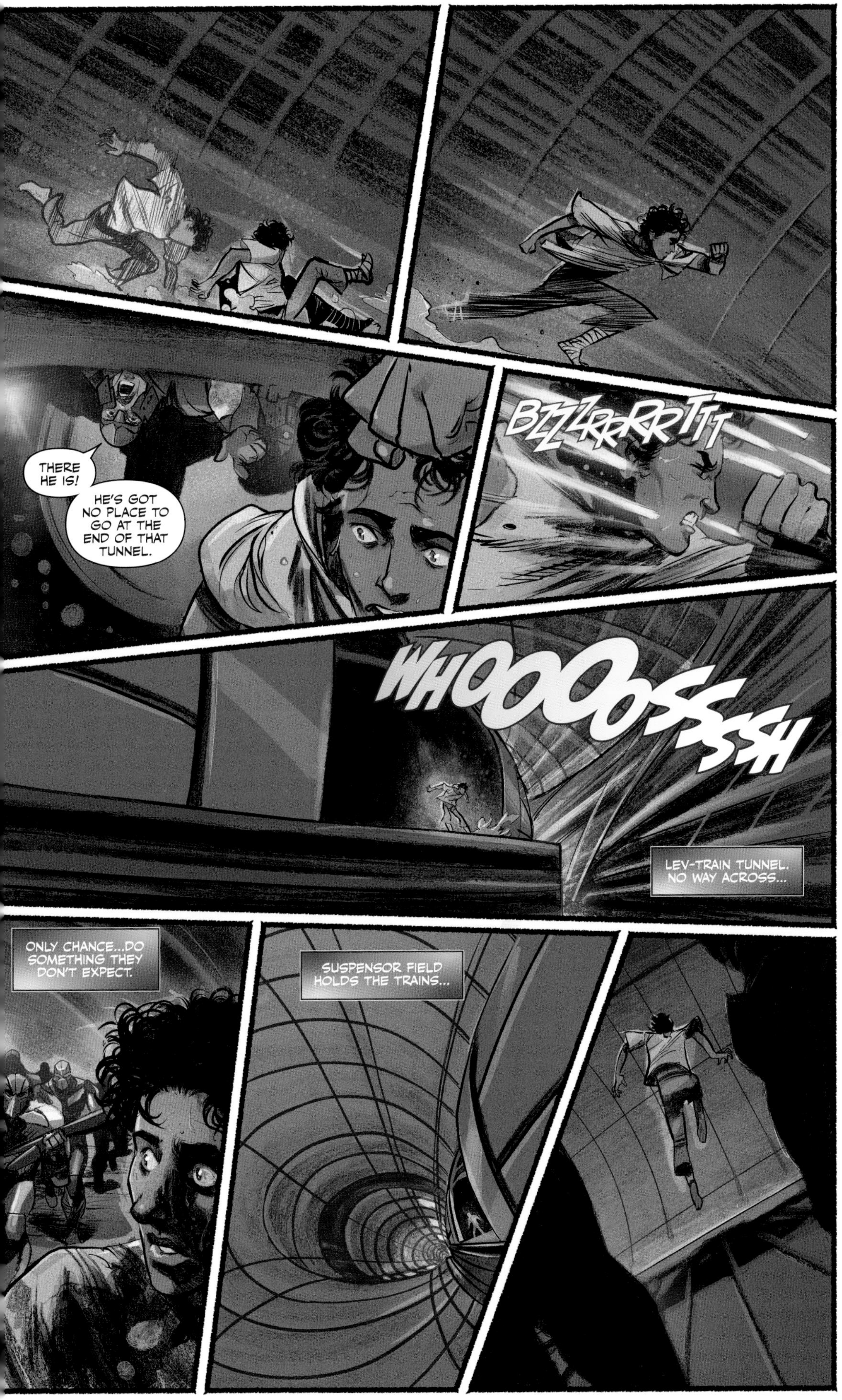
THERE HE IS!
HE'S GOT NO PLACE TO GO AT THE END OF THAT TUNNEL.
BZZZRRRRRTTT
WHOOOOSSSH
LEV-TRAIN TUNNEL. NO WAY ACROSS...
ONLY CHANCE...DO SOMETHING THEY DON'T EXPECT.
SUSPENSOR FIELD HOLDS THE TRAINS...

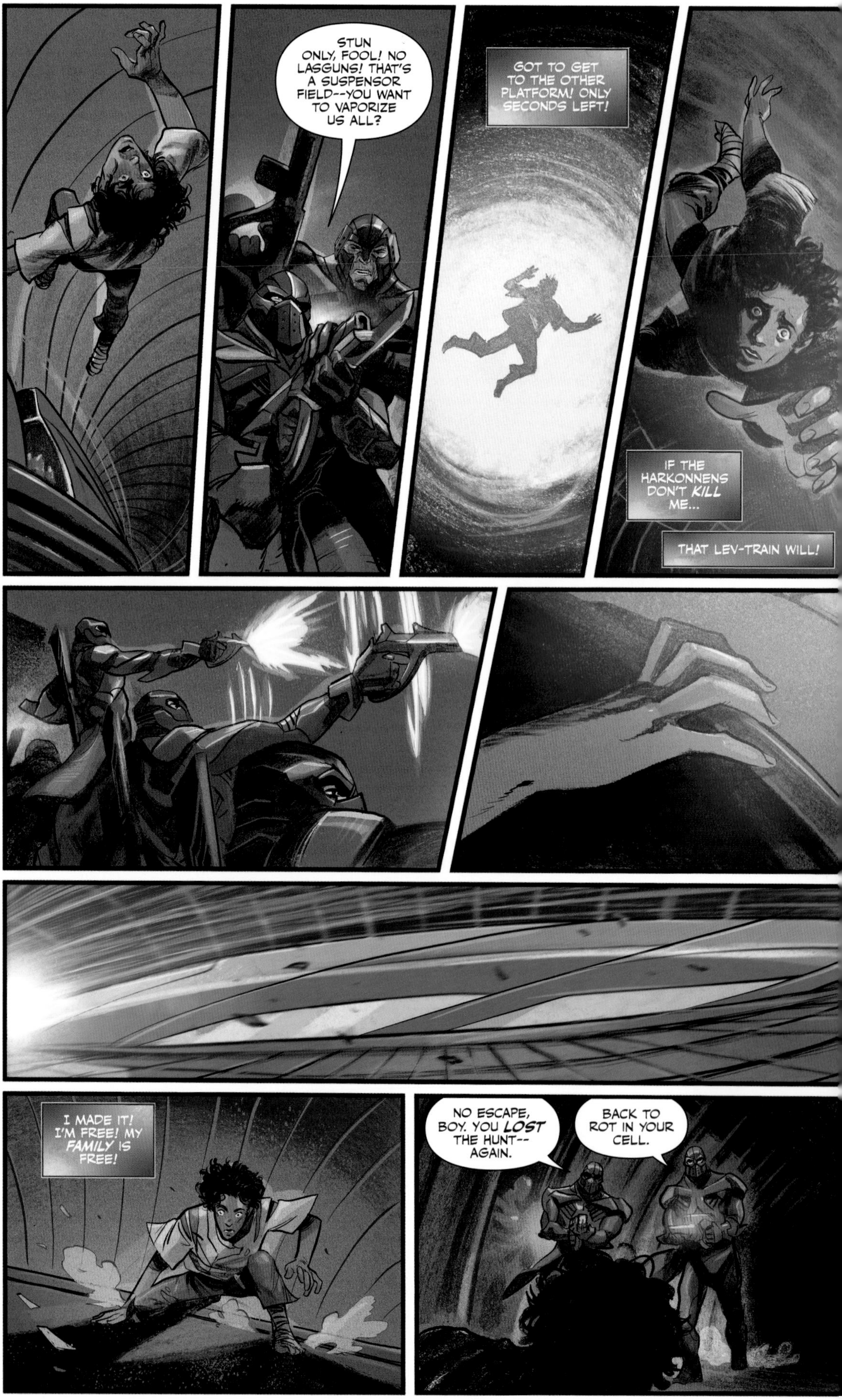
STUN ONLY, FOOL! NO LASGUNS! THAT'S A SUSPENSOR FIELD--YOU WANT TO VAPORIZE US ALL?
GOT TO GET TO THE OTHER PLATFORM! ONLY SECONDS LEFT!
IF THE HARKONNENS DON'T KILL ME...
THAT LEV-TRAIN WILL!
I MADE IT! I'M FREE! MY FAMILY IS FREE!
NO ESCAPE, BOY. YOU LOST THE HUNT-- AGAIN.
BACK TO ROT IN YOUR CELL.

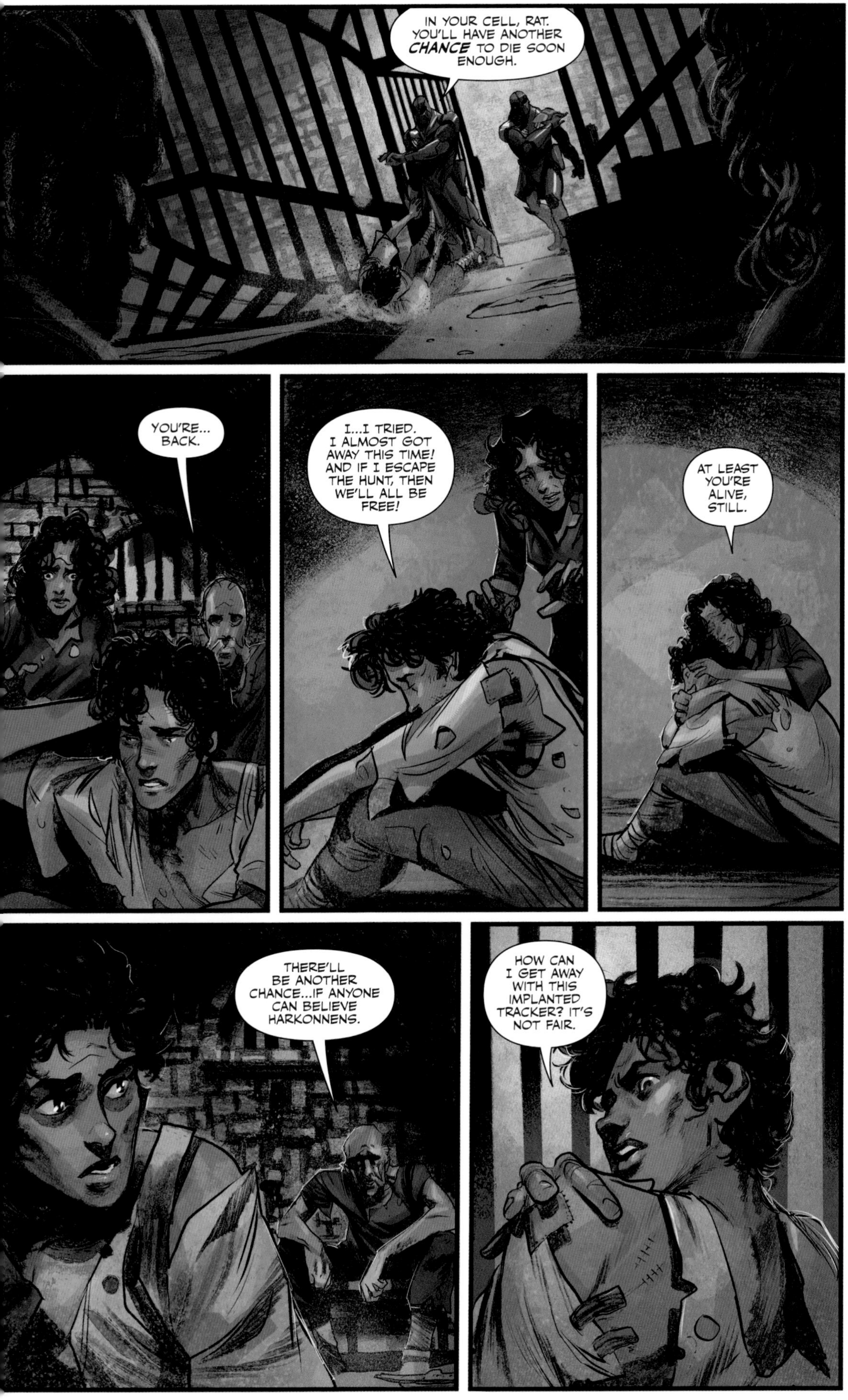
IN YOUR CELL, RAT. YOU'LL HAVE ANOTHER *CHANCE* TO DIE SOON ENOUGH.
YOU'RE... BACK.
I...I TRIED. I ALMOST GOT AWAY THIS TIME! AND IF I ESCAPE THE HUNT, THEN WE'LL ALL BE FREE!
AT LEAST YOU'RE ALIVE, STILL.
THERE'LL BE ANOTHER CHANCE...IF ANYONE CAN BELIEVE HARKONNENS.
HOW CAN I GET AWAY WITH THIS IMPLANTED TRACKER? IT'S NOT FAIR.

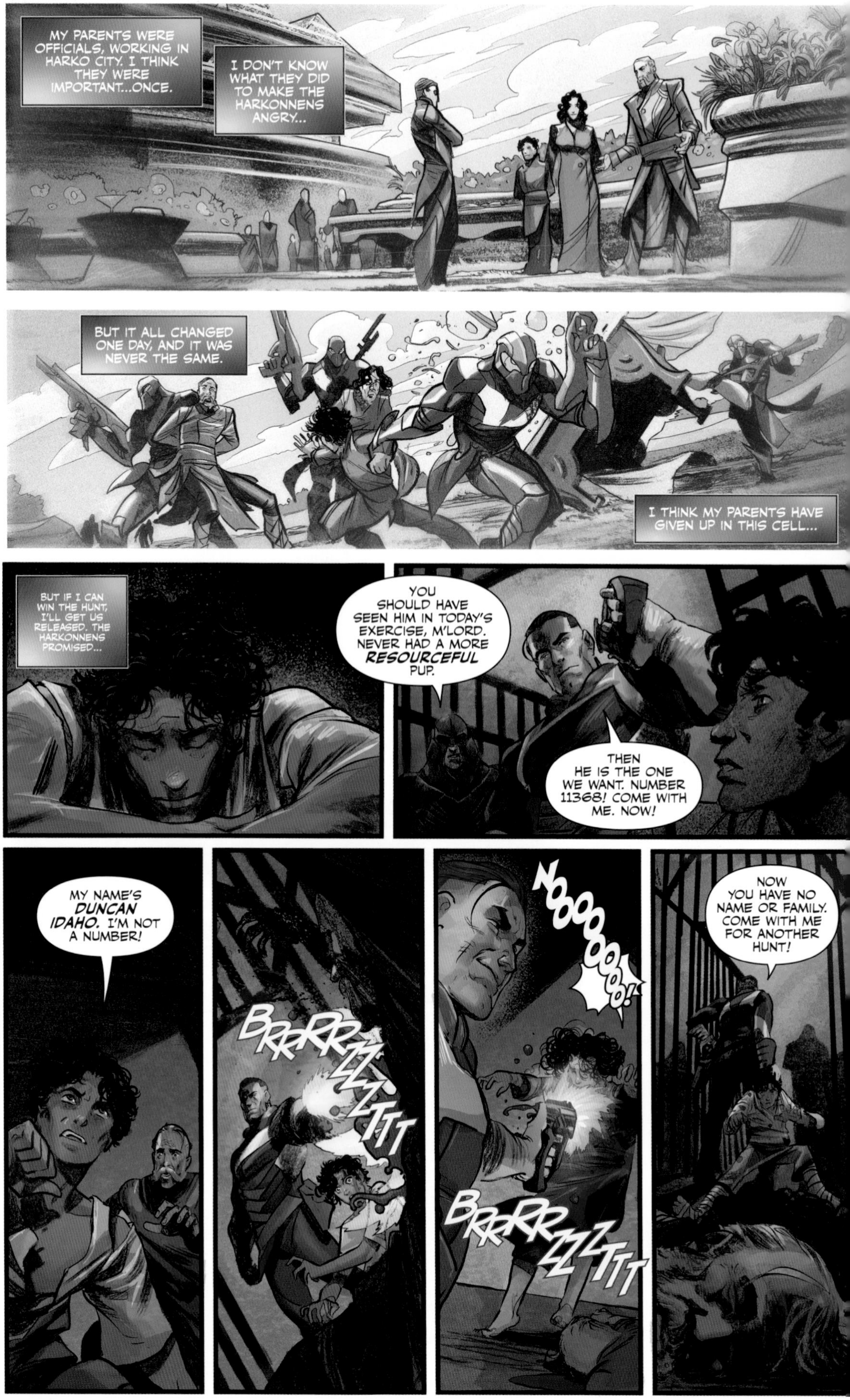
MY PARENTS WERE OFFICIALS, WORKING IN HARKO CITY. I THINK THEY WERE IMPORTANT...ONCE.
I DON'T KNOW WHAT THEY DID TO MAKE THE HARKONNENS ANGRY...
BUT IT ALL CHANGED ONE DAY, AND IT WAS NEVER THE SAME.
I THINK MY PARENTS HAVE GIVEN UP IN THIS CELL...
BUT IF I CAN WIN THE HUNT, I'LL GET US RELEASED. THE HARKONNENS PROMISED...
YOU SHOULD HAVE SEEN HIM IN TODAY'S EXERCISE, M'LORD. NEVER HAD A MORE RESOURCEFUL PUP.
THEN HE IS THE ONE WE WANT. NUMBER 11368! COME WITH ME. NOW!
MY NAME'S DUNCAN IDAHO. I'M NOT A NUMBER!
BRRRRZZZTTT
NOOOOOOO!
BRRRRZZZTTT
NOW YOU HAVE NO NAME OR FAMILY. COME WITH ME FOR ANOTHER HUNT!

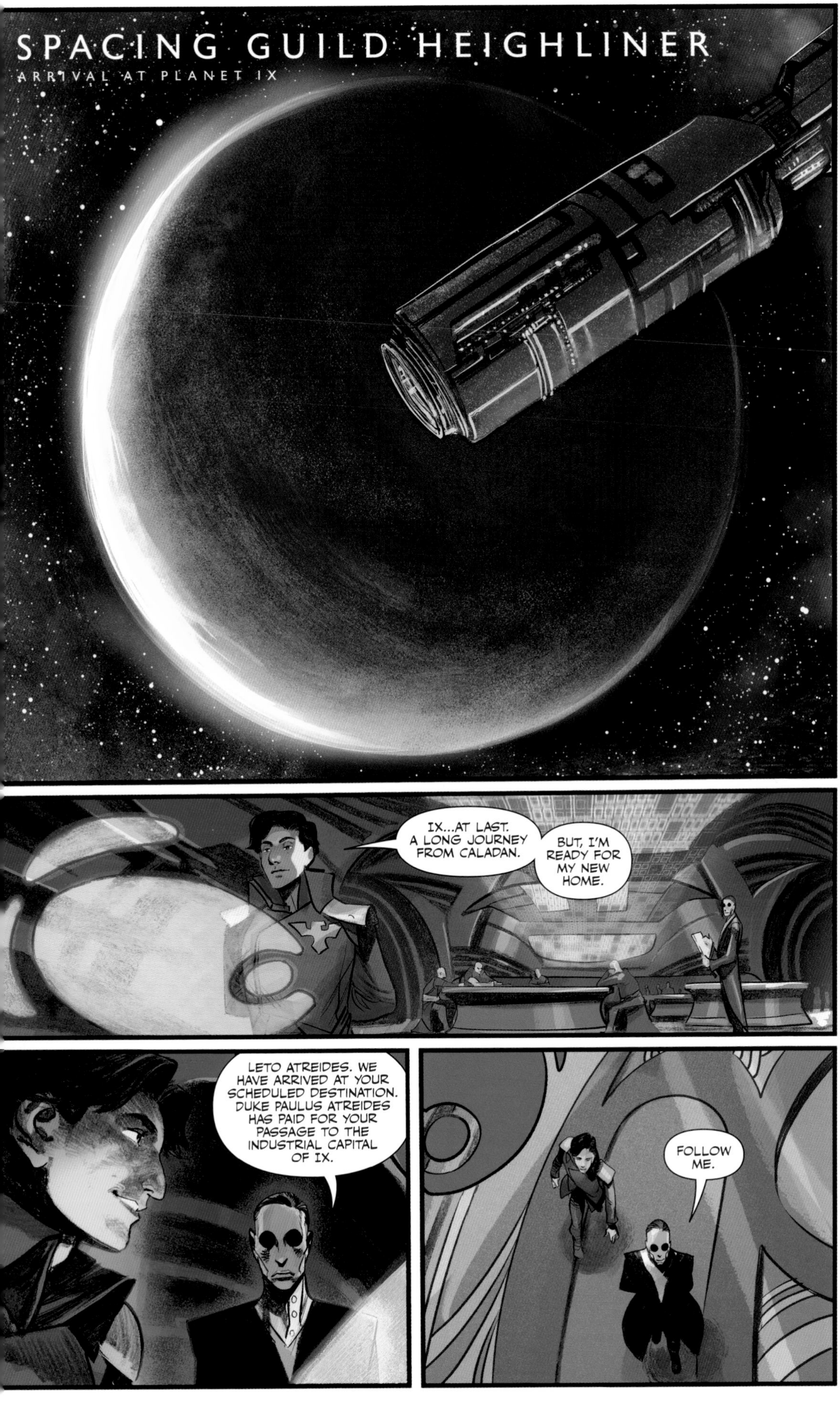
SPACING GUILD HEIGHLINER
ARRIVAL AT PLANET IX
IX...AT LAST. A LONG JOURNEY FROM CALADAN.
BUT, I'M READY FOR MY NEW HOME.
LETO ATREIDES. WE HAVE ARRIVED AT YOUR SCHEDULED DESTINATION. DUKE PAULUS ATREIDES HAS PAID FOR YOUR PASSAGE TO THE INDUSTRIAL CAPITAL OF IX.
FOLLOW ME.

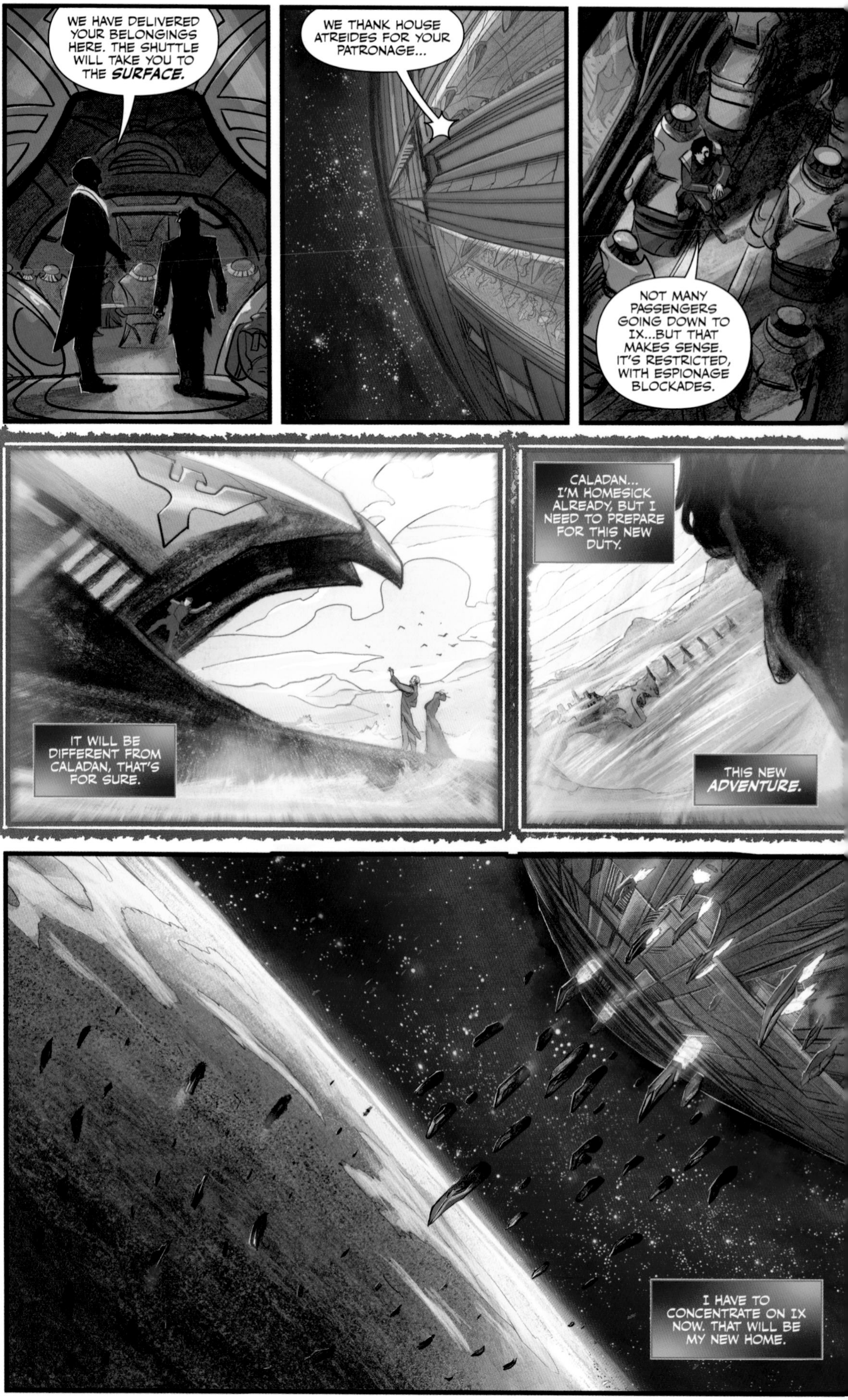
WE HAVE DELIVERED YOUR BELONGINGS HERE. THE SHUTTLE WILL TAKE YOU TO THE *SURFACE.*
WE THANK HOUSE ATREIDES FOR YOUR PATRONAGE...
NOT MANY PASSENGERS GOING DOWN TO IX...BUT THAT MAKES SENSE. IT'S RESTRICTED, WITH ESPIONAGE BLOCKADES.
IT WILL BE DIFFERENT FROM CALADAN, THAT'S FOR SURE.
CALADAN... I'M HOMESICK ALREADY, BUT I NEED TO PREPARE FOR THIS NEW DUTY.
THIS NEW *ADVENTURE.*
I HAVE TO CONCENTRATE ON IX NOW. THAT WILL BE MY NEW HOME.

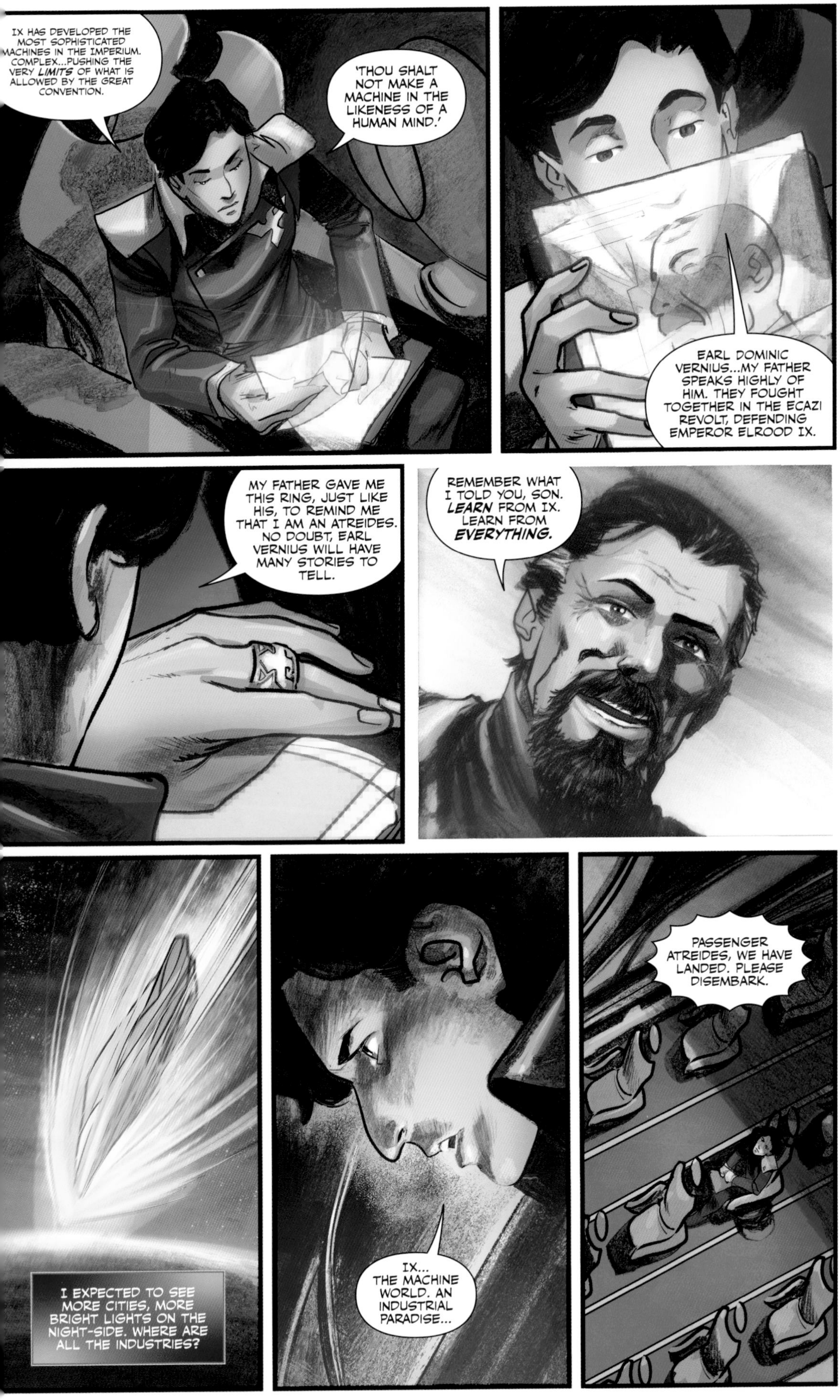
IX HAS DEVELOPED THE MOST SOPHISTICATED MACHINES IN THE IMPERIUM. COMPLEX...PUSHING THE VERY LIMITS OF WHAT IS ALLOWED BY THE GREAT CONVENTION.
'THOU SHALT NOT MAKE A MACHINE IN THE LIKENESS OF A HUMAN MIND.'
EARL DOMINIC VERNIUS...MY FATHER SPEAKS HIGHLY OF HIM. THEY FOUGHT TOGETHER IN THE ECAZI REVOLT, DEFENDING EMPEROR ELROOD IX.
MY FATHER GAVE ME THIS RING, JUST LIKE HIS, TO REMIND ME THAT I AM AN ATREIDES. NO DOUBT, EARL VERNIUS WILL HAVE MANY STORIES TO TELL.
REMEMBER WHAT I TOLD YOU, SON. LEARN FROM IX. LEARN FROM EVERYTHING.
I EXPECTED TO SEE MORE CITIES, MORE BRIGHT LIGHTS ON THE NIGHT-SIDE. WHERE ARE ALL THE INDUSTRIES?
IX... THE MACHINE WORLD. AN INDUSTRIAL PARADISE...
PASSENGER ATREIDES, WE HAVE LANDED. PLEASE DISEMBARK.

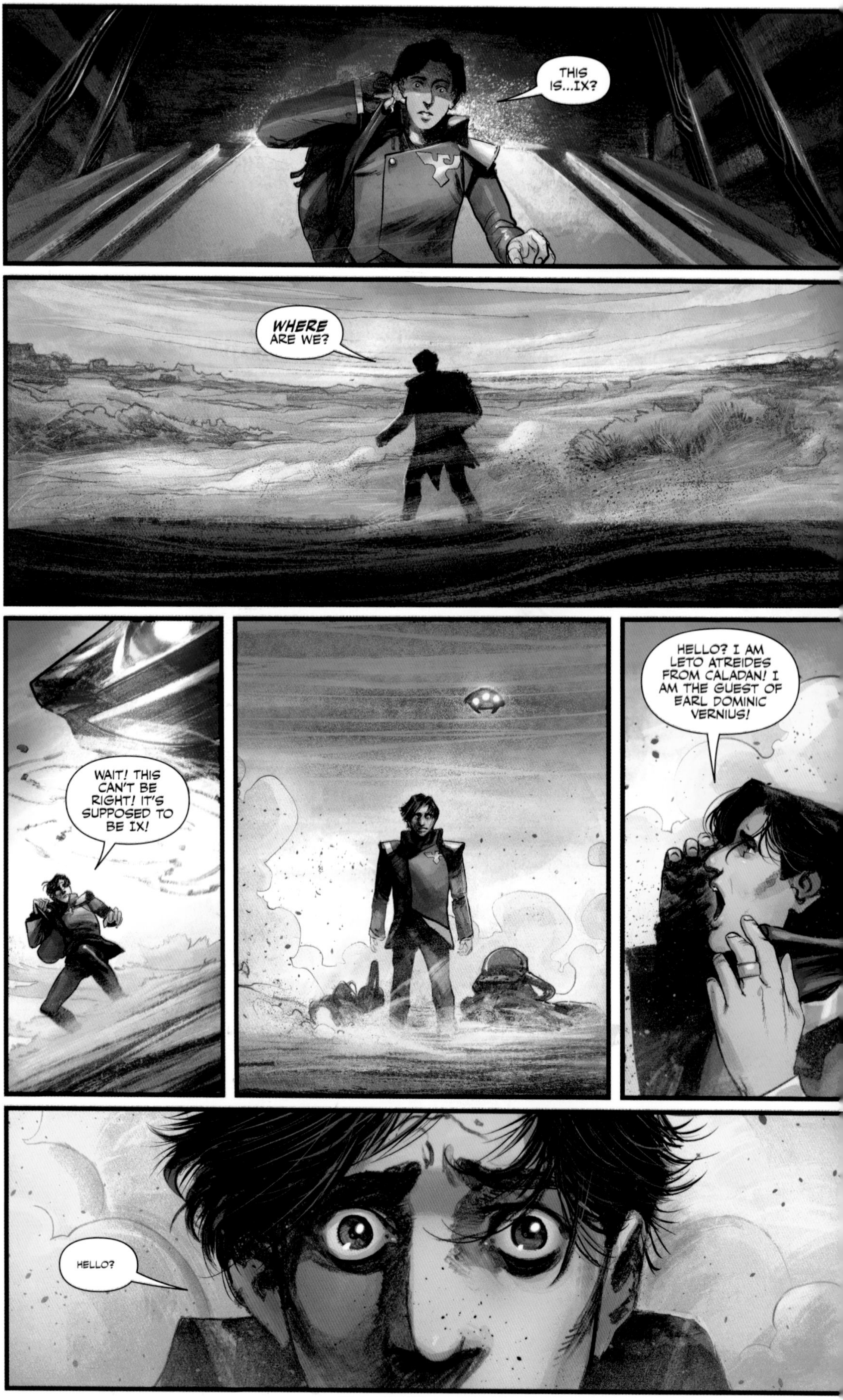
THIS IS...IX?
WHERE ARE WE?
WAIT! THIS CAN'T BE RIGHT! IT'S SUPPOSED TO BE IX!
HELLO? I AM LETO ATREIDES FROM CALADAN! I AM THE GUEST OF EARL DOMINIC VERNIUS!
HELLO?

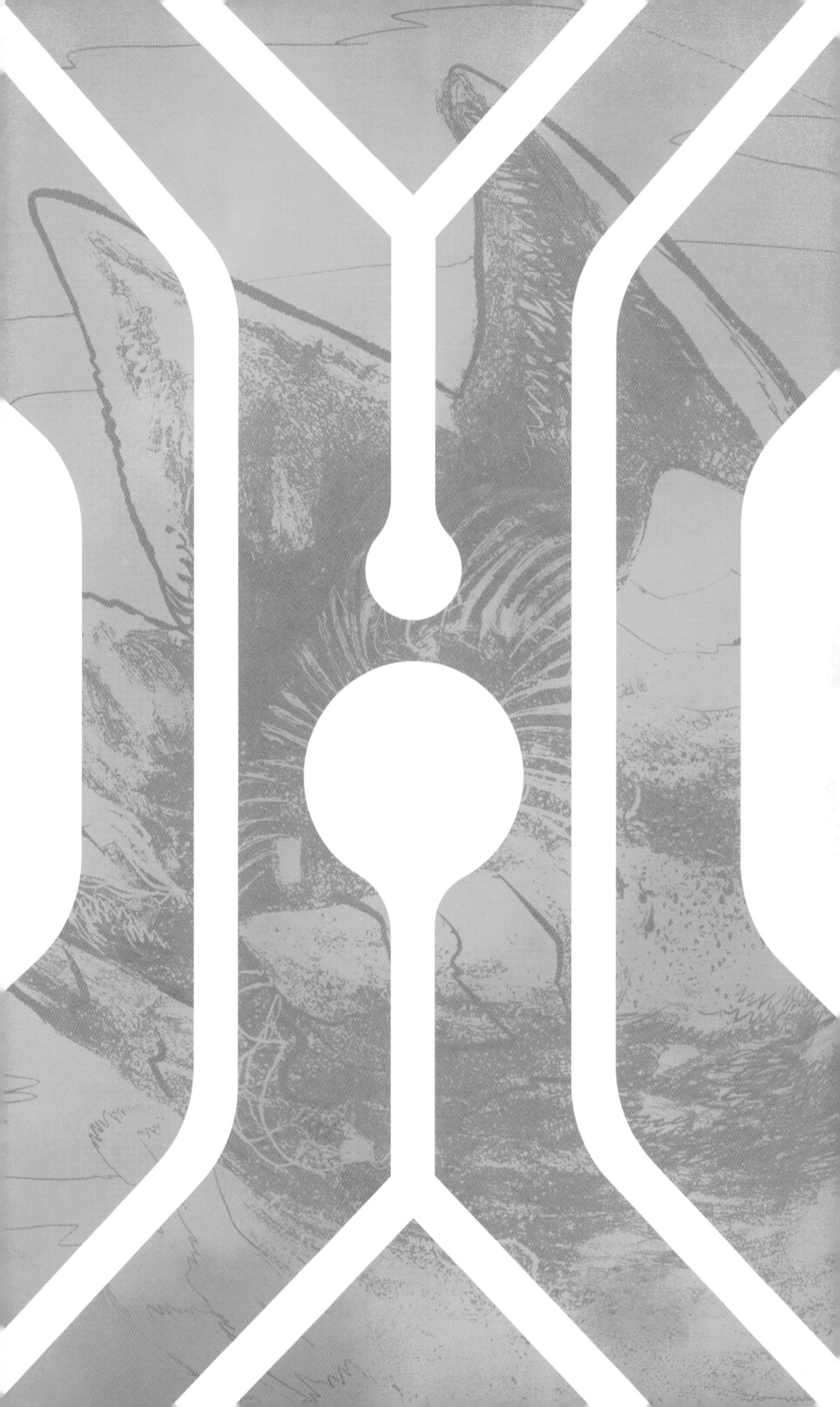

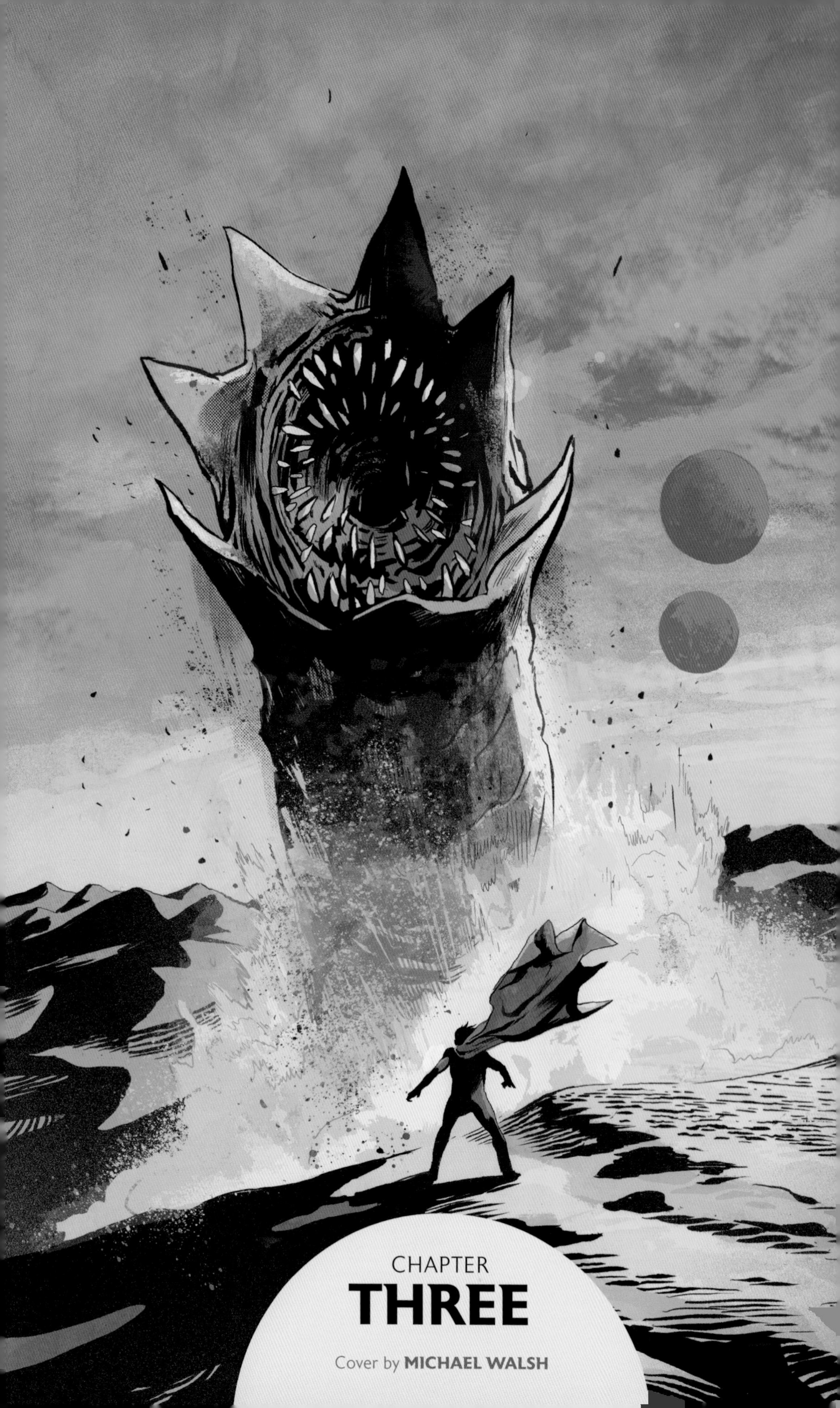

CHAPTER THREE

Cover by **MICHAEL WALSH**

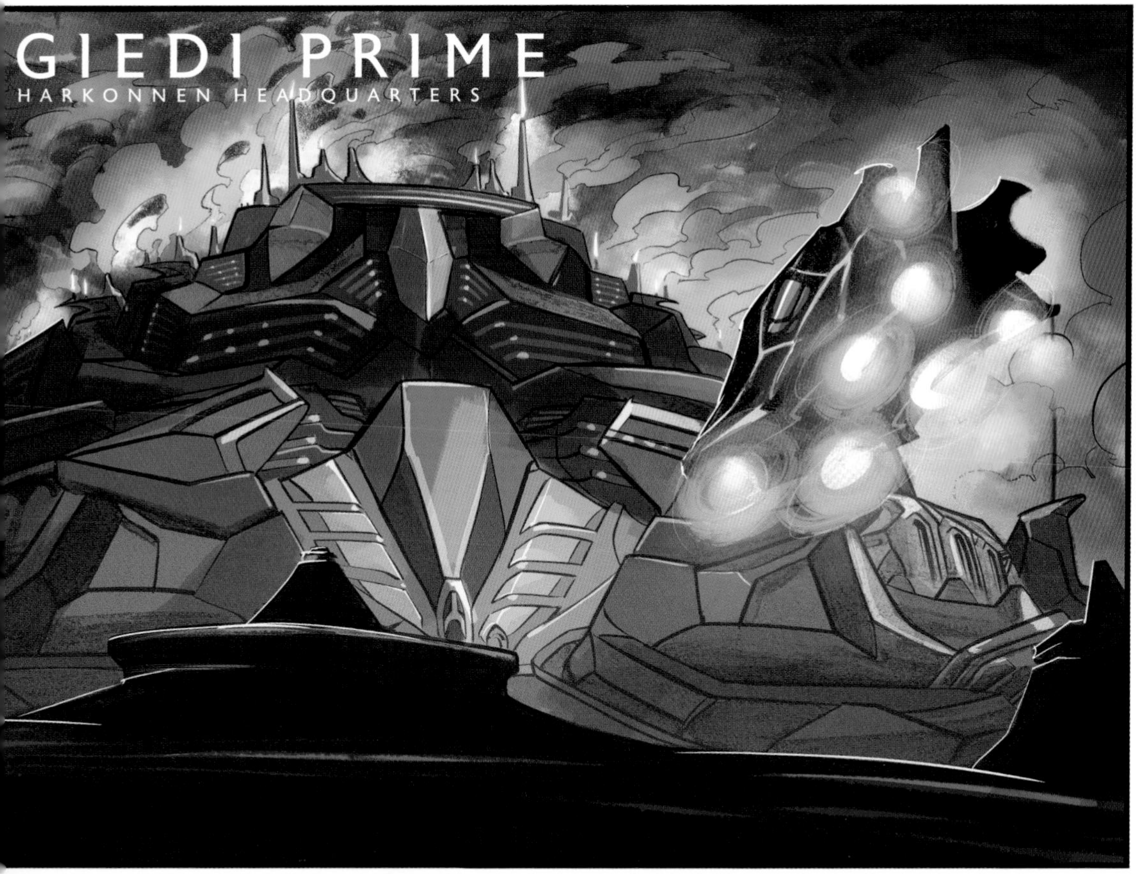
GIEDI PRIME
HARKONNEN HEADQUARTERS

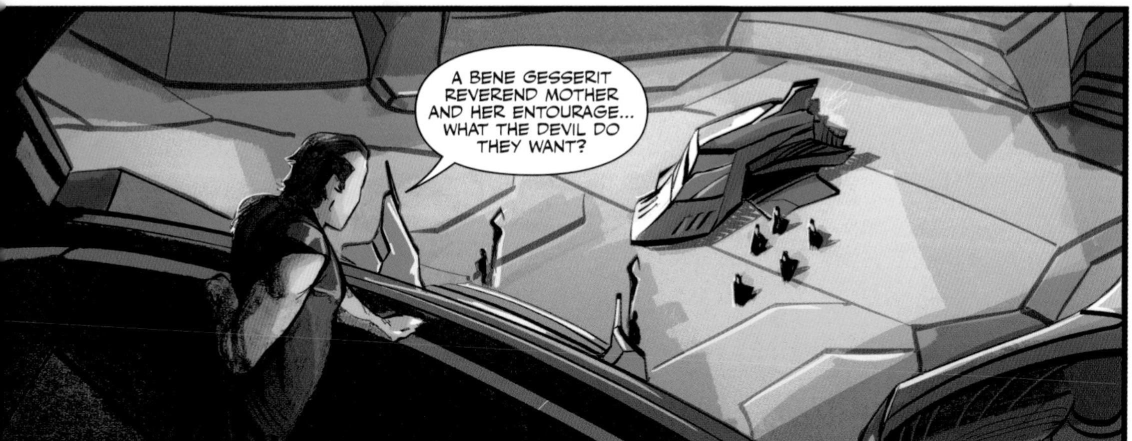
A BENE GESSERIT REVEREND MOTHER AND HER ENTOURAGE... WHAT THE DEVIL DO THEY WANT?

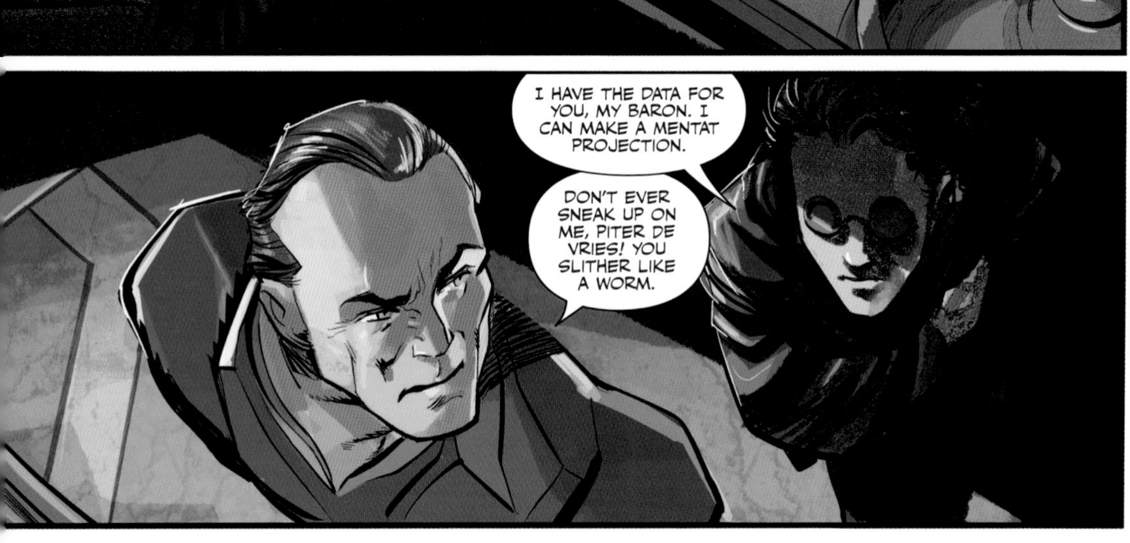
I HAVE THE DATA FOR YOU, MY BARON. I CAN MAKE A MENTAT PROJECTION.
DON'T EVER SNEAK UP ON ME, PITER DE VRIES! YOU SLITHER LIKE A WORM.

I AM REVEREND MOTHER *GAIUS HELEN MOHIAM*, AND I WILL SEE BARON HARKONNEN. WITHOUT DELAY.

I WILL MEET THE *WITCHES* HERE IN MY OFFICE, BUT THERE WILL BE NO REFRESHMENTS, NO HOSPITALITY WHATSOEVER.

I DON'T TRUST WHAT THEY WANT.

NO WEAPONS DETECTED, BARON...BUT THE BENE GESSERIT ARE NEVER WITHOUT WEAPONS.

IT'S NEVER WISE TO INCUR THE *WRATH* OF THE SISTERHOOD.

I KNOW THAT, IDIOT! DAMN THEM AND THEIR SECRETS.

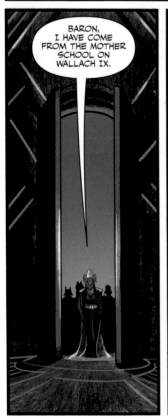

BARON, I HAVE COME FROM THE MOTHER SCHOOL ON WALLACH IX.

WE HAVE BUSINESS TO DISCUSS, YOU AND I.

I'M NOT INTERESTED IN DOING BUSINESS WITH WITCHES.

NEVERTHELESS, YOU WILL HEAR WHAT I HAVE TO SAY.

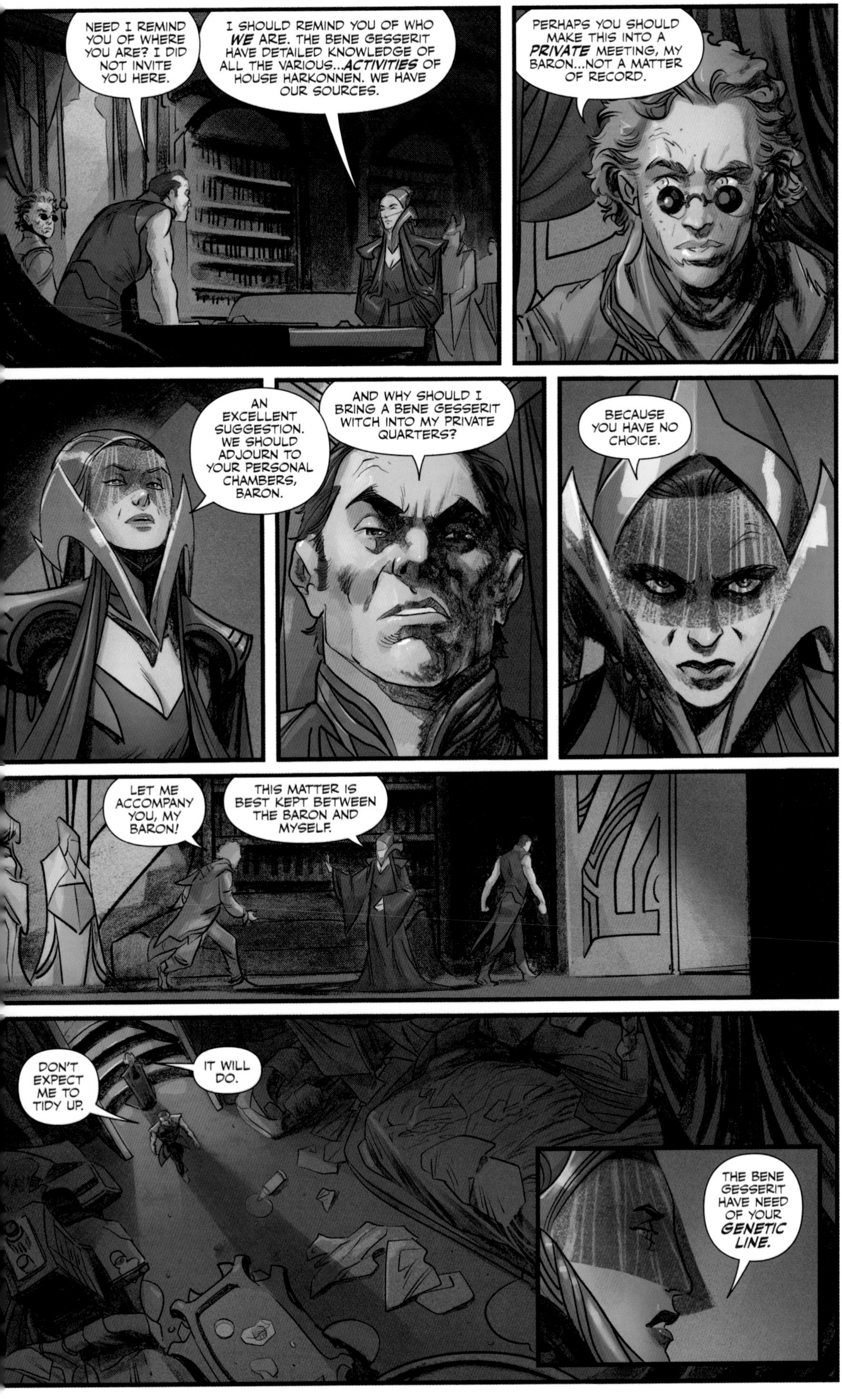
NEED I REMIND YOU OF WHERE YOU ARE? I DID NOT INVITE YOU HERE.
I SHOULD REMIND YOU OF WHO WE ARE. THE BENE GESSERIT HAVE DETAILED KNOWLEDGE OF ALL THE VARIOUS...ACTIVITIES OF HOUSE HARKONNEN. WE HAVE OUR SOURCES.
PERHAPS YOU SHOULD MAKE THIS INTO A PRIVATE MEETING, MY BARON...NOT A MATTER OF RECORD.
AN EXCELLENT SUGGESTION. WE SHOULD ADJOURN TO YOUR PERSONAL CHAMBERS, BARON.
AND WHY SHOULD I BRING A BENE GESSERIT WITCH INTO MY PRIVATE QUARTERS?
BECAUSE YOU HAVE NO CHOICE.
LET ME ACCOMPANY YOU, MY BARON!
THIS MATTER IS BEST KEPT BETWEEN THE BARON AND MYSELF.
DON'T EXPECT ME TO TIDY UP.
IT WILL DO.
THE BENE GESSERIT HAVE NEED OF YOUR GENETIC LINE.

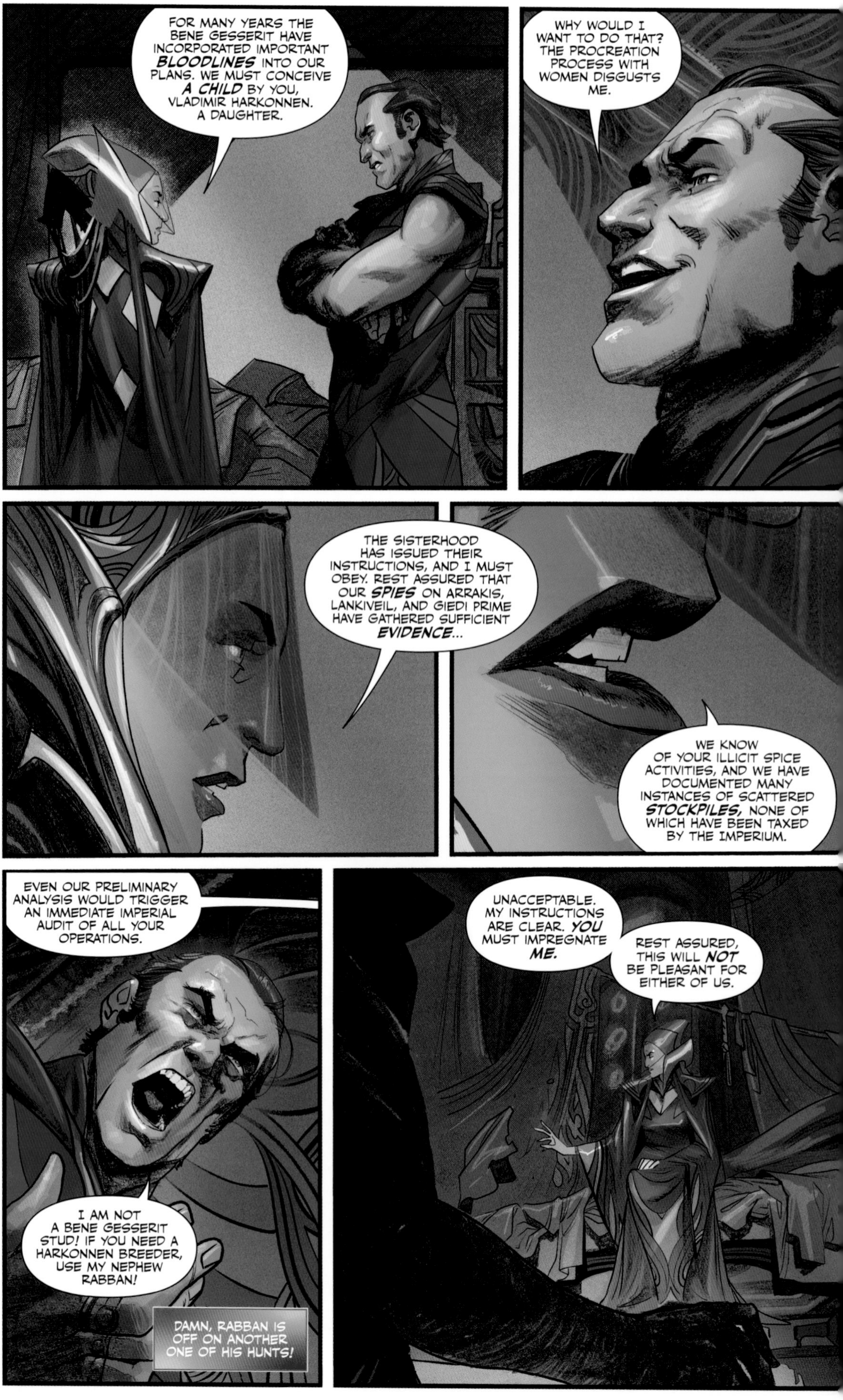
FOR MANY YEARS THE BENE GESSERIT HAVE INCORPORATED IMPORTANT BLOODLINES INTO OUR PLANS. WE MUST CONCEIVE A CHILD BY YOU, VLADIMIR HARKONNEN. A DAUGHTER.
WHY WOULD I WANT TO DO THAT? THE PROCREATION PROCESS WITH WOMEN DISGUSTS ME.
THE SISTERHOOD HAS ISSUED THEIR INSTRUCTIONS, AND I MUST OBEY. REST ASSURED THAT OUR SPIES ON ARRAKIS, LANKIVEIL, AND GIEDI PRIME HAVE GATHERED SUFFICIENT EVIDENCE...
WE KNOW OF YOUR ILLICIT SPICE ACTIVITIES, AND WE HAVE DOCUMENTED MANY INSTANCES OF SCATTERED STOCKPILES, NONE OF WHICH HAVE BEEN TAXED BY THE IMPERIUM.
EVEN OUR PRELIMINARY ANALYSIS WOULD TRIGGER AN IMMEDIATE IMPERIAL AUDIT OF ALL YOUR OPERATIONS.
I AM NOT A BENE GESSERIT STUD! IF YOU NEED A HARKONNEN BREEDER, USE MY NEPHEW RABBAN!
DAMN, RABBAN IS OFF ON ANOTHER ONE OF HIS HUNTS!
UNACCEPTABLE. MY INSTRUCTIONS ARE CLEAR. YOU MUST IMPREGNATE ME.
REST ASSURED, THIS WILL NOT BE PLEASANT FOR EITHER OF US.

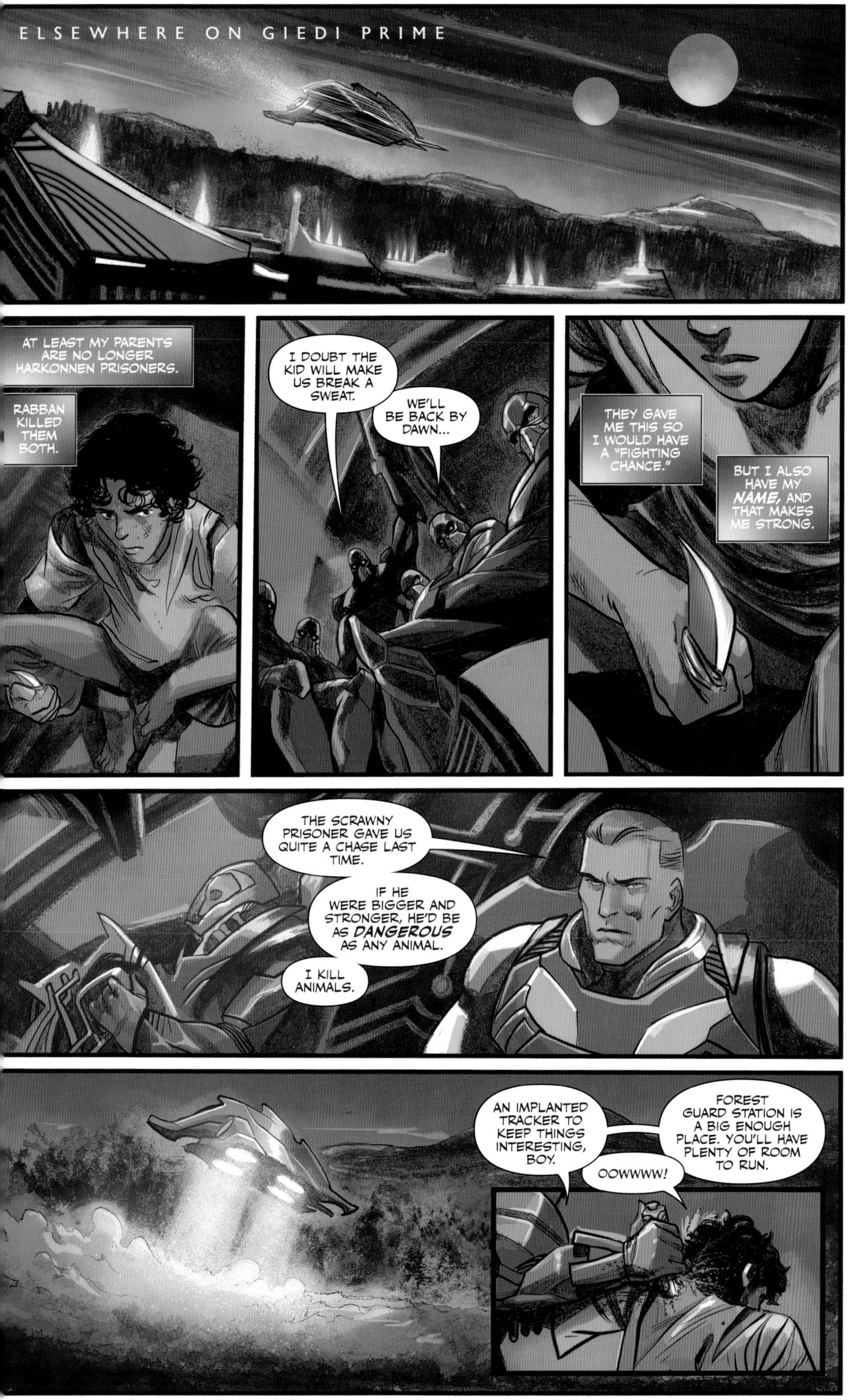
ELSEWHERE ON GIEDI PRIME
AT LEAST MY PARENTS ARE NO LONGER HARKONNEN PRISONERS.
RABBAN KILLED THEM BOTH.
I DOUBT THE KID WILL MAKE US BREAK A SWEAT.
WE'LL BE BACK BY DAWN...
THEY GAVE ME THIS SO I WOULD HAVE A "FIGHTING CHANCE."
BUT I ALSO HAVE MY NAME, AND THAT MAKES ME STRONG.
THE SCRAWNY PRISONER GAVE US QUITE A CHASE LAST TIME.
IF HE WERE BIGGER AND STRONGER, HE'D BE AS DANGEROUS AS ANY ANIMAL.
I KILL ANIMALS.
AN IMPLANTED TRACKER TO KEEP THINGS INTERESTING, BOY.
OOWWWW!
FOREST GUARD STATION IS A BIG ENOUGH PLACE. YOU'LL HAVE PLENTY OF ROOM TO RUN.

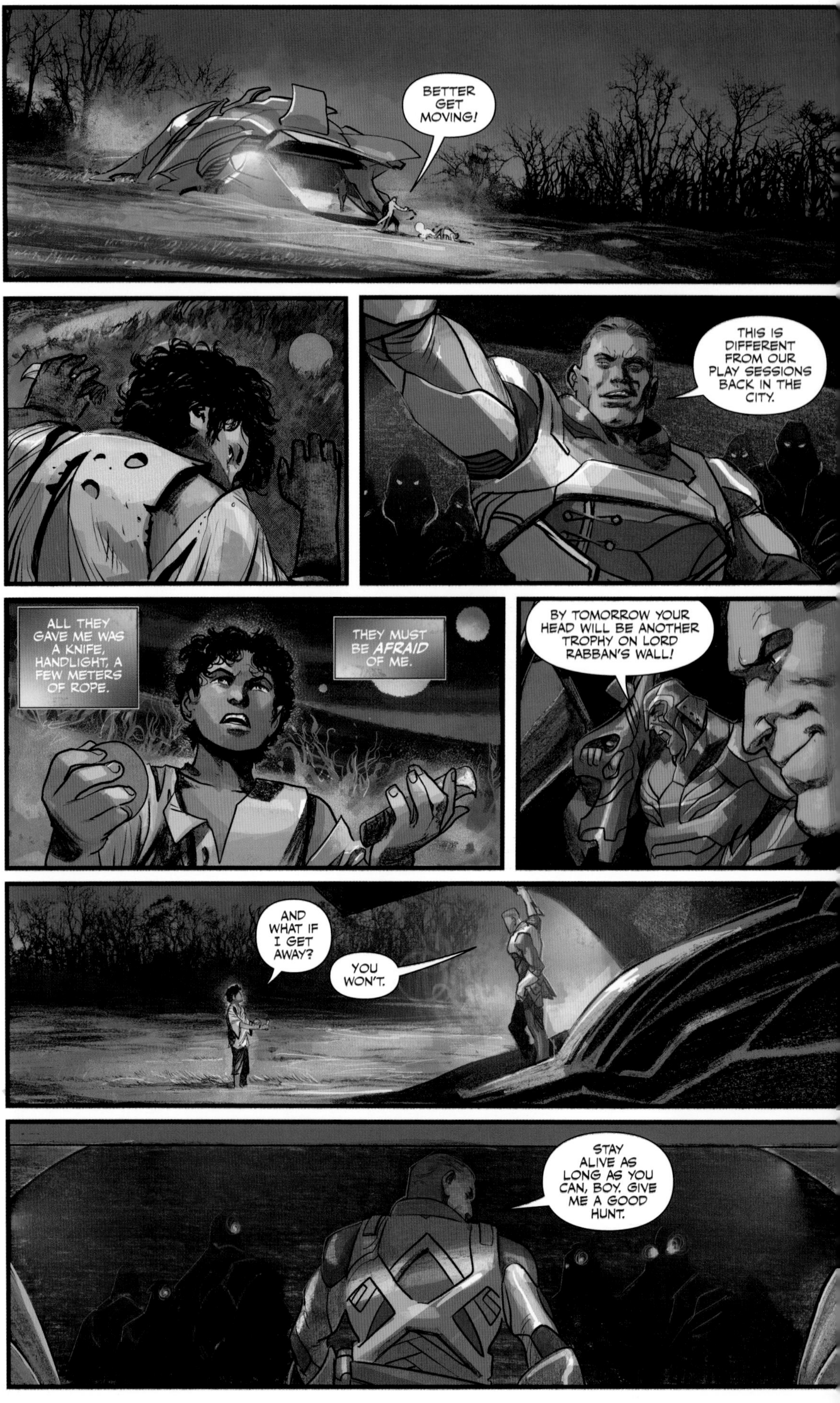
BETTER GET MOVING!
THIS IS DIFFERENT FROM OUR PLAY SESSIONS BACK IN THE CITY.
ALL THEY GAVE ME WAS A KNIFE, HANDLIGHT, A FEW METERS OF ROPE.
THEY MUST BE *AFRAID* OF ME.
BY TOMORROW YOUR HEAD WILL BE ANOTHER TROPHY ON LORD RABBAN'S WALL!
AND WHAT IF I GET AWAY?
YOU WON'T.
STAY ALIVE AS LONG AS YOU CAN, BOY. GIVE ME A GOOD HUNT.

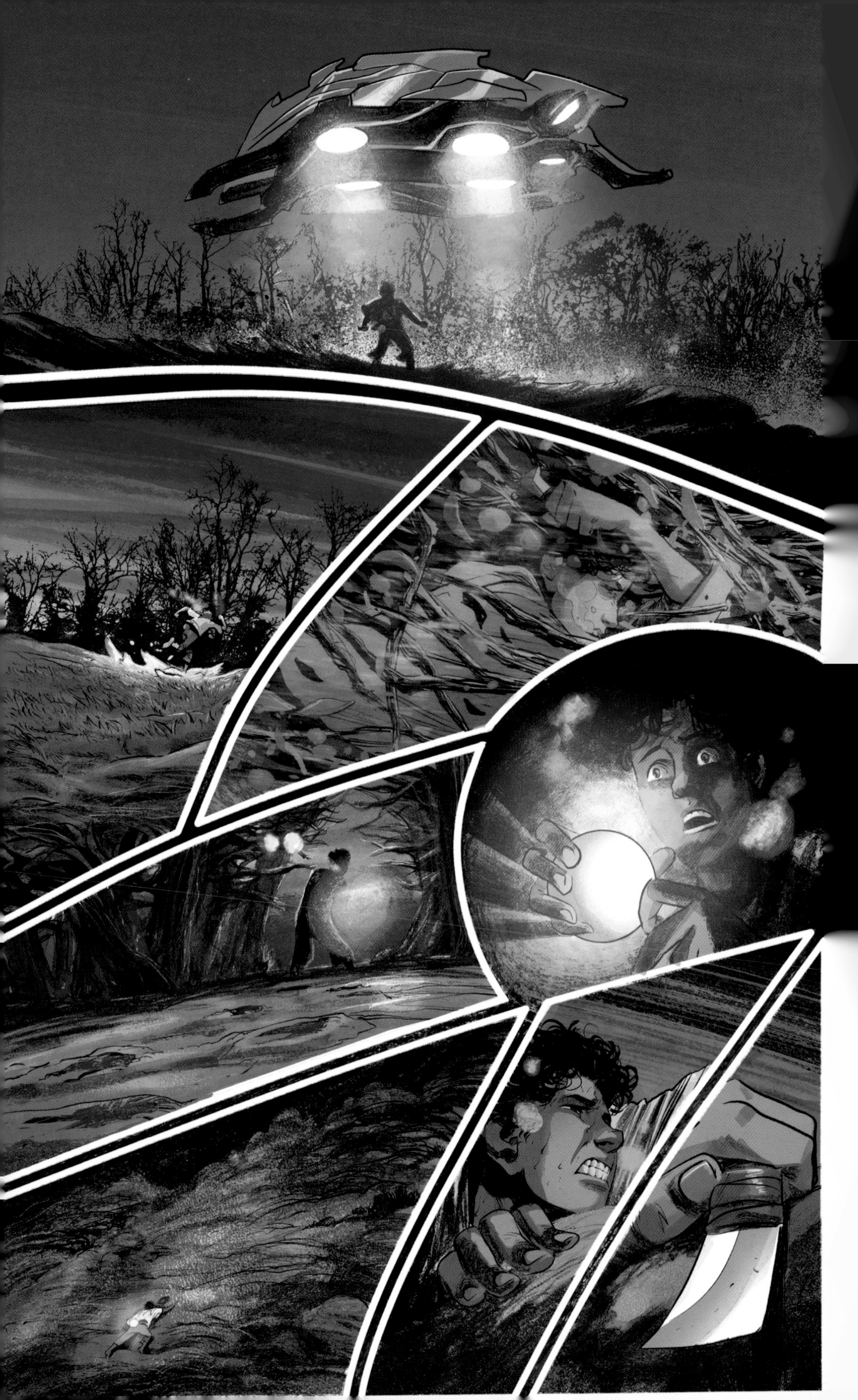

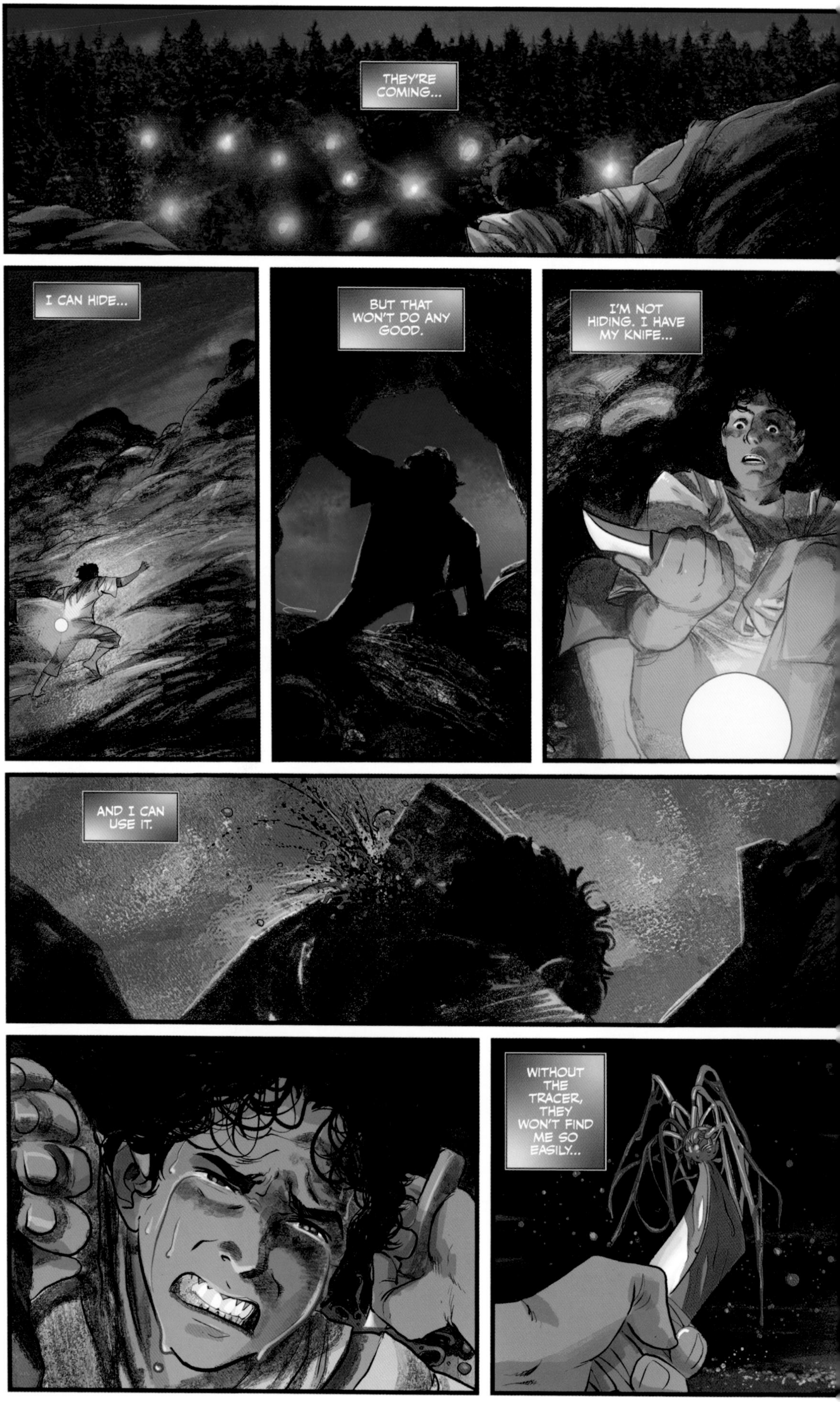
THEY'RE COMING...
I CAN HIDE...
BUT THAT WON'T DO ANY GOOD.
I'M NOT HIDING. I HAVE MY KNIFE...
AND I CAN USE IT.
WITHOUT THE TRACER, THEY WON'T FIND ME SO EASILY...

WAIT...
BETTER
IDEA

THEY'LL
FOLLOW
ANYWAY.

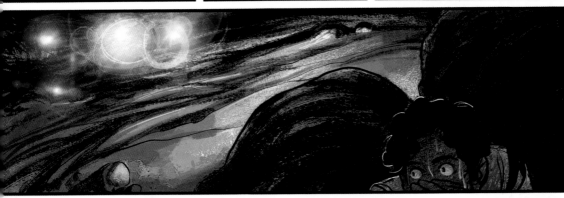

FOUND
YOU, LITTLE
RAT!

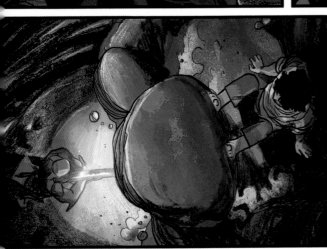

CRUNNCH

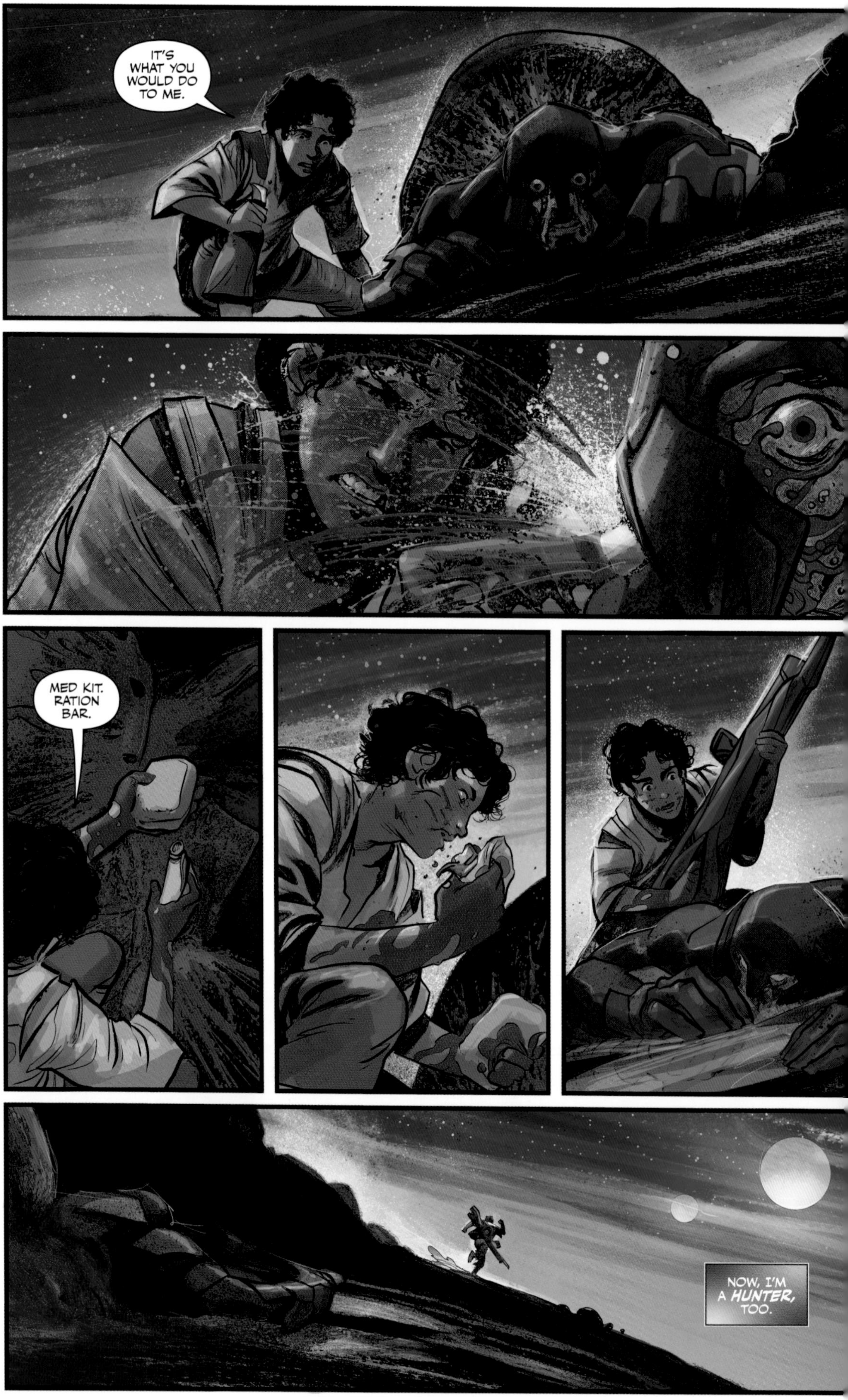
IT'S WHAT YOU WOULD DO TO ME.
MED KIT. RATION BAR.
NOW, I'M A HUNTER, TOO.

ABANDONED AND ISOLATED. JUST... LEFT HERE, ALONE.

IX IS SUPPOSED TO BE A ONE OF THE MOST *ADVANCED*, INDUSTRIAL WORLDS IN THE IMPERIUM.

NOT...THIS.

IX

HELLO? I AM LETO ATREIDES! I'M A GUEST OF *EARL DOMINIC VERNIUS!*

HELLO?

HUMMMMMMMMMMMMMMMMMM

YOU MUST BE LETO ATREIDES. I'M NOT A VERY EFFICIENT WELCOMING PARTY, AM I?

I'M RHOMBUR. *PRINCE RHOMBUR OF HOUSE VERNIUS,* IF YOU WANT THE FORMALITIES. WE'LL BE STUDYING TOGETHER. COME WITH ME. I'LL TAKE YOU TO THE GRAND PALAIS.

SO, THIS IS REALLY IX? THE *MACHINE* PLANET? NOT WHAT I EXPECTED.

IX? NO! THE REAL IX IS *UNDERGROUND,* SO WE CAN KEEP THE SURFACE PRISTINE. YOU'LL SEE!

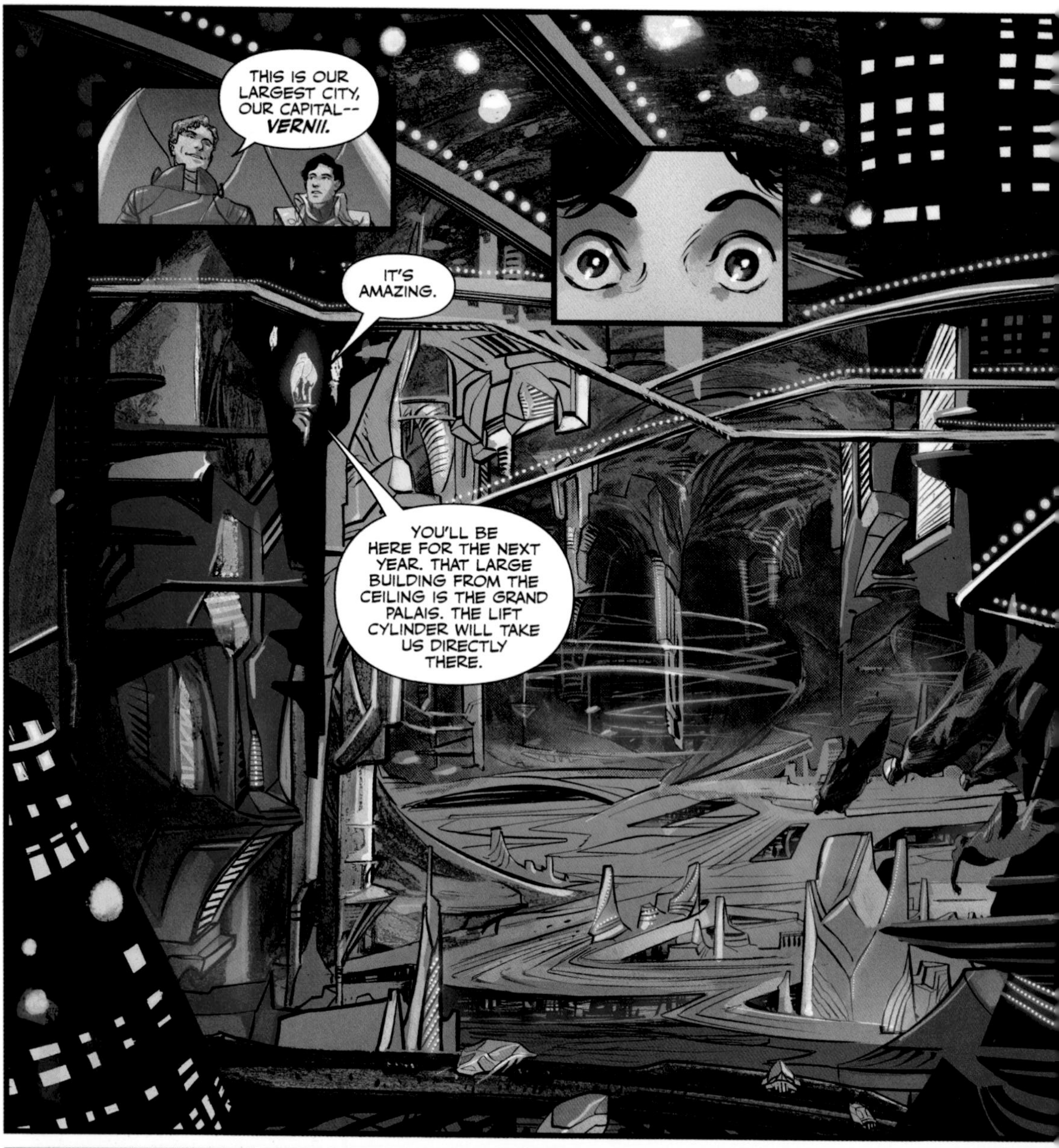
THIS IS OUR LARGEST CITY, OUR CAPITAL-- VERNII.
IT'S AMAZING.
YOU'LL BE HERE FOR THE NEXT YEAR. THAT LARGE BUILDING FROM THE CEILING IS THE GRAND PALAIS. THE LIFT CYLINDER WILL TAKE US DIRECTLY THERE.

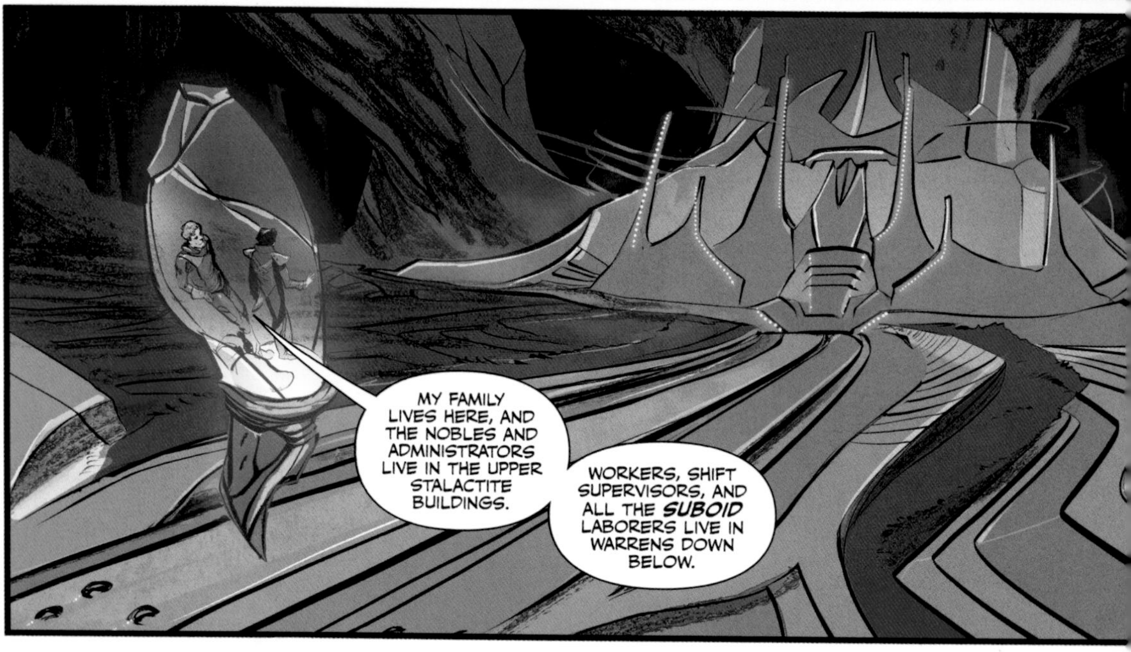
MY FAMILY LIVES HERE, AND THE NOBLES AND ADMINISTRATORS LIVE IN THE UPPER STALACTITE BUILDINGS.
WORKERS, SHIFT SUPERVISORS, AND ALL THE SUBOID LABORERS LIVE IN WARRENS DOWN BELOW.

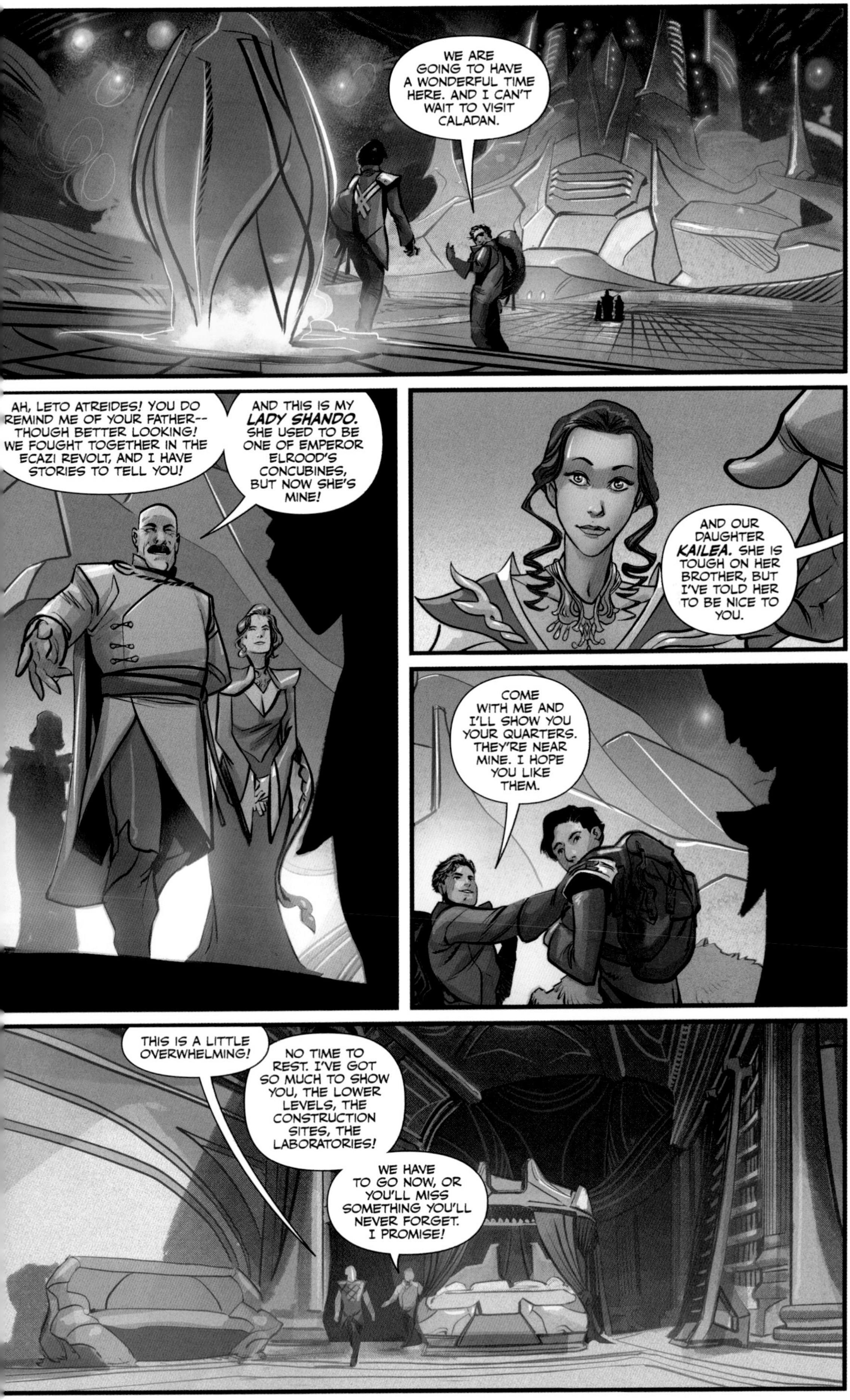
WE ARE GOING TO HAVE A WONDERFUL TIME HERE. AND I CAN'T WAIT TO VISIT CALADAN.
AH, LETO ATREIDES! YOU DO REMIND ME OF YOUR FATHER-- THOUGH BETTER LOOKING! WE FOUGHT TOGETHER IN THE ECAZI REVOLT, AND I HAVE STORIES TO TELL YOU!
AND THIS IS MY LADY SHANDO. SHE USED TO BE ONE OF EMPEROR ELROOD'S CONCUBINES, BUT NOW SHE'S MINE!
AND OUR DAUGHTER KAILEA. SHE IS TOUGH ON HER BROTHER, BUT I'VE TOLD HER TO BE NICE TO YOU.
COME WITH ME AND I'LL SHOW YOU YOUR QUARTERS. THEY'RE NEAR MINE. I HOPE YOU LIKE THEM.
THIS IS A LITTLE OVERWHELMING!
NO TIME TO REST. I'VE GOT SO MUCH TO SHOW YOU, THE LOWER LEVELS, THE CONSTRUCTION SITES, THE LABORATORIES!
WE HAVE TO GO NOW, OR YOU'LL MISS SOMETHING YOU'LL NEVER FORGET. I PROMISE!

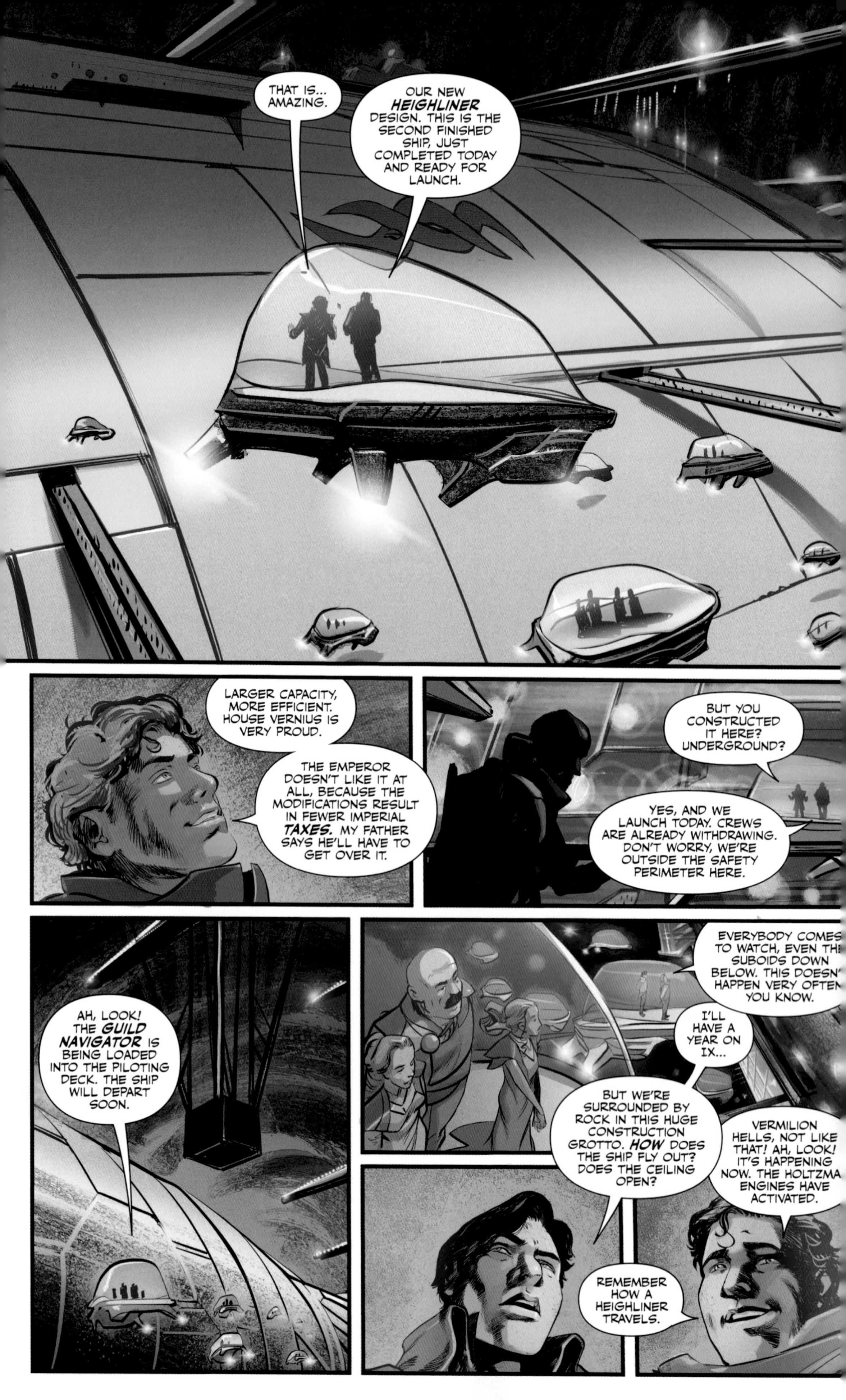
THAT IS... AMAZING.
OUR NEW HEIGHLINER DESIGN. THIS IS THE SECOND FINISHED SHIP, JUST COMPLETED TODAY AND READY FOR LAUNCH.
LARGER CAPACITY, MORE EFFICIENT. HOUSE VERNIUS IS VERY PROUD.
THE EMPEROR DOESN'T LIKE IT AT ALL, BECAUSE THE MODIFICATIONS RESULT IN FEWER IMPERIAL TAXES. MY FATHER SAYS HE'LL HAVE TO GET OVER IT.
BUT YOU CONSTRUCTED IT HERE? UNDERGROUND?
YES, AND WE LAUNCH TODAY. CREWS ARE ALREADY WITHDRAWING. DON'T WORRY, WE'RE OUTSIDE THE SAFETY PERIMETER HERE.
AH, LOOK! THE GUILD NAVIGATOR IS BEING LOADED INTO THE PILOTING DECK. THE SHIP WILL DEPART SOON.
EVERYBODY COMES TO WATCH, EVEN THE SUBOIDS DOWN BELOW. THIS DOESN'T HAPPEN VERY OFTEN, YOU KNOW.
I'LL HAVE A YEAR ON IX...
BUT WE'RE SURROUNDED BY ROCK IN THIS HUGE CONSTRUCTION GROTTO. HOW DOES THE SHIP FLY OUT? DOES THE CEILING OPEN?
VERMILION HELLS, NOT LIKE THAT! AH, LOOK! IT'S HAPPENING NOW. THE HOLTZMAN ENGINES HAVE ACTIVATED.
REMEMBER HOW A HEIGHLINER TRAVELS.

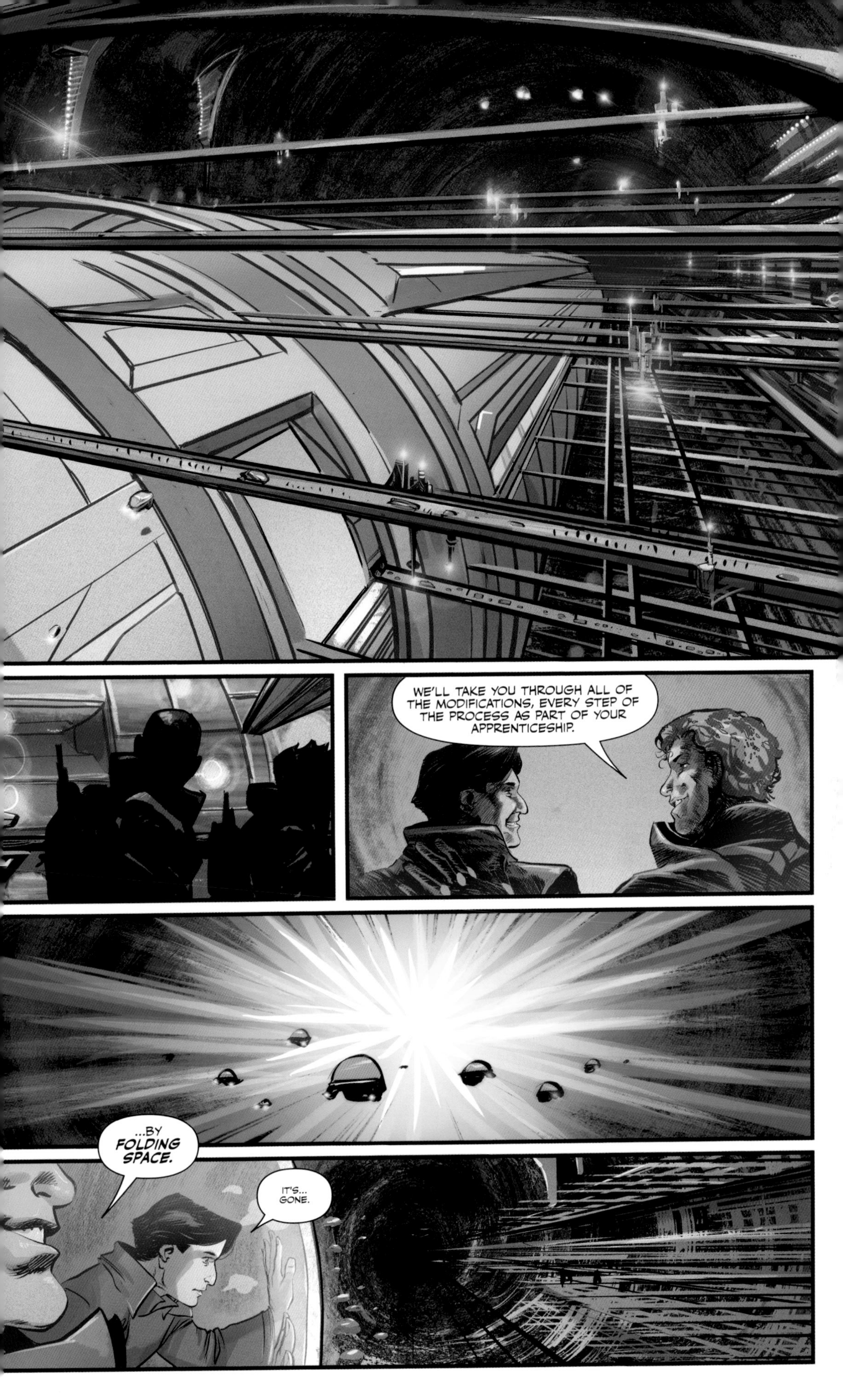
WE'LL TAKE YOU THROUGH ALL OF THE MODIFICATIONS, EVERY STEP OF THE PROCESS AS PART OF YOUR APPRENTICESHIP.
...BY FOLDING SPACE.
IT'S... GONE.

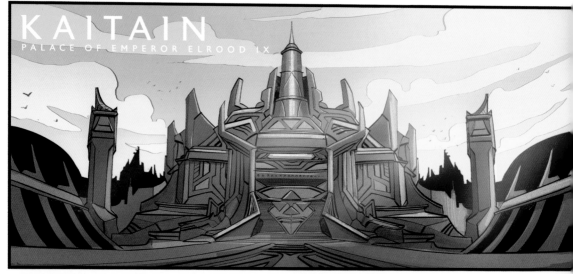

KAITAIN
PALACE OF EMPEROR ELROOD IX

PRIVATE CHAMBERS OF
CROWN PRINCE SHADDAM

IT IS TAKING MUCH TOO LONG, HASIMIR!

WE'VE POISONED THE EMPEROR. WHY WON'T HE JUST *DIE?*

QUIET, MY FRIEND! I'VE SCANNED FOR LISTENING DEVICES, BUT NOTHING IS PERFECT!

I IMPLANTED THE SUBTLE POISON INTO YOUR FATHER, BUT IT IS SLOW ACTING.

TOO SLOW.

MEANWHILE, USE THE TIME AND LEARN ABOUT YOUR IMPERIUM. MAKE PLANS...

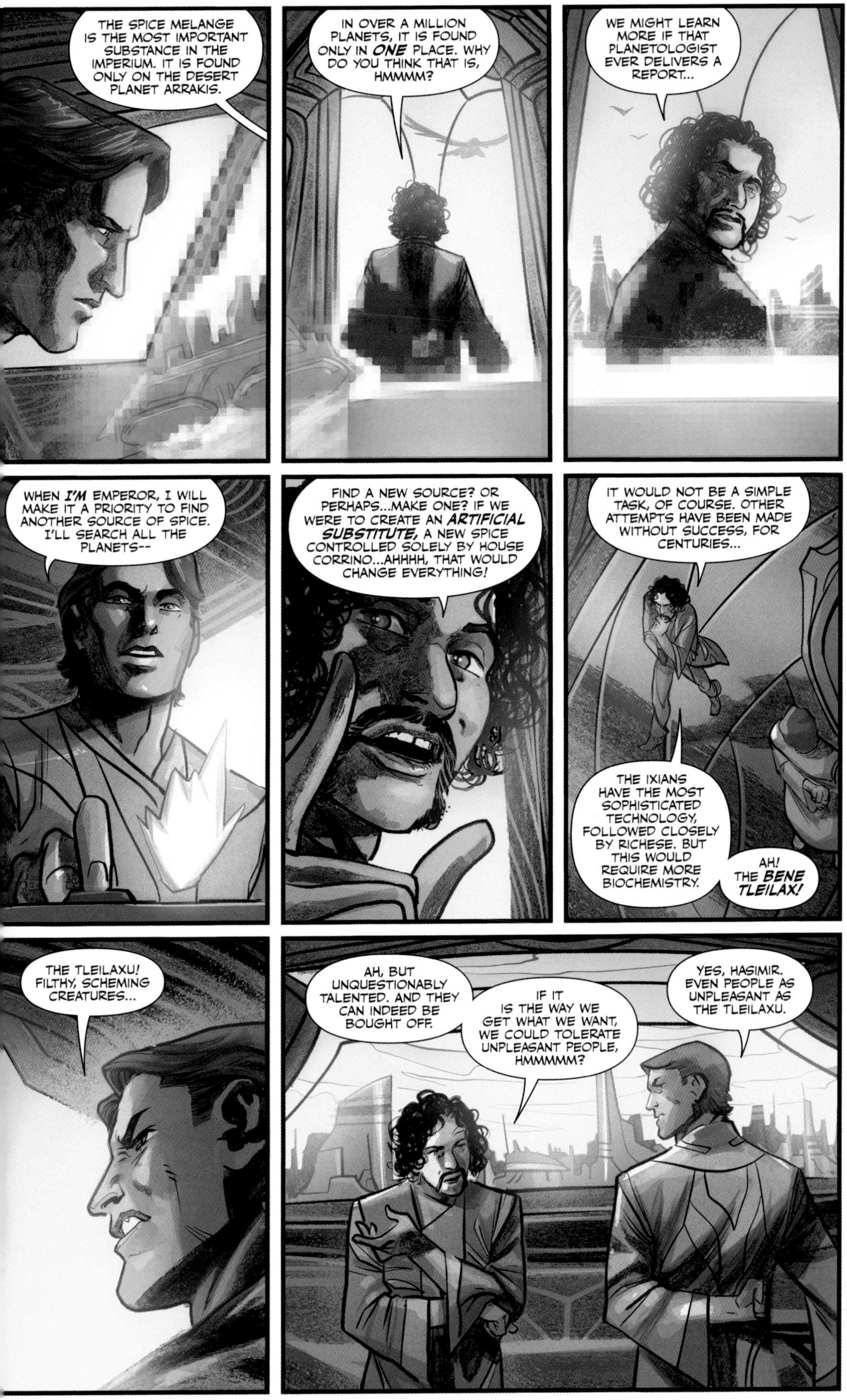
THE SPICE MELANGE IS THE MOST IMPORTANT SUBSTANCE IN THE IMPERIUM. IT IS FOUND ONLY ON THE DESERT PLANET ARRAKIS.
IN OVER A MILLION PLANETS, IT IS FOUND ONLY IN *ONE* PLACE. WHY DO YOU THINK THAT IS, HMMMM?
WE MIGHT LEARN MORE IF THAT PLANETOLOGIST EVER DELIVERS A REPORT...
WHEN *I'M* EMPEROR, I WILL MAKE IT A PRIORITY TO FIND ANOTHER SOURCE OF SPICE. I'LL SEARCH ALL THE PLANETS--
FIND A NEW SOURCE? OR PERHAPS...MAKE ONE? IF WE WERE TO CREATE AN ***ARTIFICIAL SUBSTITUTE,*** A NEW SPICE CONTROLLED SOLELY BY HOUSE CORRINO...AHHHH, THAT WOULD CHANGE EVERYTHING!
IT WOULD NOT BE A SIMPLE TASK, OF COURSE. OTHER ATTEMPTS HAVE BEEN MADE WITHOUT SUCCESS, FOR CENTURIES...
THE IXIANS HAVE THE MOST SOPHISTICATED TECHNOLOGY, FOLLOWED CLOSELY BY RICHESE. BUT THIS WOULD REQUIRE MORE BIOCHEMISTRY.
AH! THE ***BENE TLEILAX!***
THE TLEILAXU! FILTHY, SCHEMING CREATURES...
AH, BUT UNQUESTIONABLY TALENTED. AND THEY CAN INDEED BE BOUGHT OFF.
IF IT IS THE WAY WE GET WHAT WE WANT, WE COULD TOLERATE UNPLEASANT PEOPLE, HMMMMM?
YES, HASIMIR. EVEN PEOPLE AS UNPLEASANT AS THE TLEILAXU.

ARRAKIS

ALONE IN THE QUIET, STARK DESERT--EXACTLY AS IT SHOULD BE.

A PLANETOLOGIST MUST HAVE THE TIME AND PLACE TO THINK.

THE LANDSCAPE HERE IS VAST AND POORLY MAPPED.

BY VIRTUE OF MY PROFESSION, THOUGH, AN EXPLORER IS NEVER EXACTLY *LOST*.

RIMWALL WEST

CARTHAG

THESE STILLSUITS... SUCH REMARKABLE ENGINEERING.

SO MUCH TO SEE HERE ON ARRAKIS. SO MUCH TO LEARN...

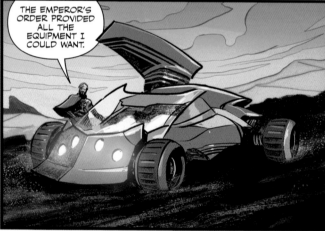

THE EMPEROR'S ORDER PROVIDED ALL THE EQUIPMENT I COULD WANT.

NOW I JUST NEED TO *UNDERSTAND* AN ENTIRE PLANET.

THE SHIELD WALL PROTECTS THE MAIN INHABITED AREAS FROM THE VAST OPEN DESERT AND THE SANDWORMS.

BUT IT IS STILL BY NO MEANS A HOSPITABLE PLACE.

HMMM, FAINT TRACES OF LICHENS HERE AND EVEN SOME RODENT DROPPINGS. *LIFE* MANAGES TO FIND A WAY, EVEN UNDER THE HARSHEST CONDITIONS.

HOW, THEN, DO THE *FREMEN* SURVIVE? AH, I WOULD LOVE TO TALK TO THEM!

THESE MARKS ARE NOT NATURAL... ARTIFICIAL STEPS! THE FREMEN HAVE BEEN HERE!

I HAVE COLLECTED SO MUCH DATA, BUT IT IS ONLY THE BEGINNING.

I SUPPOSE I AM OVERDUE TO FILE A REPORT TO EMPEROR ELROOD...BUT THERE'S SO MUCH TO DO.

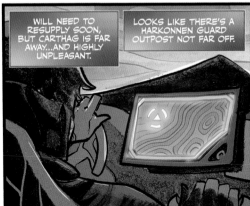

WILL NEED TO RESUPPLY SOON, BUT CARTHAG IS FAR AWAY...AND HIGHLY UNPLEASANT.

LOOKS LIKE THERE'S A HARKONNEN GUARD OUTPOST NOT FAR OFF.

I WISH I COULD AT LEAST INTERVIEW A FEW FREMEN BEFORE I MAKE MY INITIAL REPORT...

HERE NOW, WHAT'S THAT UP AHEAD?

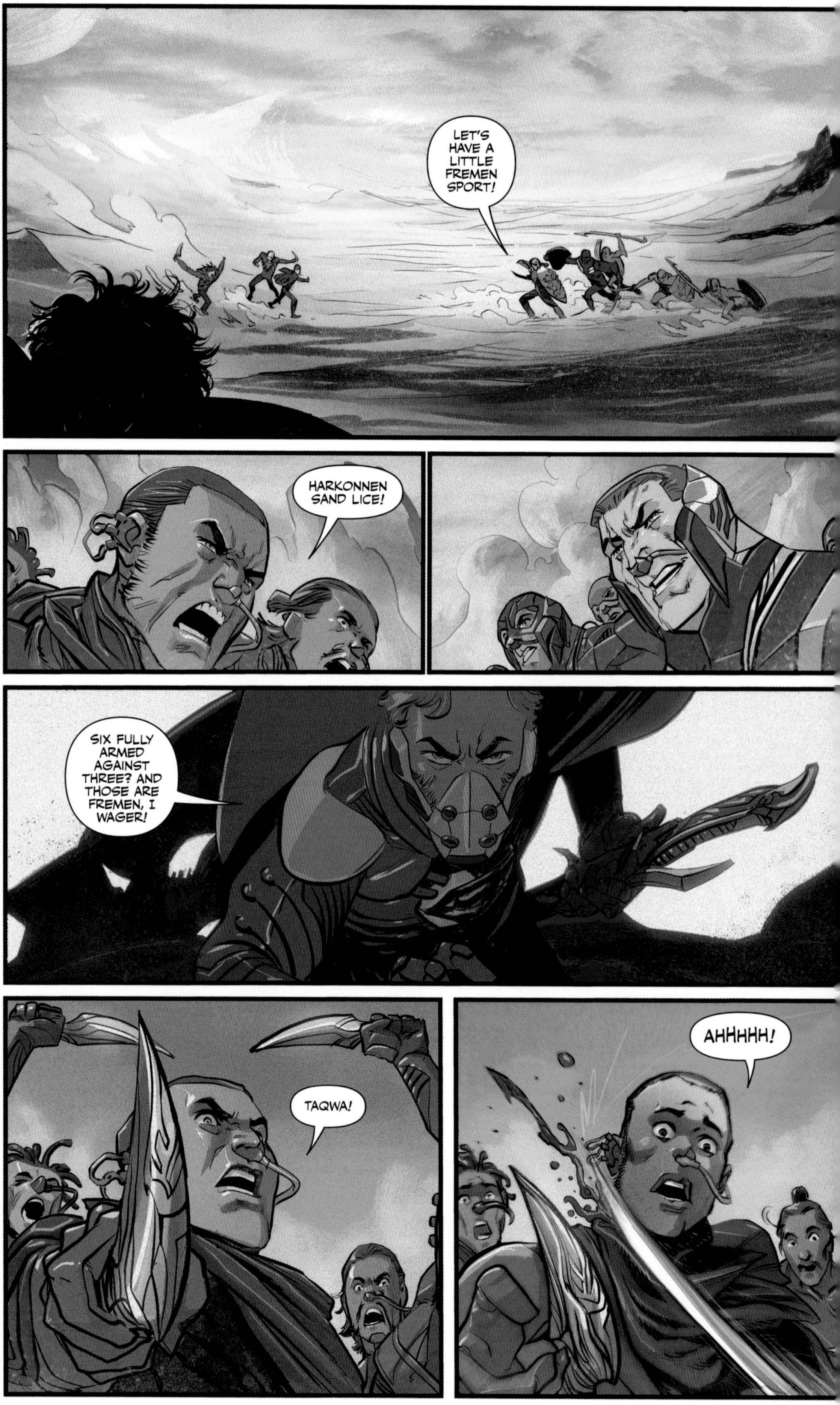
LET'S HAVE A LITTLE FREMEN SPORT!
HARKONNEN SAND LICE!
SIX FULLY ARMED AGAINST THREE? AND THOSE ARE FREMEN, I WAGER!
TAQWA!
AHHHHH!

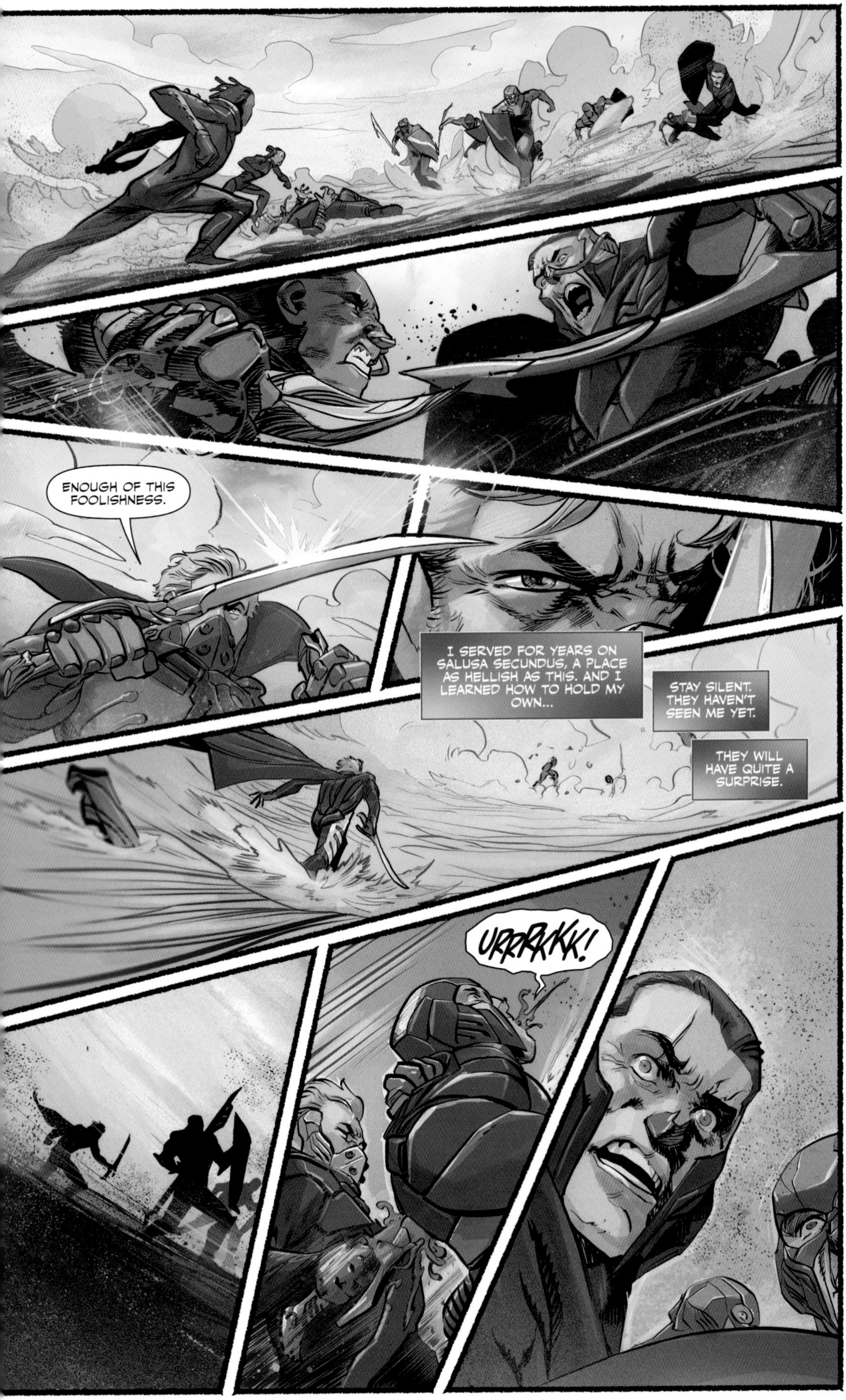
ENOUGH OF THIS FOOLISHNESS.
I SERVED FOR YEARS ON SALUSA SECUNDUS, A PLACE AS HELLISH AS THIS. AND I LEARNED HOW TO HOLD MY OWN...
STAY SILENT. THEY HAVEN'T SEEN ME YET.
THEY WILL HAVE QUITE A SURPRISE.
URRRKKK!

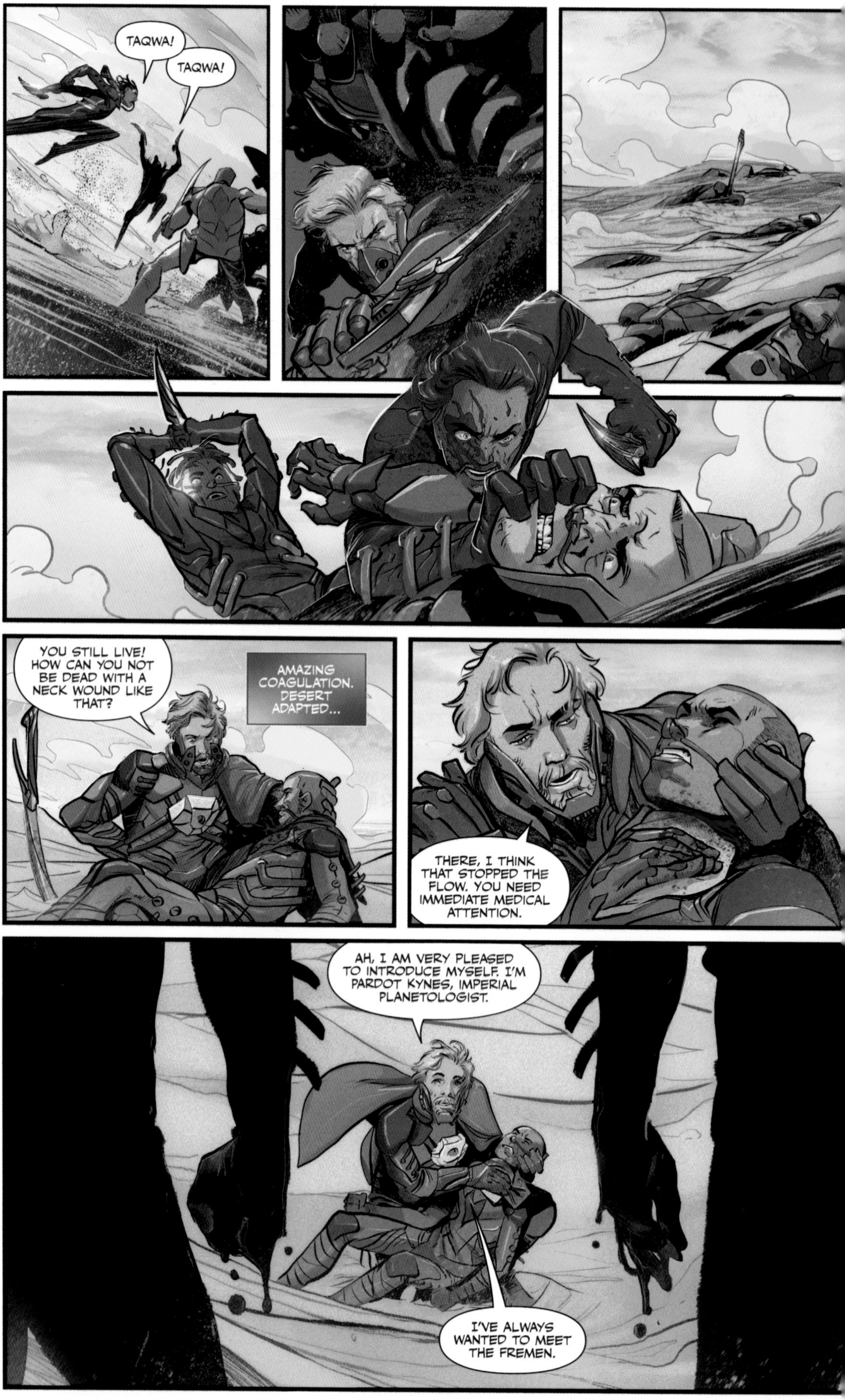
TAQWA!
TAQWA!
YOU STILL LIVE! HOW CAN YOU NOT BE DEAD WITH A NECK WOUND LIKE THAT?
AMAZING COAGULATION. DESERT ADAPTED...
THERE, I THINK THAT STOPPED THE FLOW. YOU NEED IMMEDIATE MEDICAL ATTENTION.
AH, I AM VERY PLEASED TO INTRODUCE MYSELF. I'M PARDOT KYNES, IMPERIAL PLANETOLOGIST.
I'VE ALWAYS WANTED TO MEET THE FREMEN.

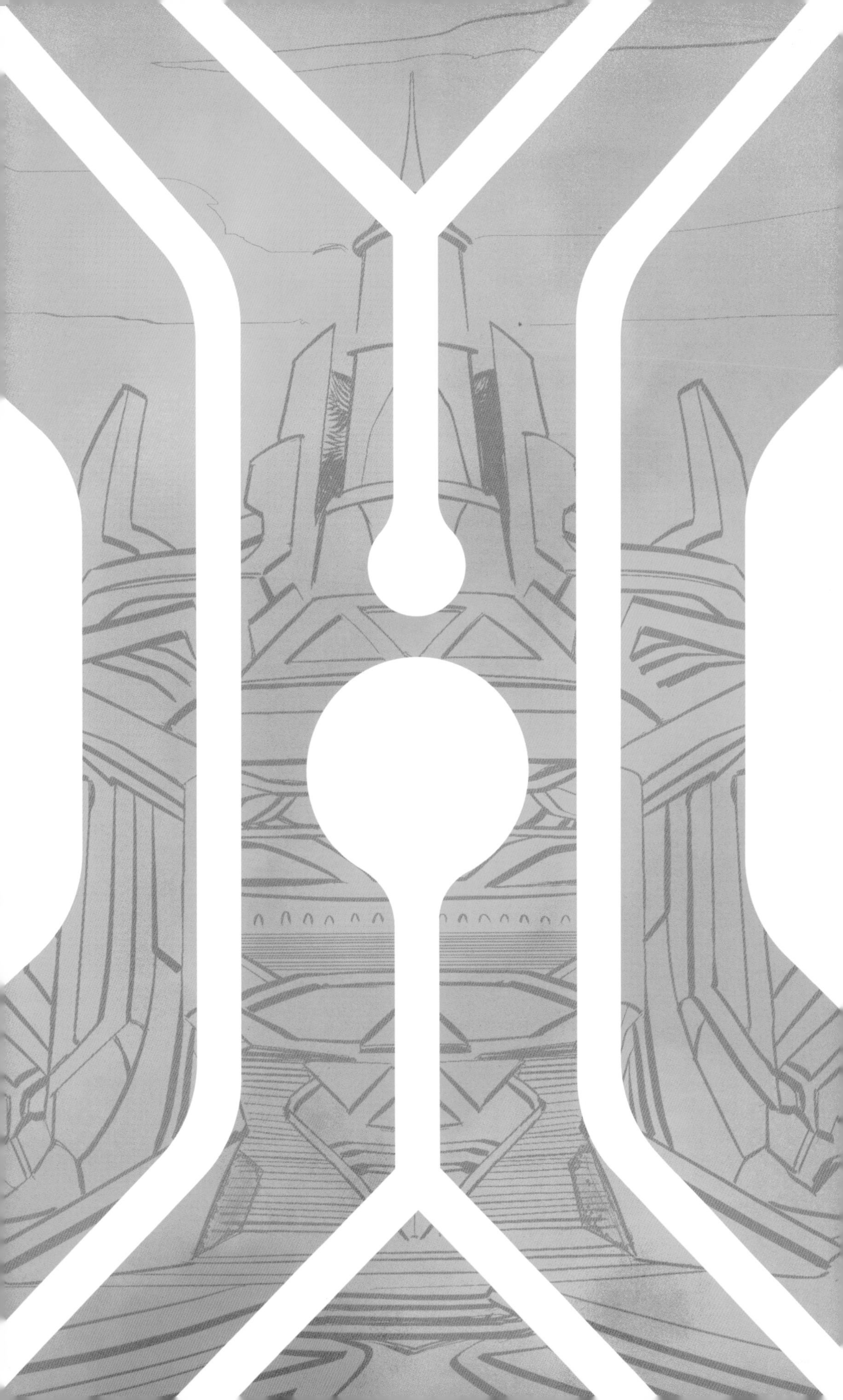

CHAPTER
FOUR

Cover by
Lorenzo De Felici

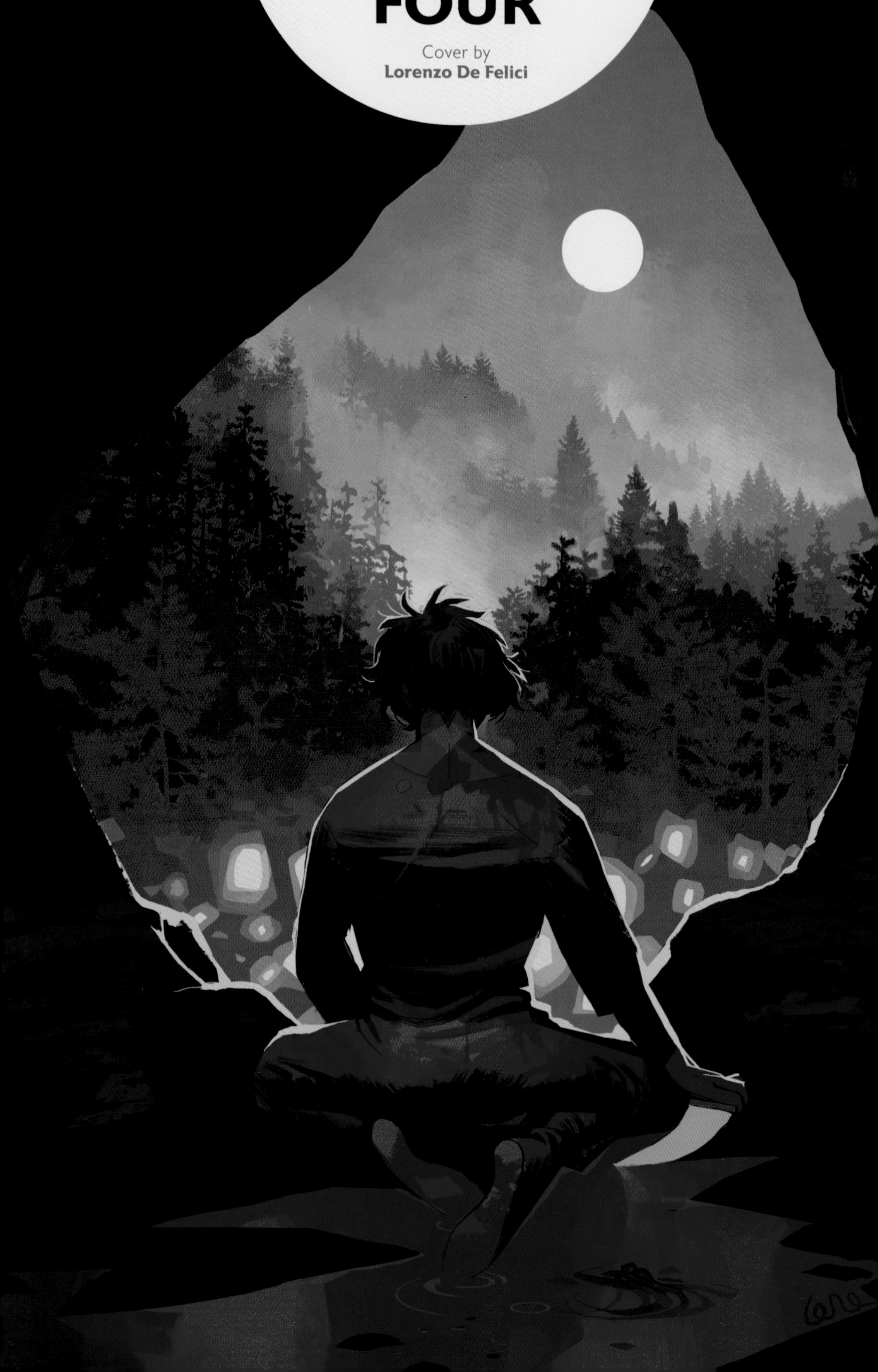

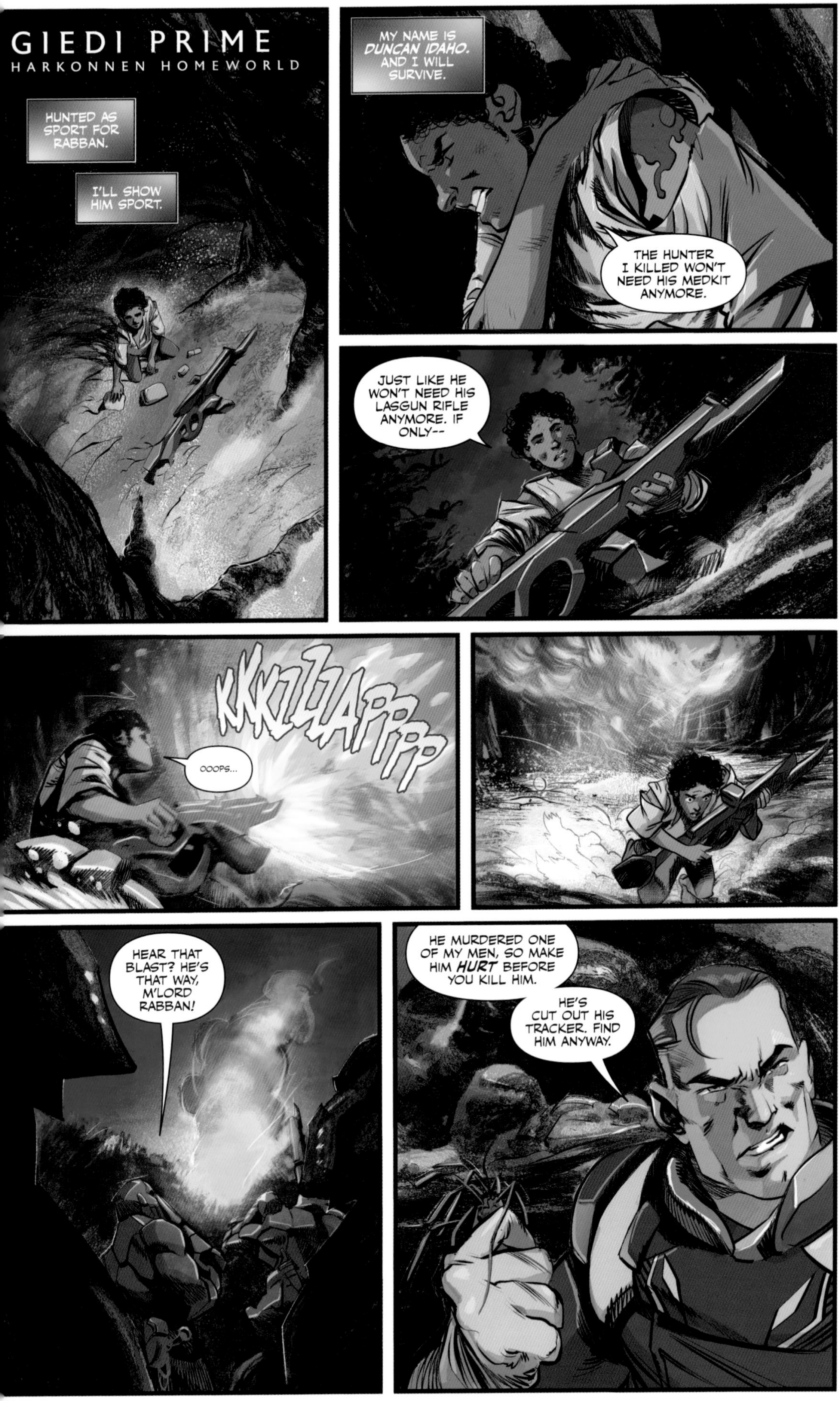
GIEDI PRIME
HARKONNEN HOMEWORLD
HUNTED AS SPORT FOR RABBAN.
I'LL SHOW HIM SPORT.
MY NAME IS DUNCAN IDAHO. AND I WILL SURVIVE.
THE HUNTER I KILLED WON'T NEED HIS MEDKIT ANYMORE.
JUST LIKE HE WON'T NEED HIS LASGUN RIFLE ANYMORE. IF ONLY--
KKKZZZZAPPPP
OOOPS...
HEAR THAT BLAST? HE'S THAT WAY, M'LORD RABBAN!
HE MURDERED ONE OF MY MEN, SO MAKE HIM HURT BEFORE YOU KILL HIM.
HE'S CUT OUT HIS TRACKER. FIND HIM ANYWAY.

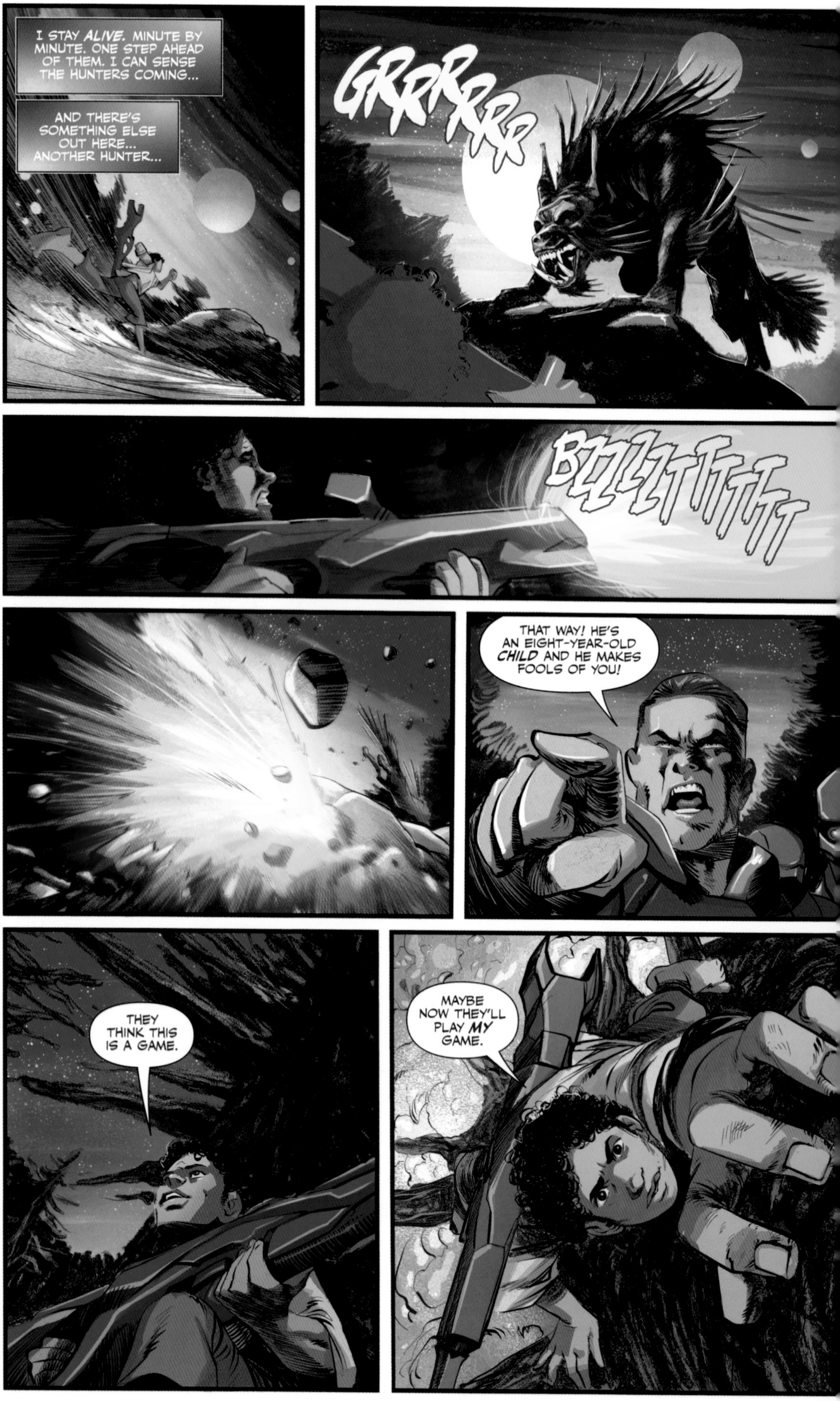
I STAY ALIVE. MINUTE BY MINUTE. ONE STEP AHEAD OF THEM. I CAN SENSE THE HUNTERS COMING...
AND THERE'S SOMETHING ELSE OUT HERE... ANOTHER HUNTER...
GRRRRRR
BZZZTTTTTTT
THAT WAY! HE'S AN EIGHT-YEAR-OLD CHILD AND HE MAKES FOOLS OF YOU!
THEY THINK THIS IS A GAME.
MAYBE NOW THEY'LL PLAY MY GAME.

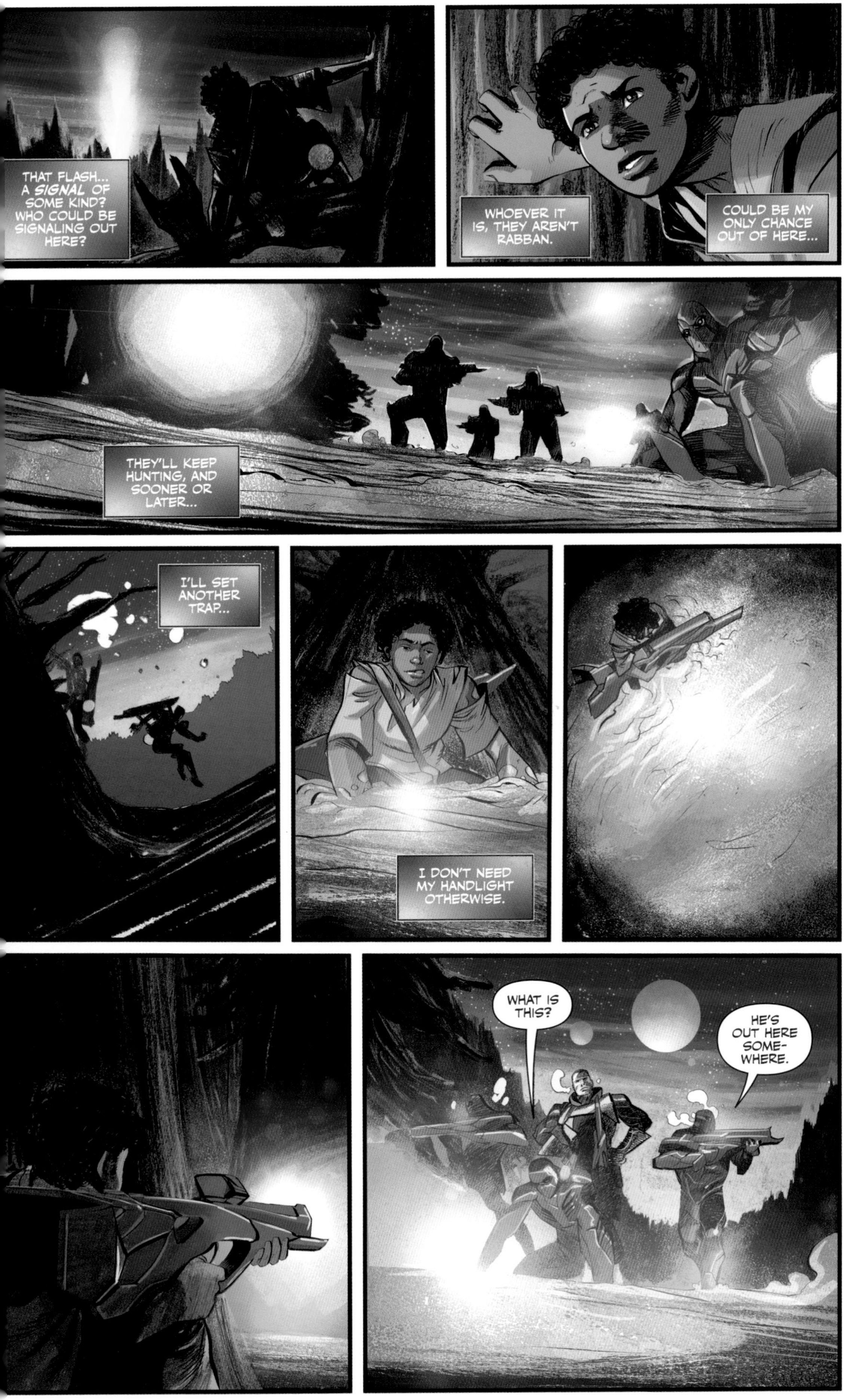
THAT FLASH... A SIGNAL OF SOME KIND? WHO COULD BE SIGNALING OUT HERE?
WHOEVER IT IS, THEY AREN'T RABBAN.
COULD BE MY ONLY CHANCE OUT OF HERE...
THEY'LL KEEP HUNTING, AND SOONER OR LATER...
I'LL SET ANOTHER TRAP...
I DON'T NEED MY HANDLIGHT OTHERWISE.
WHAT IS THIS?
HE'S OUT HERE SOME-WHERE.

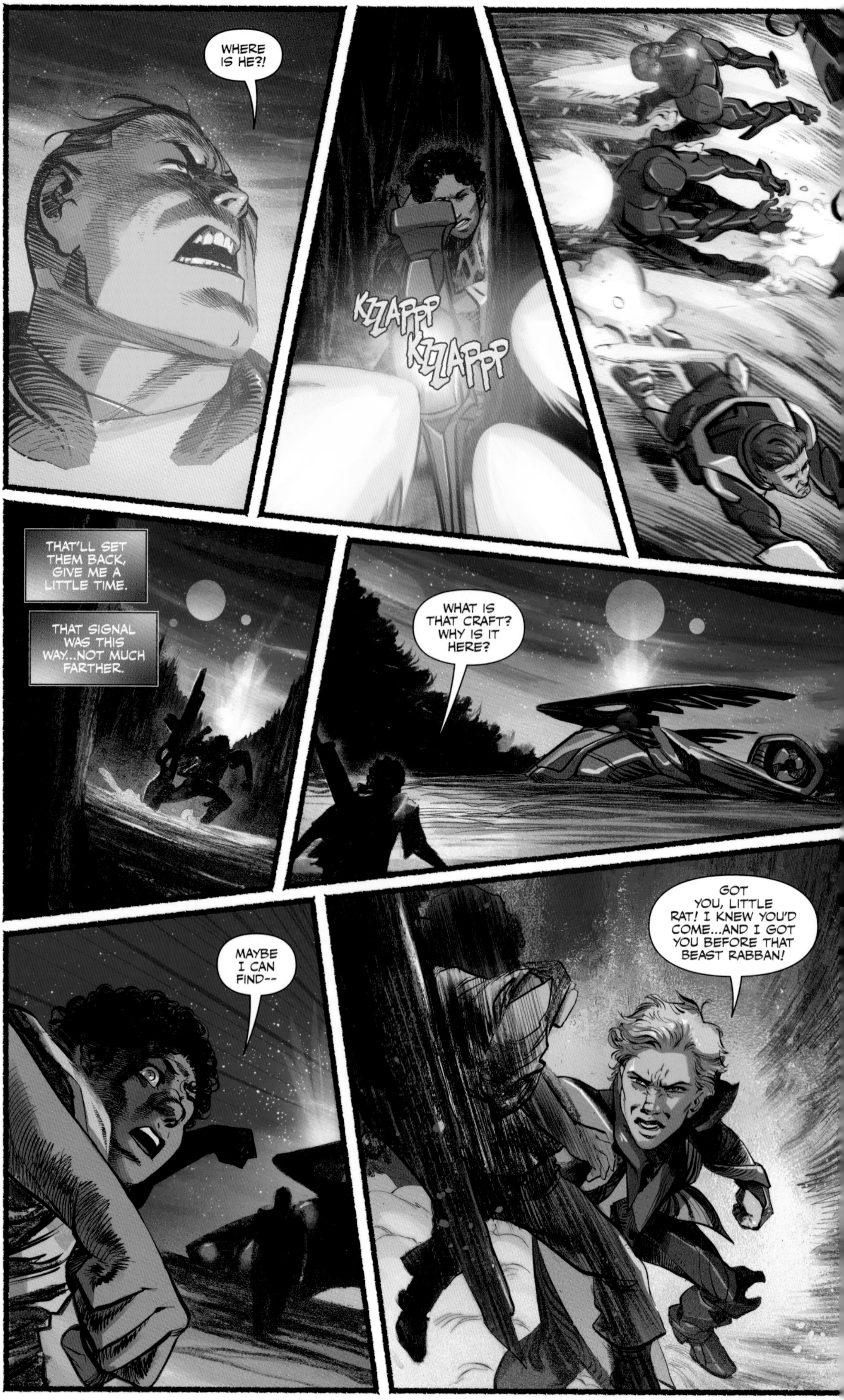
WHERE IS HE?!
KZZAPPP KZZAPPP
THAT'LL SET THEM BACK, GIVE ME A LITTLE TIME.
THAT SIGNAL WAS THIS WAY...NOT MUCH FARTHER.
WHAT IS THAT CRAFT? WHY IS IT HERE?
MAYBE I CAN FIND--
GOT YOU, LITTLE RAT! I KNEW YOU'D COME...AND I GOT YOU BEFORE THAT BEAST RABBAN!

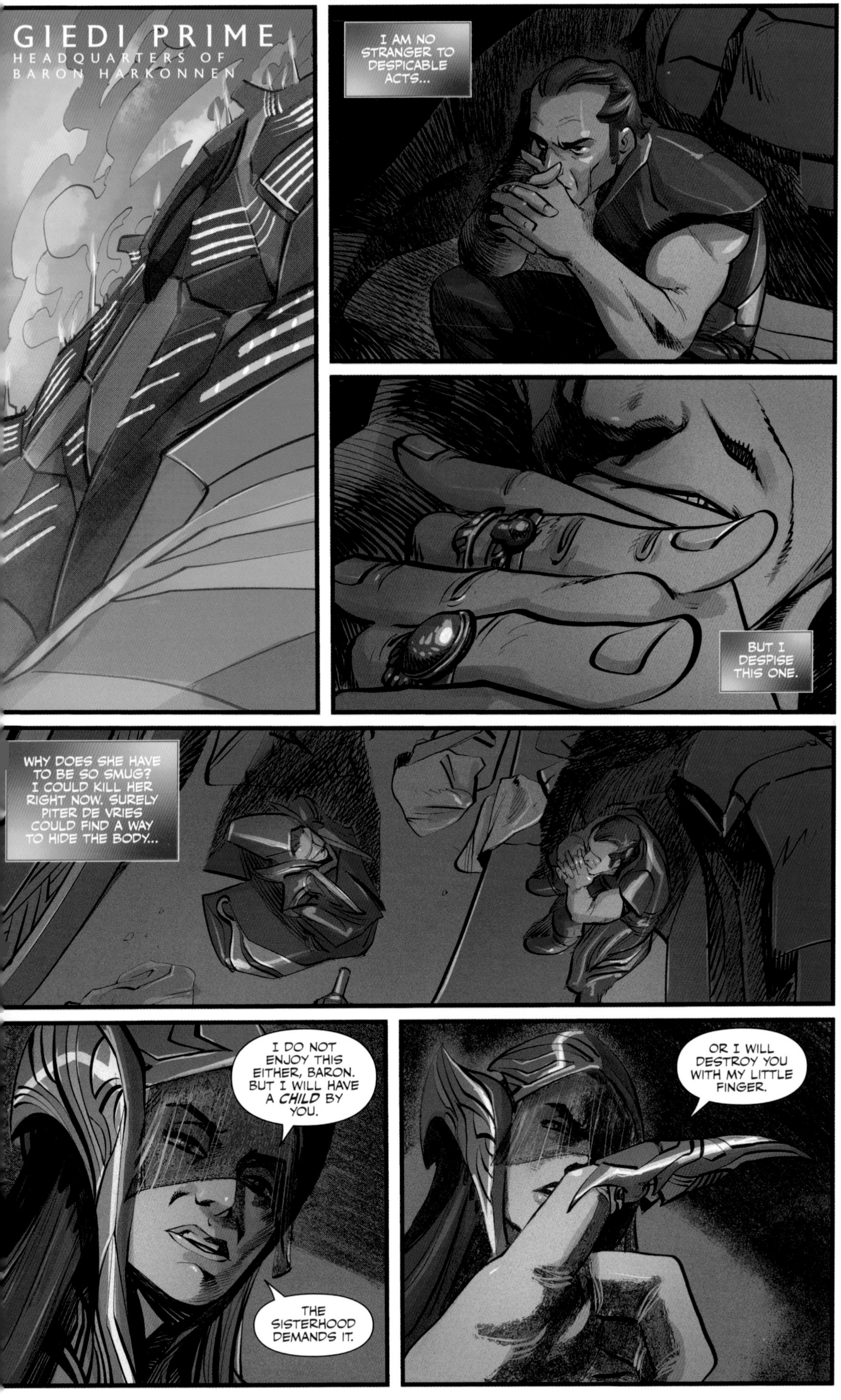
GIEDI PRIME
HEADQUARTERS OF BARON HARKONNEN
I AM NO STRANGER TO DESPICABLE ACTS...
BUT I DESPISE THIS ONE.
WHY DOES SHE HAVE TO BE SO SMUG? I COULD KILL HER RIGHT NOW. SURELY PITER DE VRIES COULD FIND A WAY TO HIDE THE BODY...
I DO NOT ENJOY THIS EITHER, BARON. BUT I WILL HAVE A *CHILD* BY YOU.
THE SISTERHOOD DEMANDS IT.
OR I WILL DESTROY YOU WITH MY LITTLE FINGER.

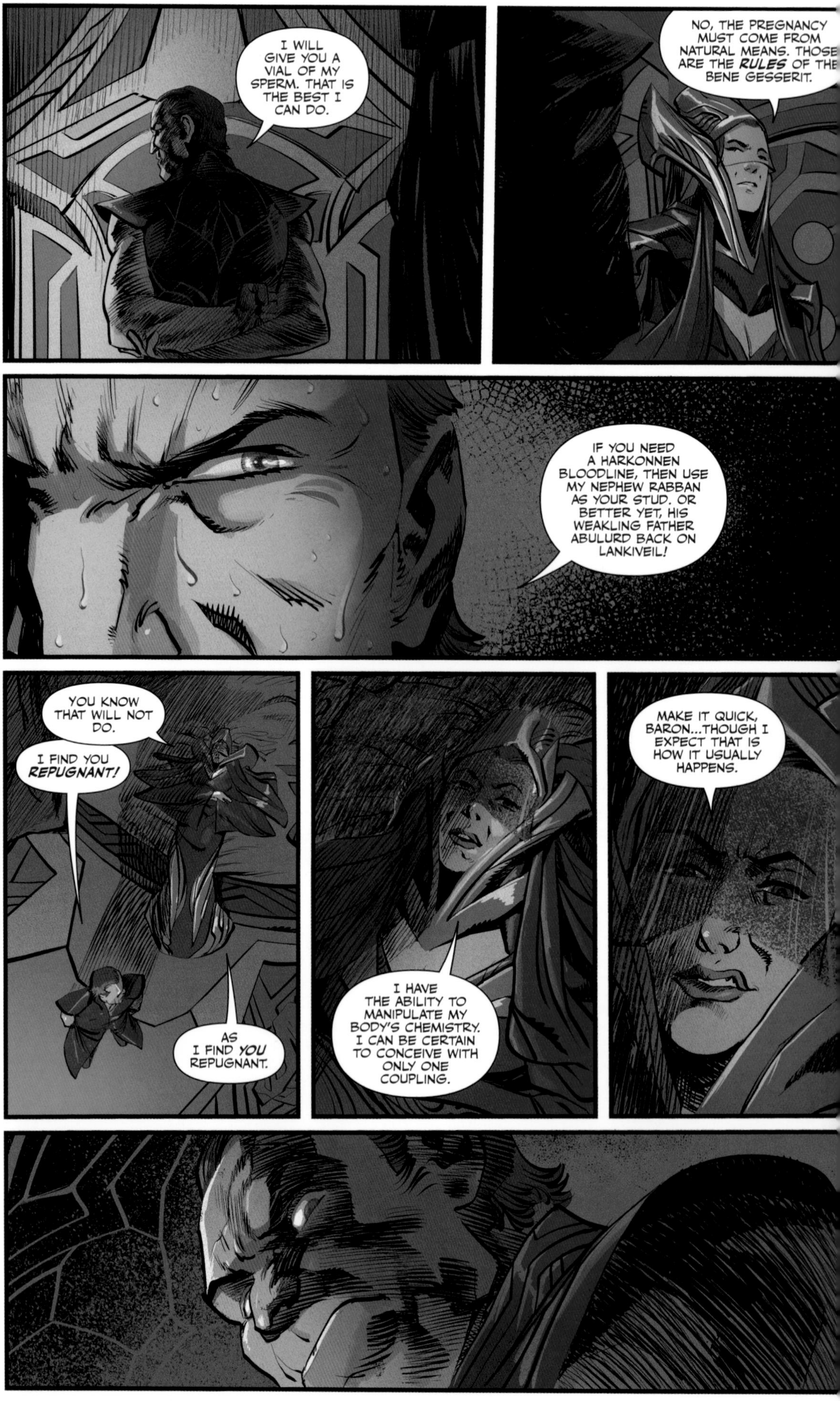
I WILL GIVE YOU A VIAL OF MY SPERM. THAT IS THE BEST I CAN DO.
NO, THE PREGNANCY MUST COME FROM NATURAL MEANS. THOSE ARE THE *RULES* OF THE BENE GESSERIT.
IF YOU NEED A HARKONNEN BLOODLINE, THEN USE MY NEPHEW RABBAN AS YOUR STUD. OR BETTER YET, HIS WEAKLING FATHER ABULURD BACK ON LANKIVEIL!
YOU KNOW THAT WILL NOT DO.
I FIND YOU *REPUGNANT!*
AS I FIND *YOU* REPUGNANT.
I HAVE THE ABILITY TO MANIPULATE MY BODY'S CHEMISTRY. I CAN BE CERTAIN TO CONCEIVE WITH ONLY ONE COUPLING.
MAKE IT QUICK, BARON...THOUGH I EXPECT THAT IS HOW IT USUALLY HAPPENS.

WITCH!

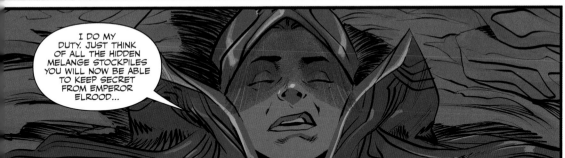

I DO MY DUTY. JUST THINK OF ALL THE HIDDEN MELANGE STOCKPILES YOU WILL NOW BE ABLE TO KEEP SECRET FROM EMPEROR ELROOD...

AHHH, MY POOR BARON!

I HAVE SPIED ON MANY OF YOUR OUTRAGEOUS ESCAPADES, BARON, BUT NOT LIKE THIS...

AHH, IF ONLY I HAD SET UP RECORDING DEVICES...

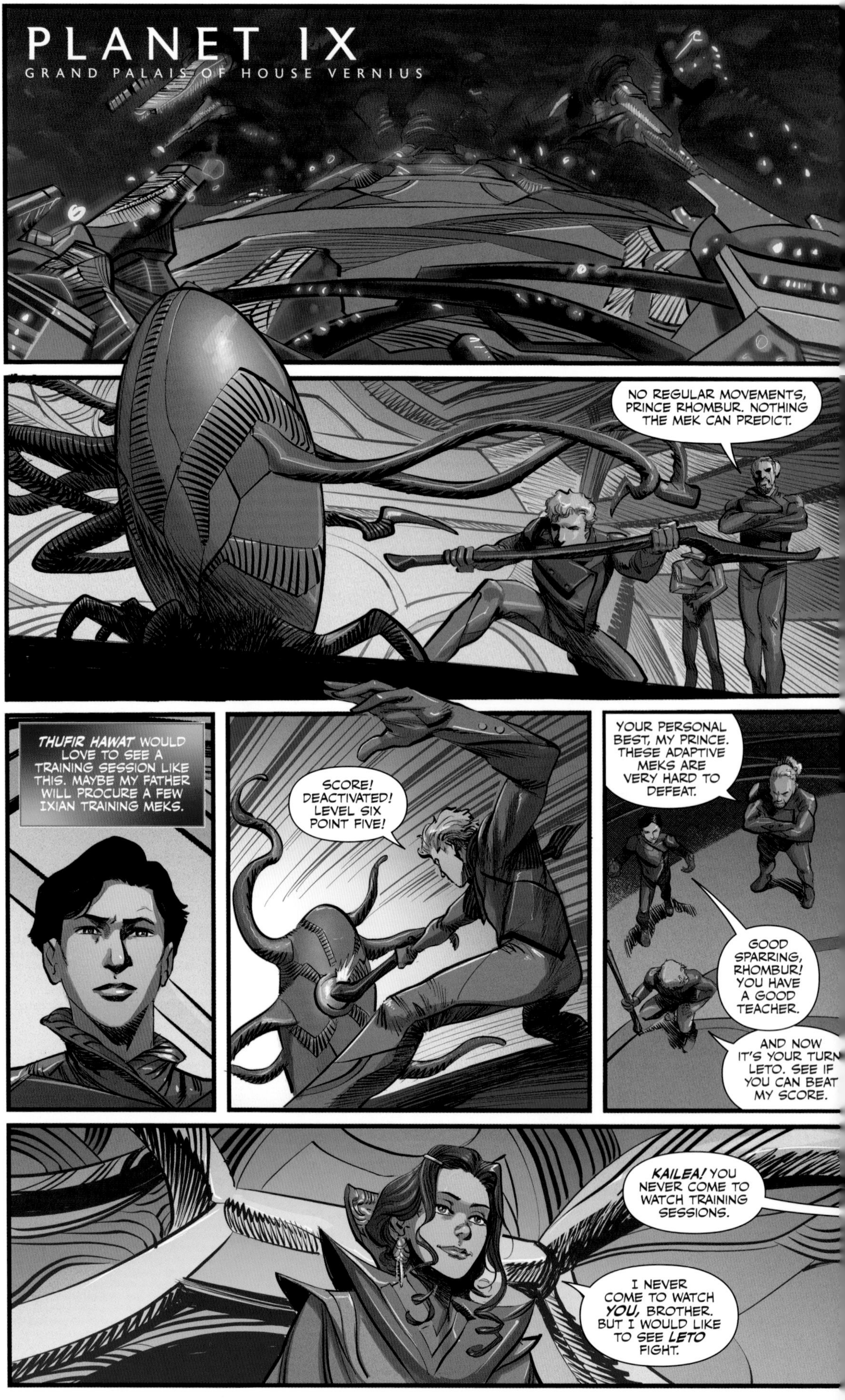
PLANET IX
GRAND PALAIS OF HOUSE VERNIUS
NO REGULAR MOVEMENTS, PRINCE RHOMBUR. NOTHING THE MEK CAN PREDICT.
THUFIR HAWAT WOULD LOVE TO SEE A TRAINING SESSION LIKE THIS. MAYBE MY FATHER WILL PROCURE A FEW IXIAN TRAINING MEKS.
SCORE! DEACTIVATED! LEVEL SIX POINT FIVE!
YOUR PERSONAL BEST, MY PRINCE. THESE ADAPTIVE MEKS ARE VERY HARD TO DEFEAT.
GOOD SPARRING, RHOMBUR! YOU HAVE A GOOD TEACHER.
AND NOW IT'S YOUR TURN LETO. SEE IF YOU CAN BEAT MY SCORE.
KAILEA! YOU NEVER COME TO WATCH TRAINING SESSIONS.
I NEVER COME TO WATCH YOU, BROTHER. BUT I WOULD LIKE TO SEE LETO FIGHT.

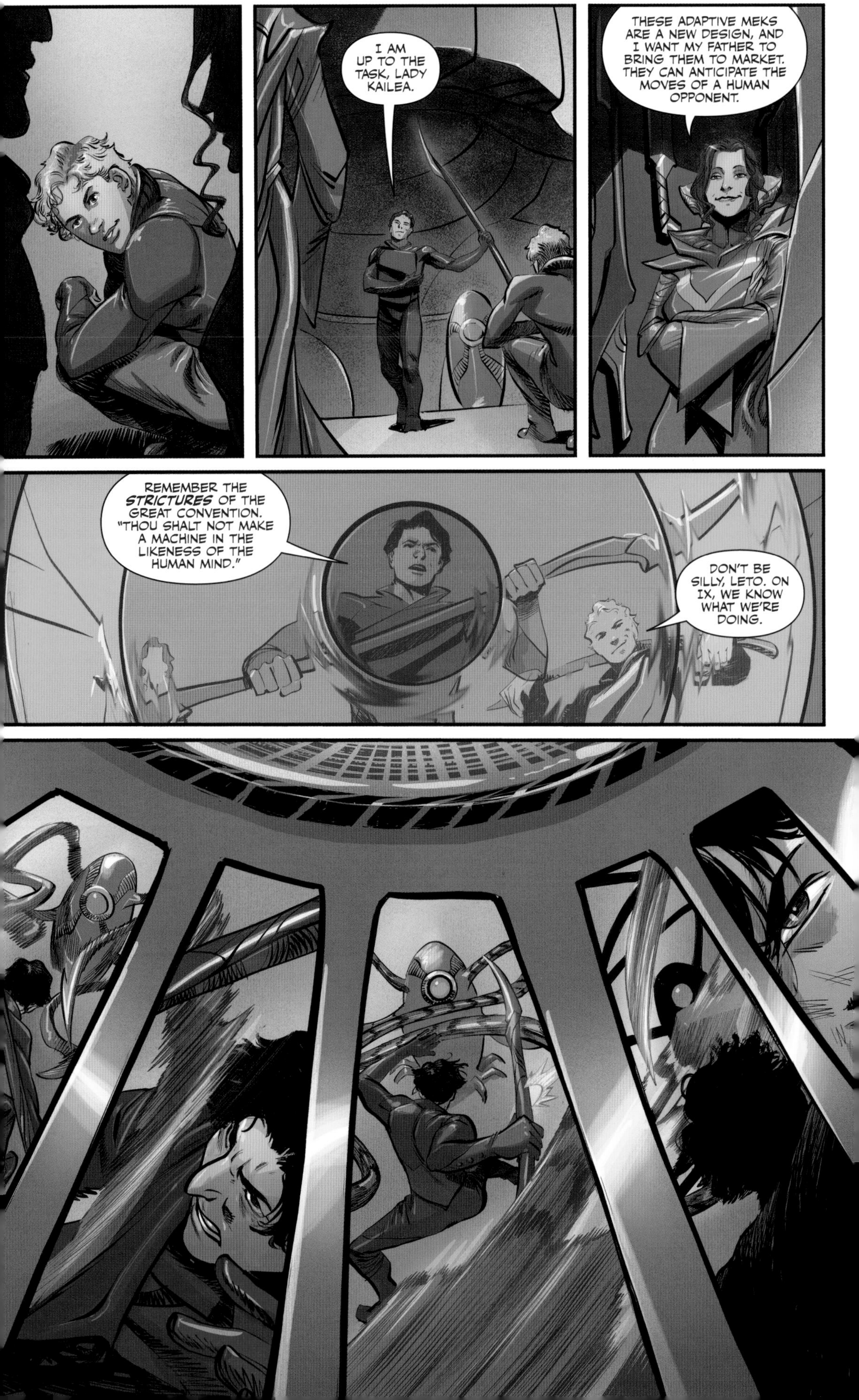
I AM UP TO THE TASK, LADY KAILEA.
THESE ADAPTIVE MEKS ARE A NEW DESIGN, AND I WANT MY FATHER TO BRING THEM TO MARKET. THEY CAN ANTICIPATE THE MOVES OF A HUMAN OPPONENT.
REMEMBER THE *STRICTURES* OF THE GREAT CONVENTION. "THOU SHALT NOT MAKE A MACHINE IN THE LIKENESS OF THE HUMAN MIND."
DON'T BE SILLY, LETO. ON IX, WE KNOW WHAT WE'RE DOING.

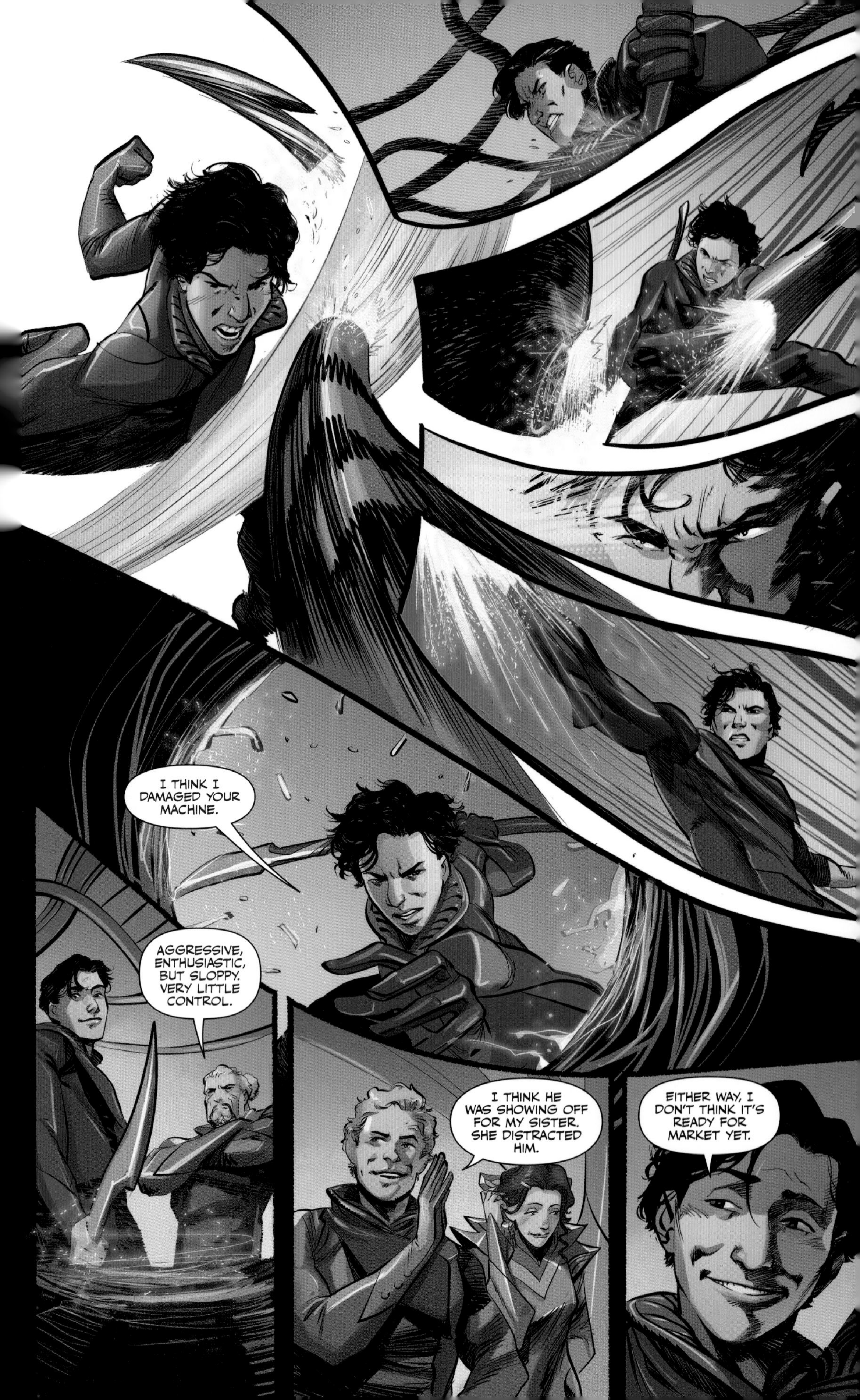
I THINK I DAMAGED YOUR MACHINE.
AGGRESSIVE, ENTHUSIASTIC, BUT SLOPPY. VERY LITTLE CONTROL.
I THINK HE WAS SHOWING OFF FOR MY SISTER. SHE DISTRACTED HIM.
EITHER WAY, I DON'T THINK IT'S READY FOR MARKET YET.

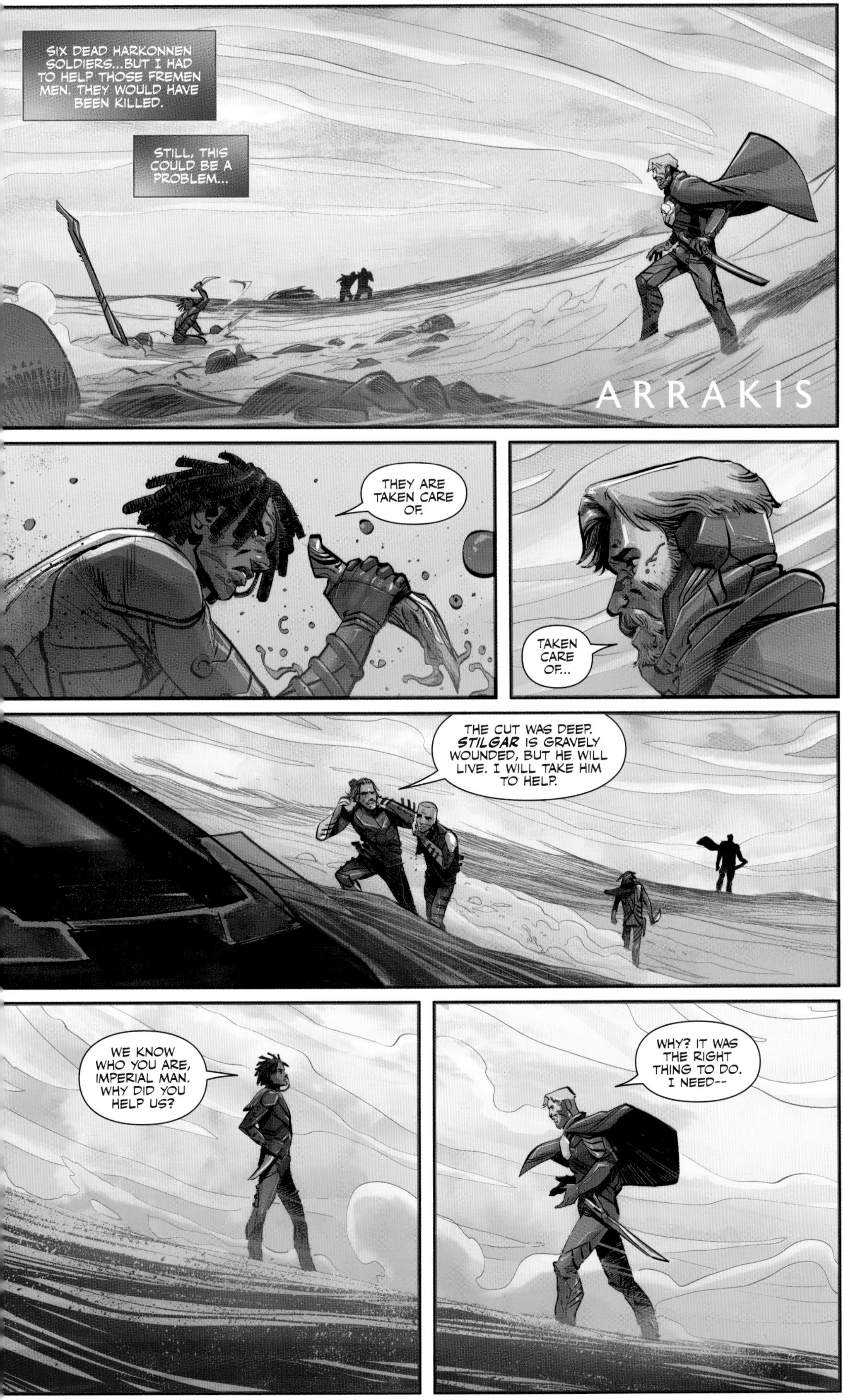

SIX DEAD HARKONNEN SOLDIERS...BUT I HAD TO HELP THOSE FREMEN MEN. THEY WOULD HAVE BEEN KILLED.
STILL, THIS COULD BE A PROBLEM...
ARRAKIS
THEY ARE TAKEN CARE OF.
TAKEN CARE OF...
THE CUT WAS DEEP. STILGAR IS GRAVELY WOUNDED, BUT HE WILL LIVE. I WILL TAKE HIM TO HELP.
WE KNOW WHO YOU ARE, IMPERIAL MAN. WHY DID YOU HELP US?
WHY? IT WAS THE RIGHT THING TO DO. I NEED--

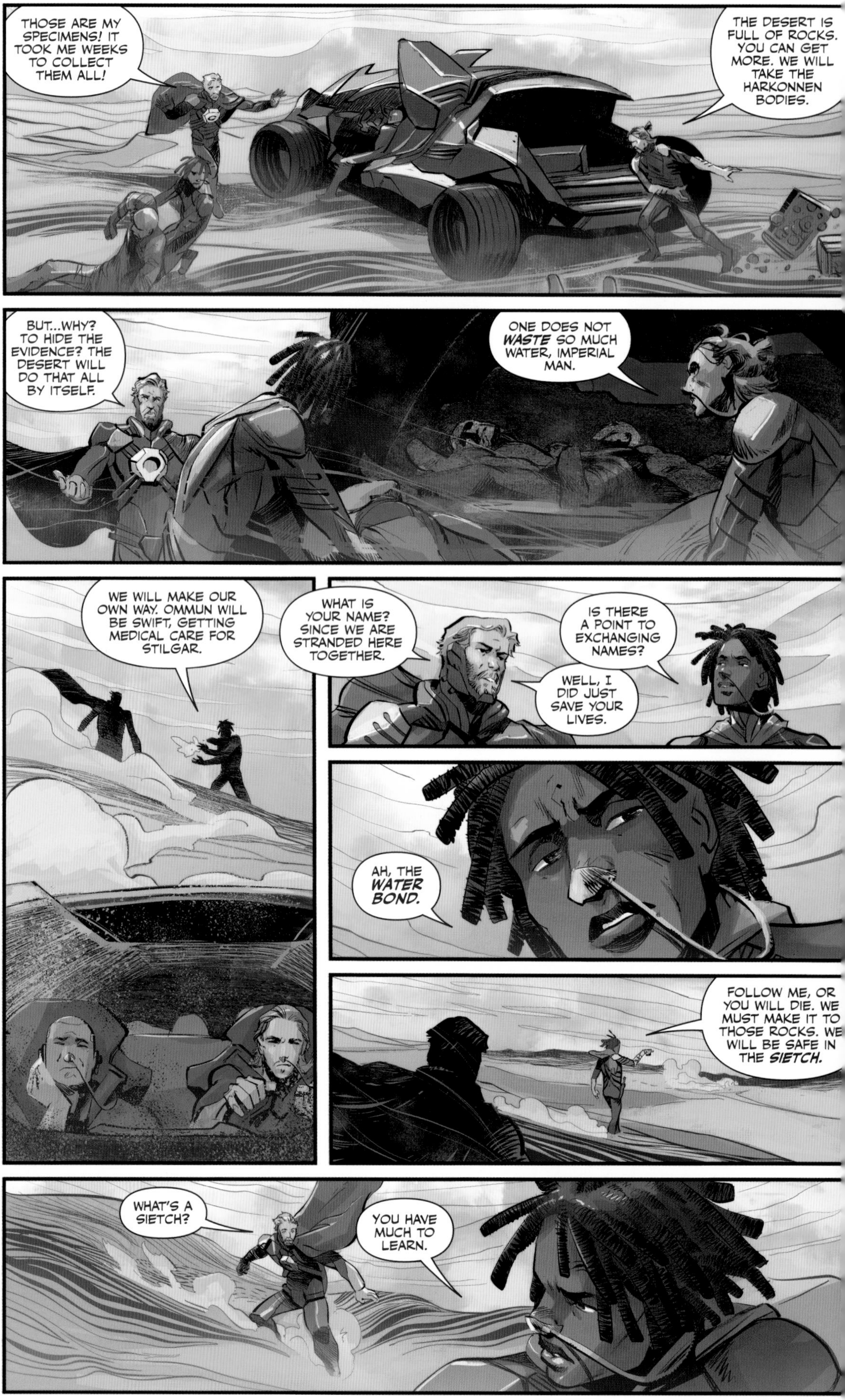

THOSE ARE MY SPECIMENS! IT TOOK ME WEEKS TO COLLECT THEM ALL!
THE DESERT IS FULL OF ROCKS. YOU CAN GET MORE. WE WILL TAKE THE HARKONNEN BODIES.
BUT...WHY? TO HIDE THE EVIDENCE? THE DESERT WILL DO THAT ALL BY ITSELF.
ONE DOES NOT WASTE SO MUCH WATER, IMPERIAL MAN.
WE WILL MAKE OUR OWN WAY. OMMUN WILL BE SWIFT, GETTING MEDICAL CARE FOR STILGAR.
WHAT IS YOUR NAME? SINCE WE ARE STRANDED HERE TOGETHER.
IS THERE A POINT TO EXCHANGING NAMES?
WELL, I DID JUST SAVE YOUR LIVES.
AH, THE WATER BOND.
FOLLOW ME, OR YOU WILL DIE. WE MUST MAKE IT TO THOSE ROCKS. WE WILL BE SAFE IN THE SIETCH.
WHAT'S A SIETCH?
YOU HAVE MUCH TO LEARN.

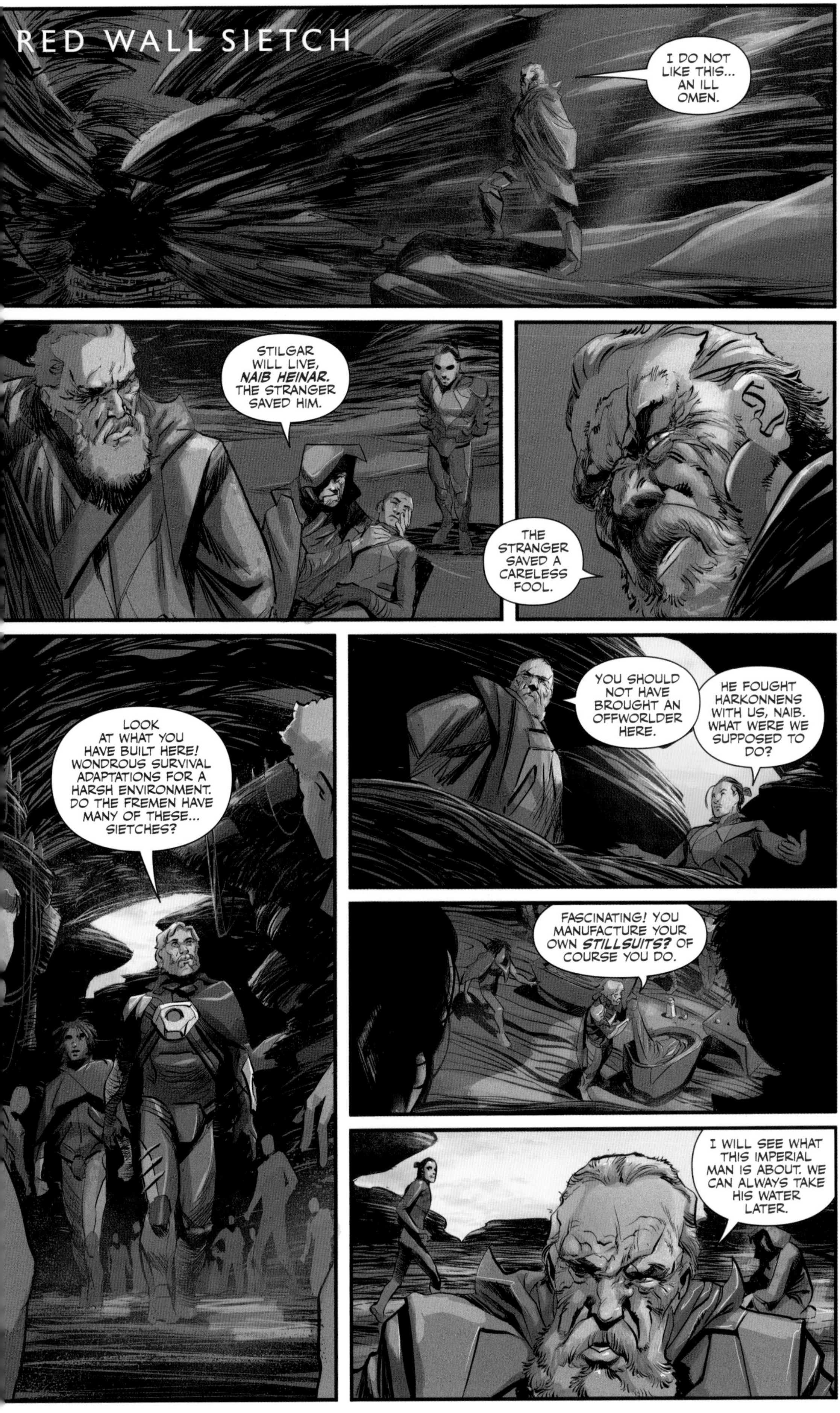
RED WALL SIETCH
I DO NOT LIKE THIS... AN ILL OMEN.
STILGAR WILL LIVE, NAIB HEINAR. THE STRANGER SAVED HIM.
THE STRANGER SAVED A CARELESS FOOL.
LOOK AT WHAT YOU HAVE BUILT HERE! WONDROUS SURVIVAL ADAPTATIONS FOR A HARSH ENVIRONMENT. DO THE FREMEN HAVE MANY OF THESE... SIETCHES?
YOU SHOULD NOT HAVE BROUGHT AN OFFWORLDER HERE.
HE FOUGHT HARKONNENS WITH US, NAIB. WHAT WERE WE SUPPOSED TO DO?
FASCINATING! YOU MANUFACTURE YOUR OWN STILLSUITS? OF COURSE YOU DO.
I WILL SEE WHAT THIS IMPERIAL MAN IS ABOUT. WE CAN ALWAYS TAKE HIS WATER LATER.

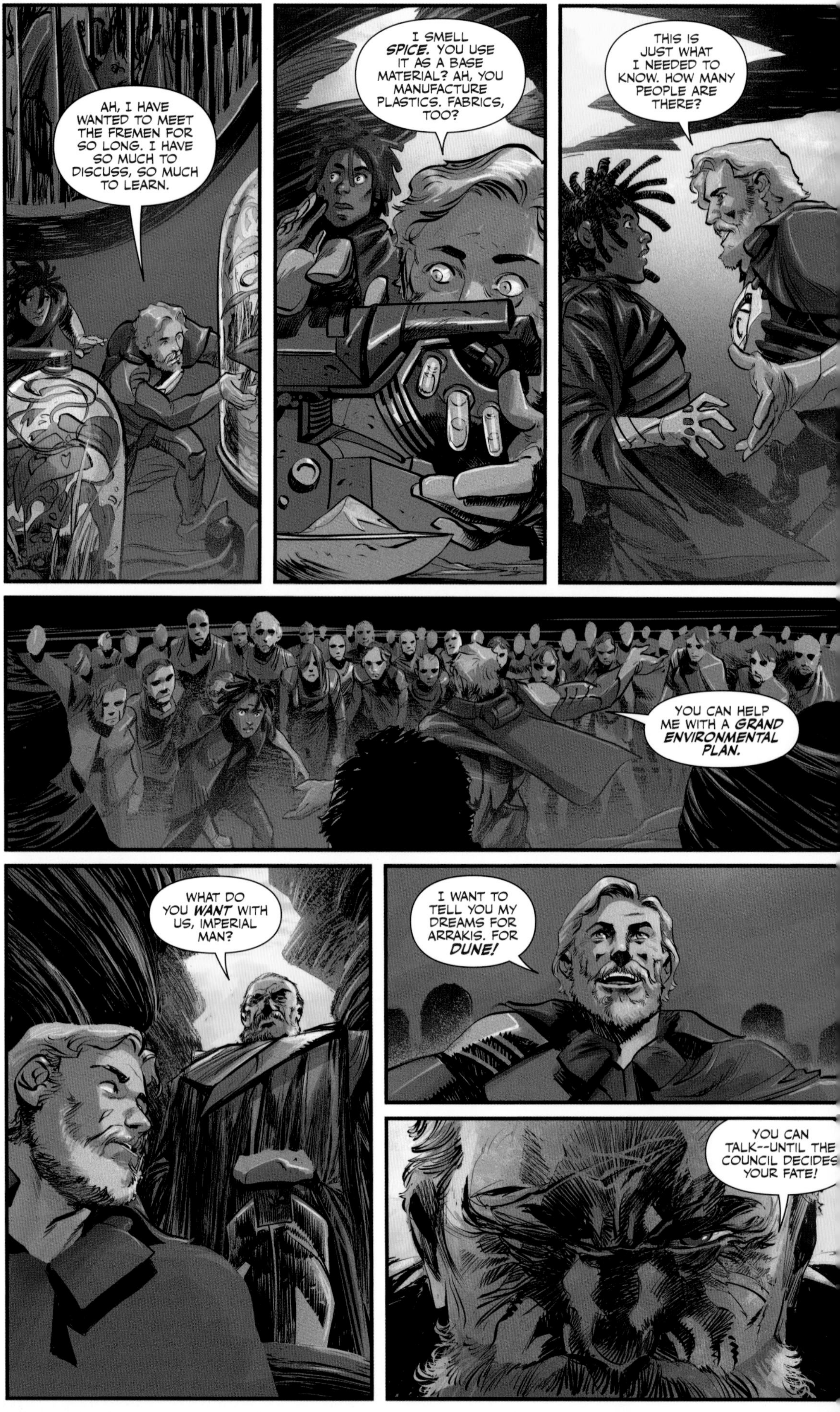
AH, I HAVE WANTED TO MEET THE FREMEN FOR SO LONG. I HAVE SO MUCH TO DISCUSS, SO MUCH TO LEARN.
I SMELL *SPICE.* YOU USE IT AS A BASE MATERIAL? AH, YOU MANUFACTURE PLASTICS. FABRICS, TOO?
THIS IS JUST WHAT I NEEDED TO KNOW. HOW MANY PEOPLE ARE THERE?
YOU CAN HELP ME WITH A ***GRAND ENVIRONMENTAL PLAN.***
WHAT DO YOU ***WANT*** WITH US, IMPERIAL MAN?
I WANT TO TELL YOU MY DREAMS FOR ARRAKIS. FOR ***DUNE!***
YOU CAN TALK--UNTIL THE COUNCIL DECIDES YOUR FATE!

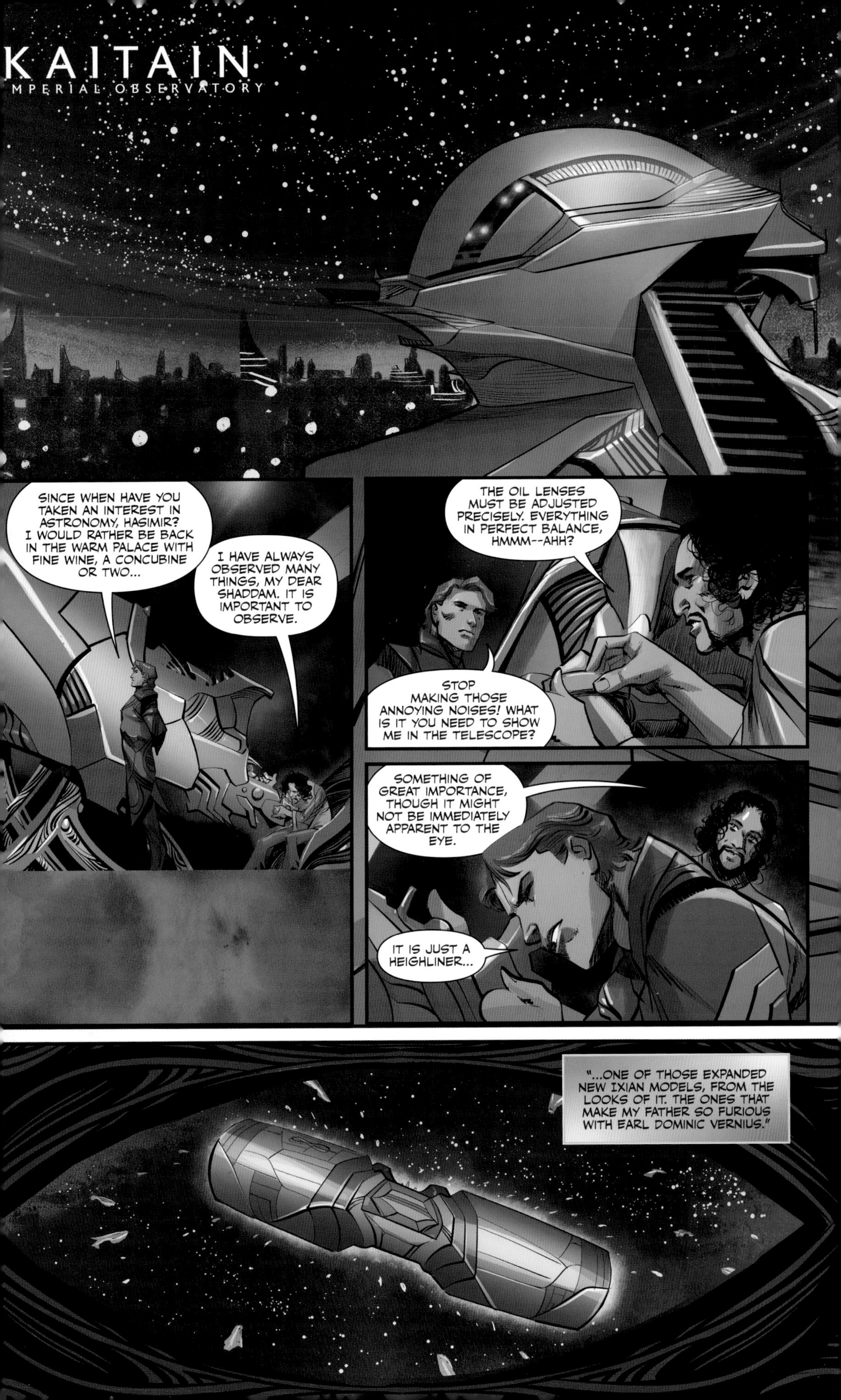
KAITAIN
IMPERIAL OBSERVATORY
SINCE WHEN HAVE YOU TAKEN AN INTEREST IN ASTRONOMY, HASIMIR? I WOULD RATHER BE BACK IN THE WARM PALACE WITH FINE WINE, A CONCUBINE OR TWO...
I HAVE ALWAYS OBSERVED MANY THINGS, MY DEAR SHADDAM. IT IS IMPORTANT TO OBSERVE.
THE OIL LENSES MUST BE ADJUSTED PRECISELY. EVERYTHING IN PERFECT BALANCE, HMMM--AHH?
STOP MAKING THOSE ANNOYING NOISES! WHAT IS IT YOU NEED TO SHOW ME IN THE TELESCOPE?
SOMETHING OF GREAT IMPORTANCE, THOUGH IT MIGHT NOT BE IMMEDIATELY APPARENT TO THE EYE.
IT IS JUST A HEIGHLINER...
"...ONE OF THOSE EXPANDED NEW IXIAN MODELS, FROM THE LOOKS OF IT. THE ONES THAT MAKE MY FATHER SO FURIOUS WITH EARL DOMINIC VERNIUS."

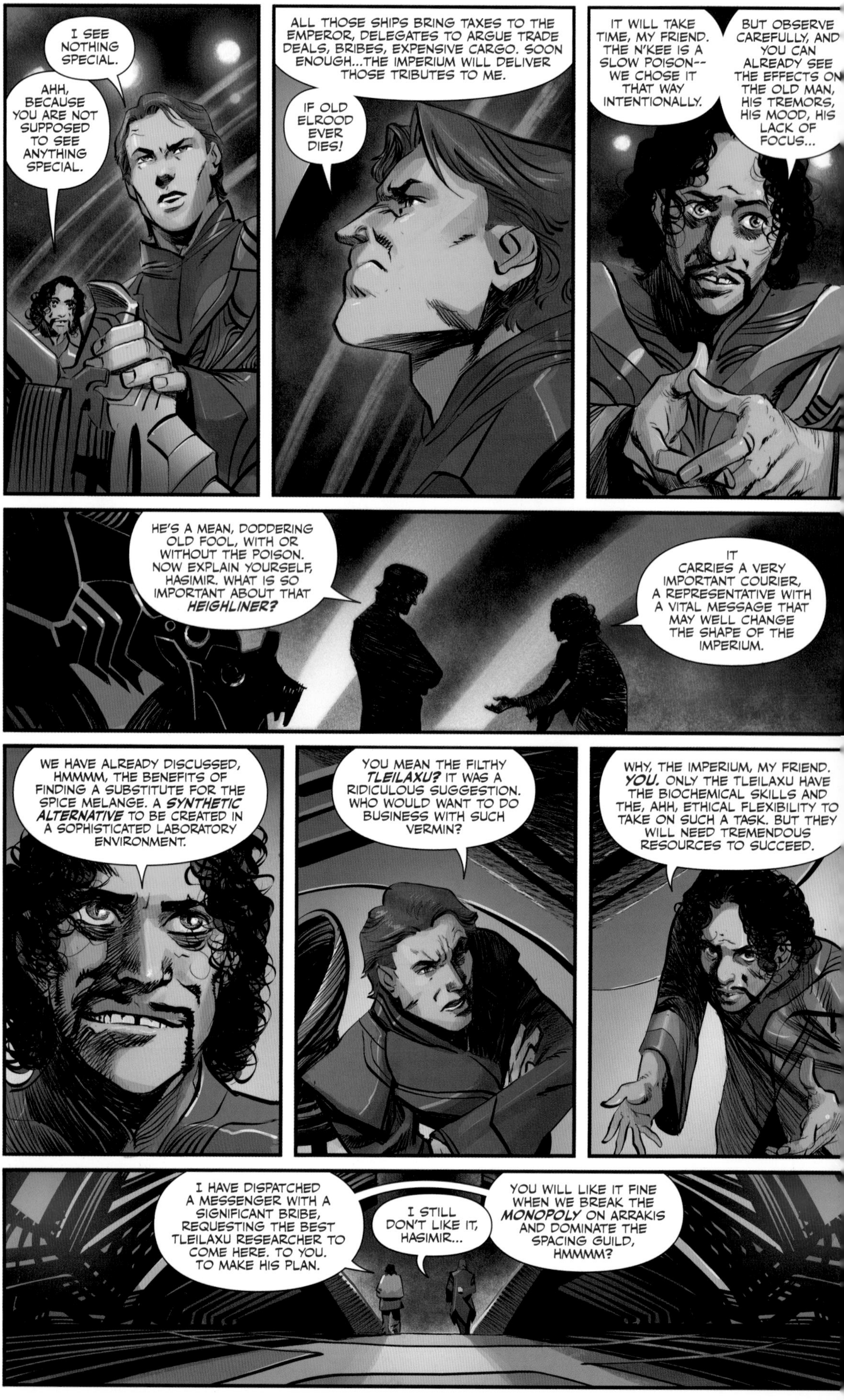
I SEE NOTHING SPECIAL.
AHH, BECAUSE YOU ARE NOT SUPPOSED TO SEE ANYTHING SPECIAL.
ALL THOSE SHIPS BRING TAXES TO THE EMPEROR, DELEGATES TO ARGUE TRADE DEALS, BRIBES, EXPENSIVE CARGO. SOON ENOUGH...THE IMPERIUM WILL DELIVER THOSE TRIBUTES TO ME.
IF OLD ELROOD EVER DIES!
IT WILL TAKE TIME, MY FRIEND. THE N'KEE IS A SLOW POISON-- WE CHOSE IT THAT WAY INTENTIONALLY.
BUT OBSERVE CAREFULLY, AND YOU CAN ALREADY SEE THE EFFECTS ON THE OLD MAN, HIS TREMORS, HIS MOOD, HIS LACK OF FOCUS...
HE'S A MEAN, DODDERING OLD FOOL, WITH OR WITHOUT THE POISON. NOW EXPLAIN YOURSELF, HASIMIR. WHAT IS SO IMPORTANT ABOUT THAT *HEIGHLINER?*
IT CARRIES A VERY IMPORTANT COURIER, A REPRESENTATIVE WITH A VITAL MESSAGE THAT MAY WELL CHANGE THE SHAPE OF THE IMPERIUM.
WE HAVE ALREADY DISCUSSED, HMMMM, THE BENEFITS OF FINDING A SUBSTITUTE FOR THE SPICE MELANGE. A *SYNTHETIC ALTERNATIVE* TO BE CREATED IN A SOPHISTICATED LABORATORY ENVIRONMENT.
YOU MEAN THE FILTHY *TLEILAXU?* IT WAS A RIDICULOUS SUGGESTION. WHO WOULD WANT TO DO BUSINESS WITH SUCH VERMIN?
WHY, THE IMPERIUM, MY FRIEND. *YOU.* ONLY THE TLEILAXU HAVE THE BIOCHEMICAL SKILLS AND THE, AHH, ETHICAL FLEXIBILITY TO TAKE ON SUCH A TASK. BUT THEY WILL NEED TREMENDOUS RESOURCES TO SUCCEED.
I HAVE DISPATCHED A MESSENGER WITH A SIGNIFICANT BRIBE, REQUESTING THE BEST TLEILAXU RESEARCHER TO COME HERE. TO YOU. TO MAKE HIS PLAN.
I STILL DON'T LIKE IT, HASIMIR...
YOU WILL LIKE IT FINE WHEN WE BREAK THE *MONOPOLY* ON ARRAKIS AND DOMINATE THE SPACING GUILD, HMMMM?

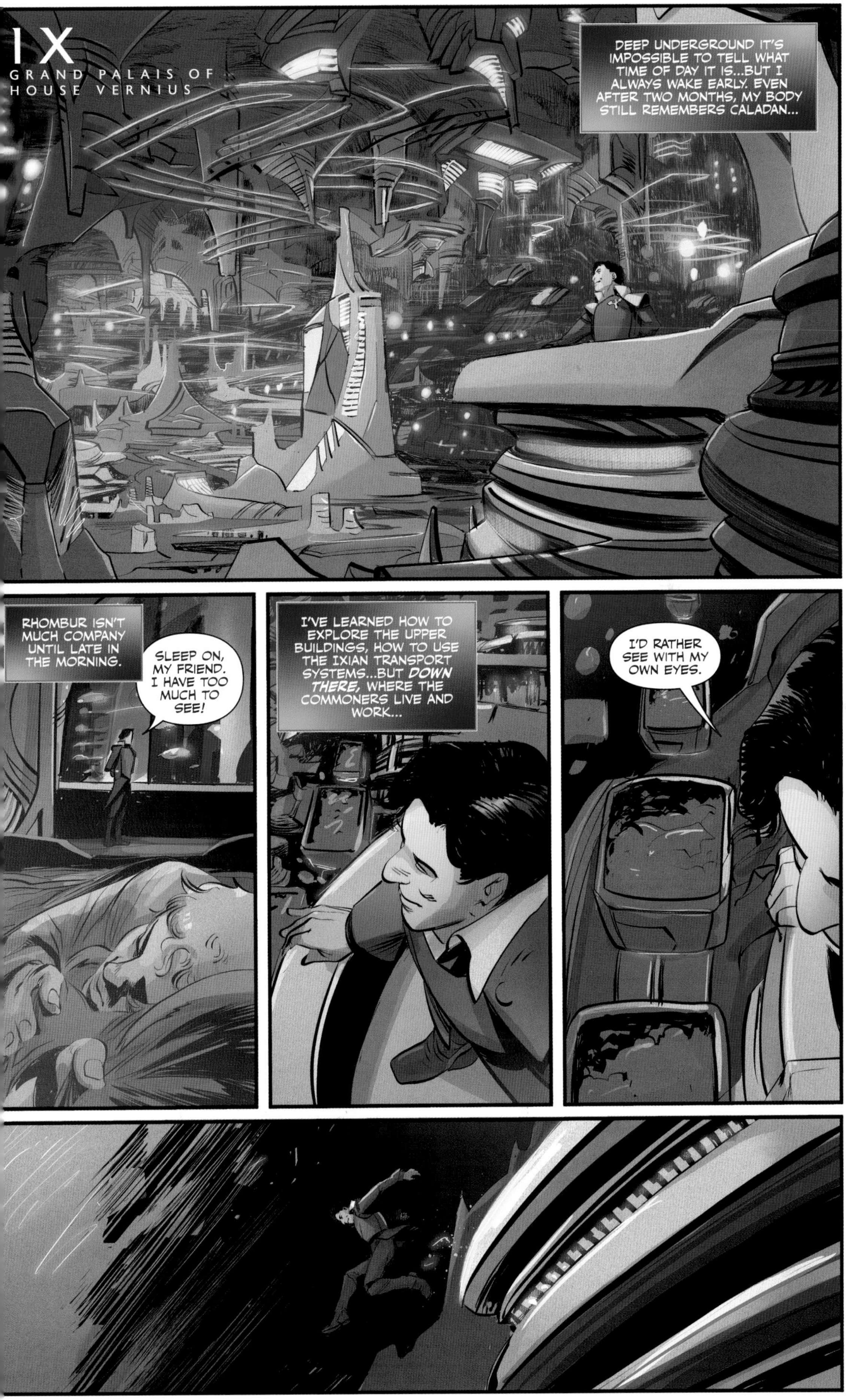
IX
GRAND PALAIS OF HOUSE VERNIUS
DEEP UNDERGROUND IT'S IMPOSSIBLE TO TELL WHAT TIME OF DAY IT IS...BUT I ALWAYS WAKE EARLY. EVEN AFTER TWO MONTHS, MY BODY STILL REMEMBERS CALADAN...
RHOMBUR ISN'T MUCH COMPANY UNTIL LATE IN THE MORNING.
SLEEP ON, MY FRIEND. I HAVE TOO MUCH TO SEE!
I'VE LEARNED HOW TO EXPLORE THE UPPER BUILDINGS, HOW TO USE THE IXIAN TRANSPORT SYSTEMS...BUT *DOWN THERE,* WHERE THE COMMONERS LIVE AND WORK...
I'D RATHER SEE WITH MY OWN EYES.

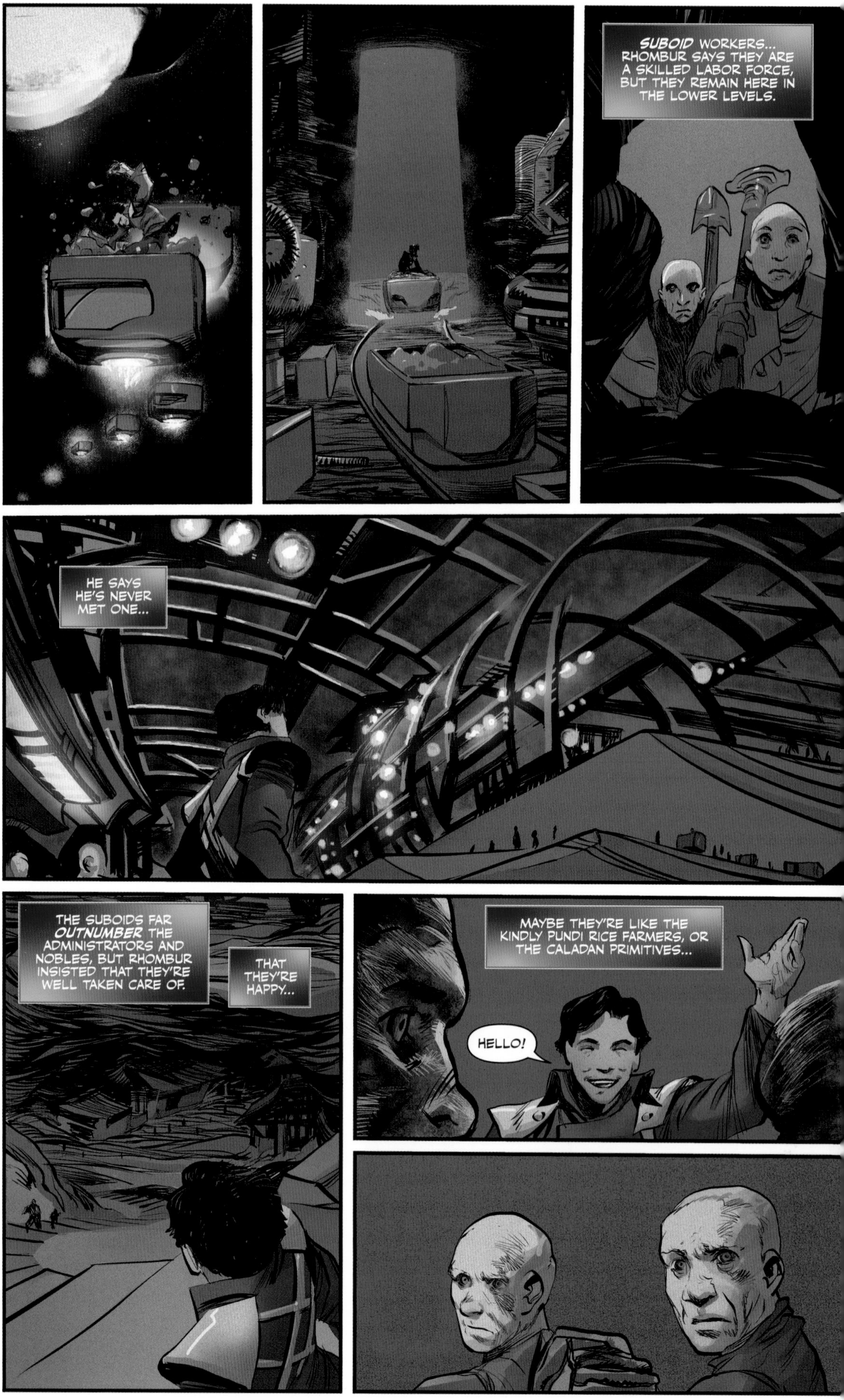
SUBOID WORKERS... RHOMBUR SAYS THEY ARE A SKILLED LABOR FORCE, BUT THEY REMAIN HERE IN THE LOWER LEVELS.
HE SAYS HE'S NEVER MET ONE...
THE SUBOIDS FAR OUTNUMBER THE ADMINISTRATORS AND NOBLES, BUT RHOMBUR INSISTED THAT THEY'RE WELL TAKEN CARE OF.
THAT THEY'RE HAPPY...
MAYBE THEY'RE LIKE THE KINDLY PUNDI RICE FARMERS, OR THE CALADAN PRIMITIVES...
HELLO!

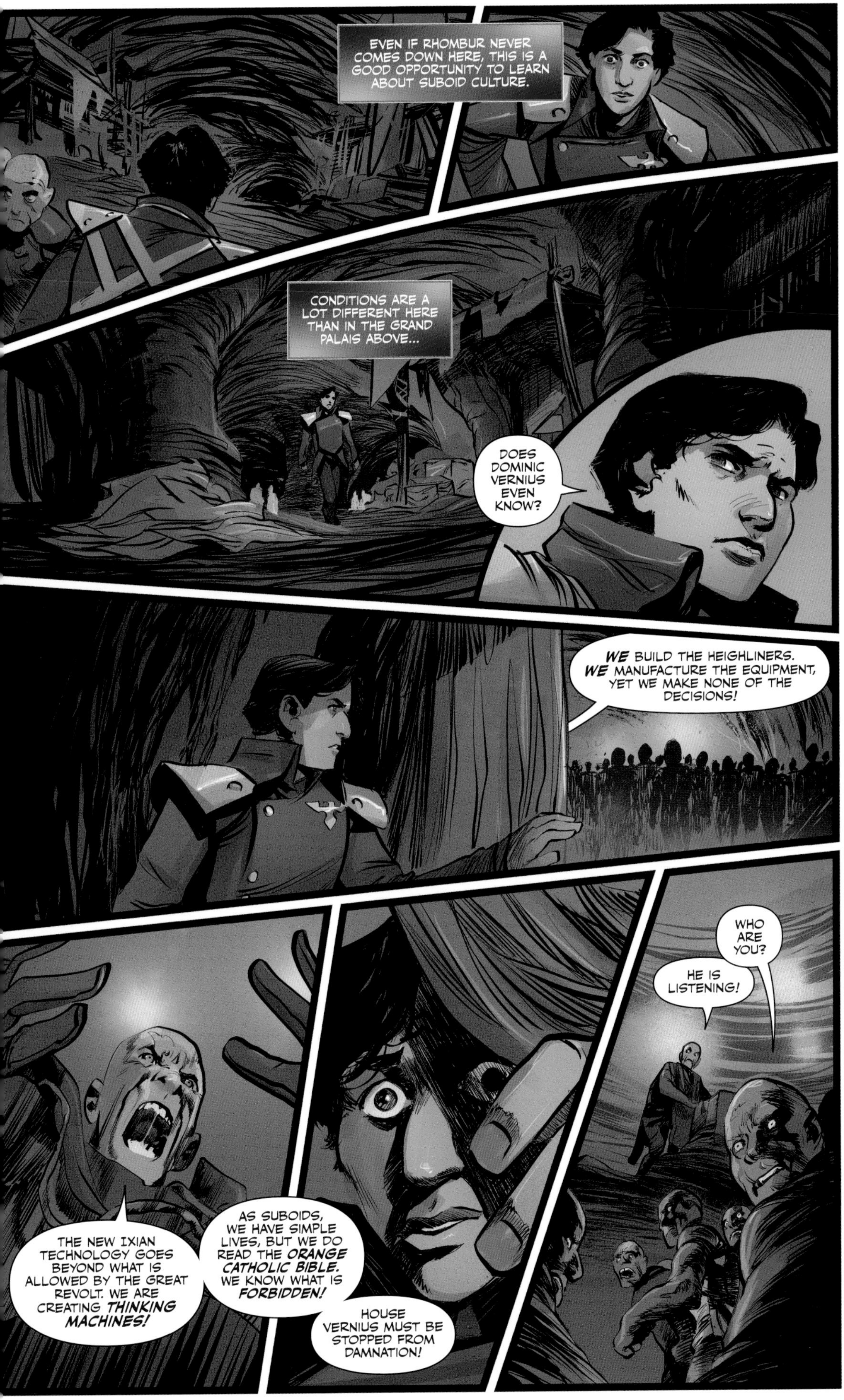
EVEN IF RHOMBUR NEVER COMES DOWN HERE, THIS IS A GOOD OPPORTUNITY TO LEARN ABOUT SUBOID CULTURE.
CONDITIONS ARE A LOT DIFFERENT HERE THAN IN THE GRAND PALAIS ABOVE...
DOES DOMINIC VERNIUS EVEN KNOW?
WE BUILD THE HEIGHLINERS. WE MANUFACTURE THE EQUIPMENT, YET WE MAKE NONE OF THE DECISIONS!
WHO ARE YOU?
HE IS LISTENING!
THE NEW IXIAN TECHNOLOGY GOES BEYOND WHAT IS ALLOWED BY THE GREAT REVOLT. WE ARE CREATING THINKING MACHINES!
AS SUBOIDS, WE HAVE SIMPLE LIVES, BUT WE DO READ THE ORANGE CATHOLIC BIBLE. WE KNOW WHAT IS FORBIDDEN!
HOUSE VERNIUS MUST BE STOPPED FROM DAMNATION!

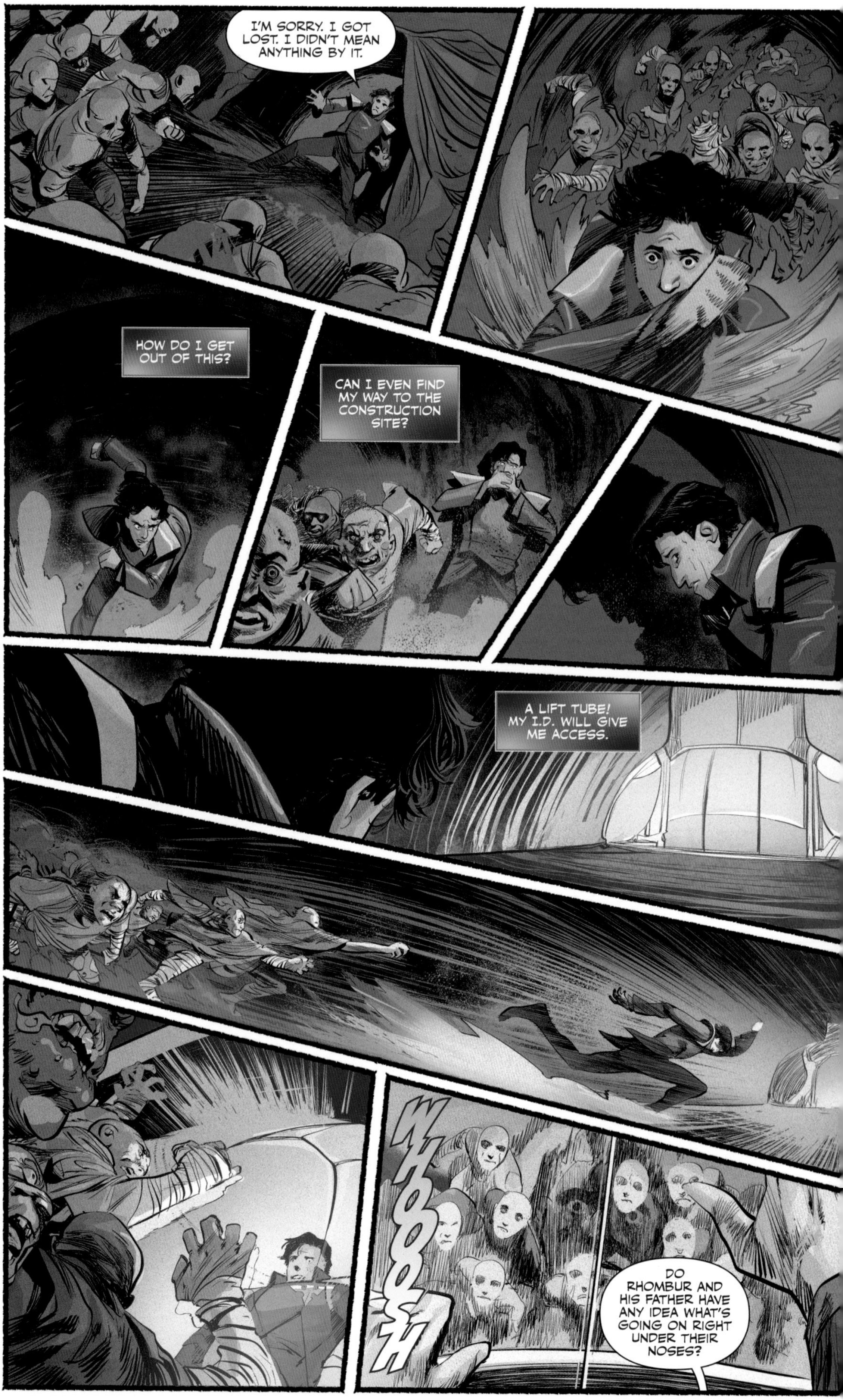
I'M SORRY. I GOT LOST. I DIDN'T MEAN ANYTHING BY IT.
HOW DO I GET OUT OF THIS?
CAN I EVEN FIND MY WAY TO THE CONSTRUCTION SITE?
A LIFT TUBE! MY I.D. WILL GIVE ME ACCESS.
WHOOOOSH
DO RHOMBUR AND HIS FATHER HAVE ANY IDEA WHAT'S GOING ON RIGHT UNDER THEIR NOSES?

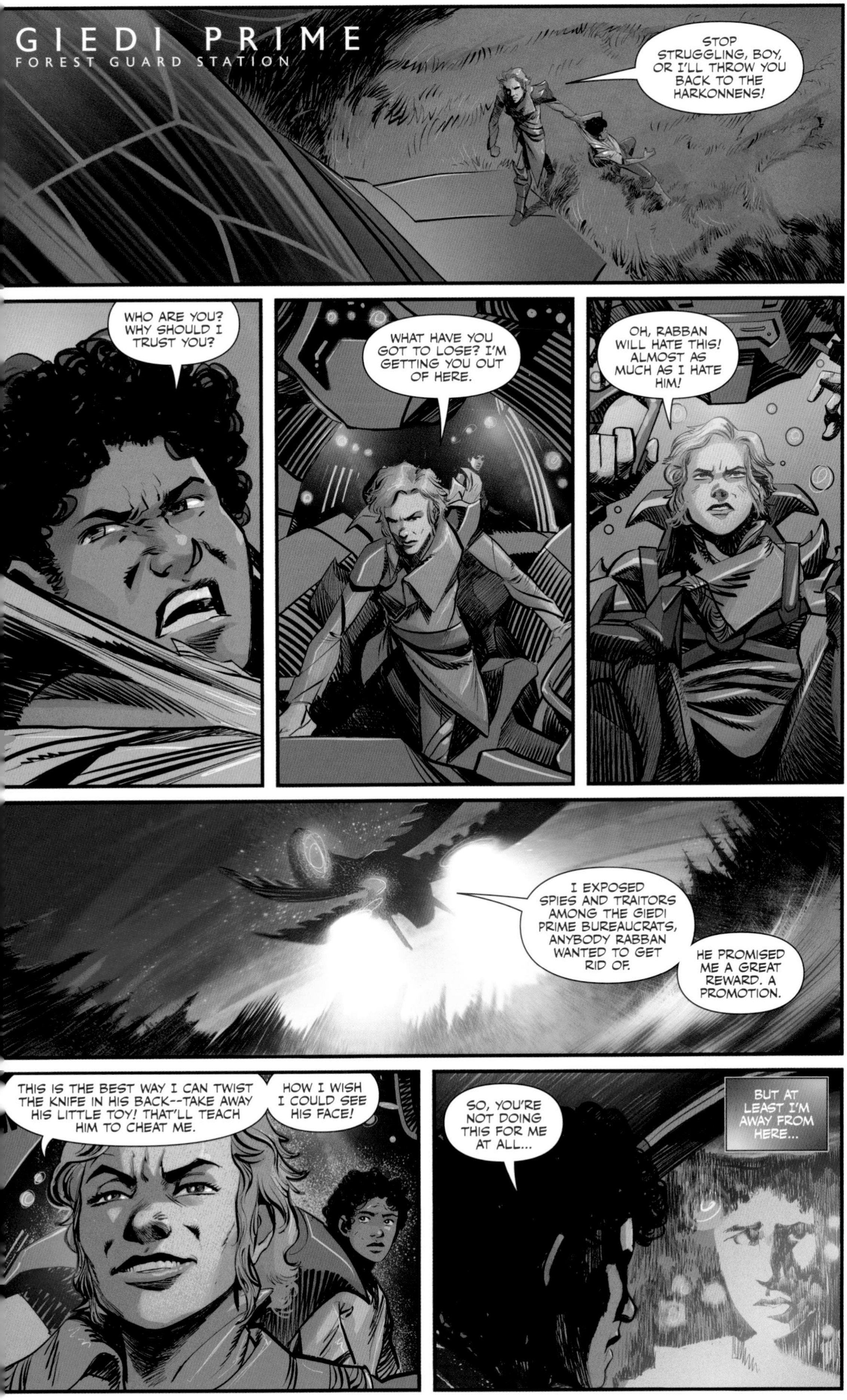
GIEDI PRIME
FOREST GUARD STATION
STOP STRUGGLING, BOY, OR I'LL THROW YOU BACK TO THE HARKONNENS!
WHO ARE YOU? WHY SHOULD I TRUST YOU?
WHAT HAVE YOU GOT TO LOSE? I'M GETTING YOU OUT OF HERE.
OH, RABBAN WILL HATE THIS! ALMOST AS MUCH AS I HATE HIM!
I EXPOSED SPIES AND TRAITORS AMONG THE GIEDI PRIME BUREAUCRATS, ANYBODY RABBAN WANTED TO GET RID OF.
HE PROMISED ME A GREAT REWARD. A PROMOTION.
THIS IS THE BEST WAY I CAN TWIST THE KNIFE IN HIS BACK--TAKE AWAY HIS LITTLE TOY! THAT'LL TEACH HIM TO CHEAT ME.
HOW I WISH I COULD SEE HIS FACE!
SO, YOU'RE NOT DOING THIS FOR ME AT ALL...
BUT AT LEAST I'M AWAY FROM HERE...

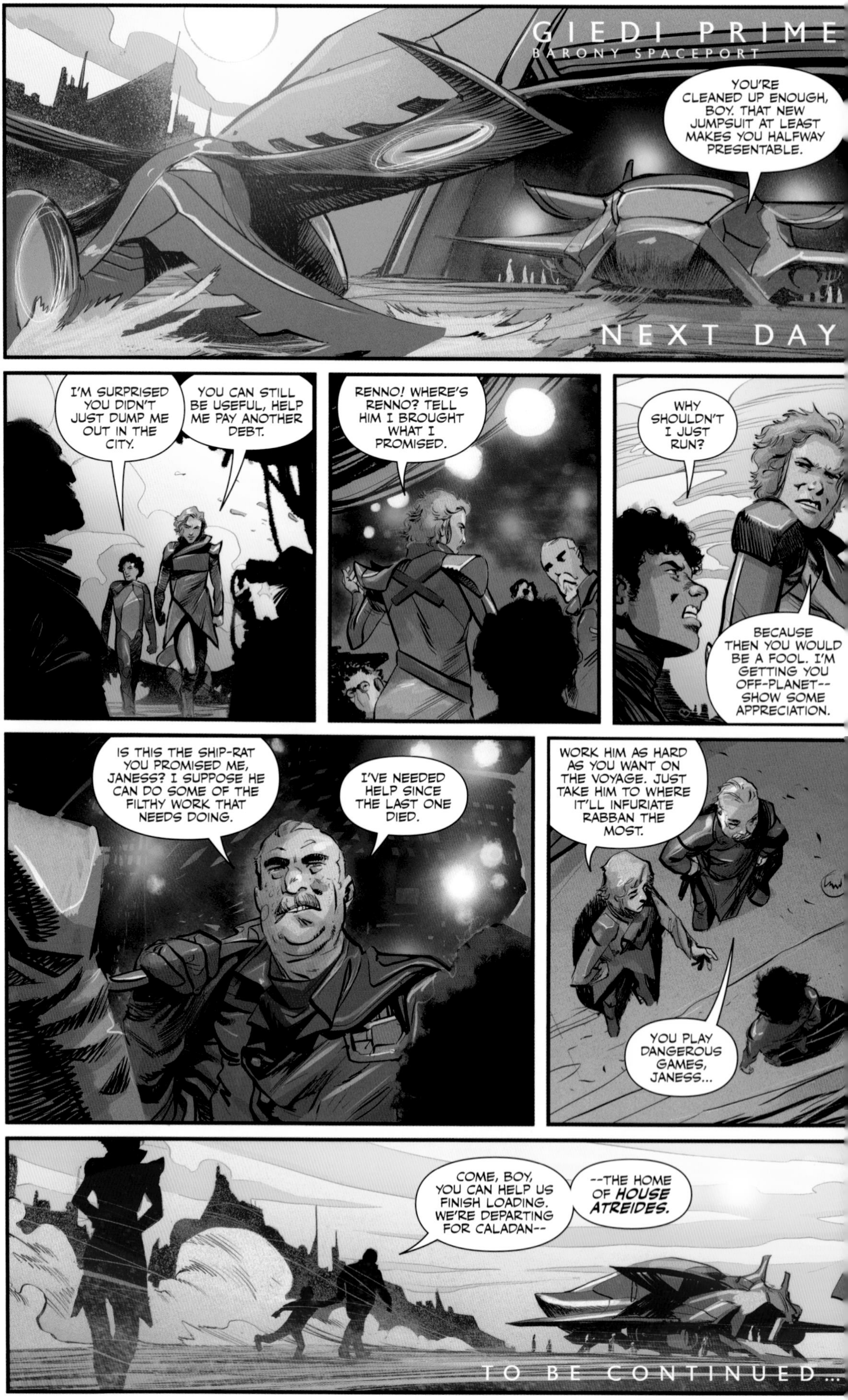
GIEDI PRIME
BARONY SPACEPORT
YOU'RE CLEANED UP ENOUGH, BOY. THAT NEW JUMPSUIT AT LEAST MAKES YOU HALFWAY PRESENTABLE.
NEXT DAY
I'M SURPRISED YOU DIDN'T JUST DUMP ME OUT IN THE CITY.
YOU CAN STILL BE USEFUL, HELP ME PAY ANOTHER DEBT.
RENNO! WHERE'S RENNO? TELL HIM I BROUGHT WHAT I PROMISED.
WHY SHOULDN'T I JUST RUN?
BECAUSE THEN YOU WOULD BE A FOOL. I'M GETTING YOU OFF-PLANET-- SHOW SOME APPRECIATION.
IS THIS THE SHIP-RAT YOU PROMISED ME, JANESS? I SUPPOSE HE CAN DO SOME OF THE FILTHY WORK THAT NEEDS DOING.
I'VE NEEDED HELP SINCE THE LAST ONE DIED.
WORK HIM AS HARD AS YOU WANT ON THE VOYAGE. JUST TAKE HIM TO WHERE IT'LL INFURIATE RABBAN THE MOST.
YOU PLAY DANGEROUS GAMES, JANESS...
COME, BOY, YOU CAN HELP US FINISH LOADING. WE'RE DEPARTING FOR CALADAN--
--THE HOME OF HOUSE ATREIDES.
TO BE CONTINUED...

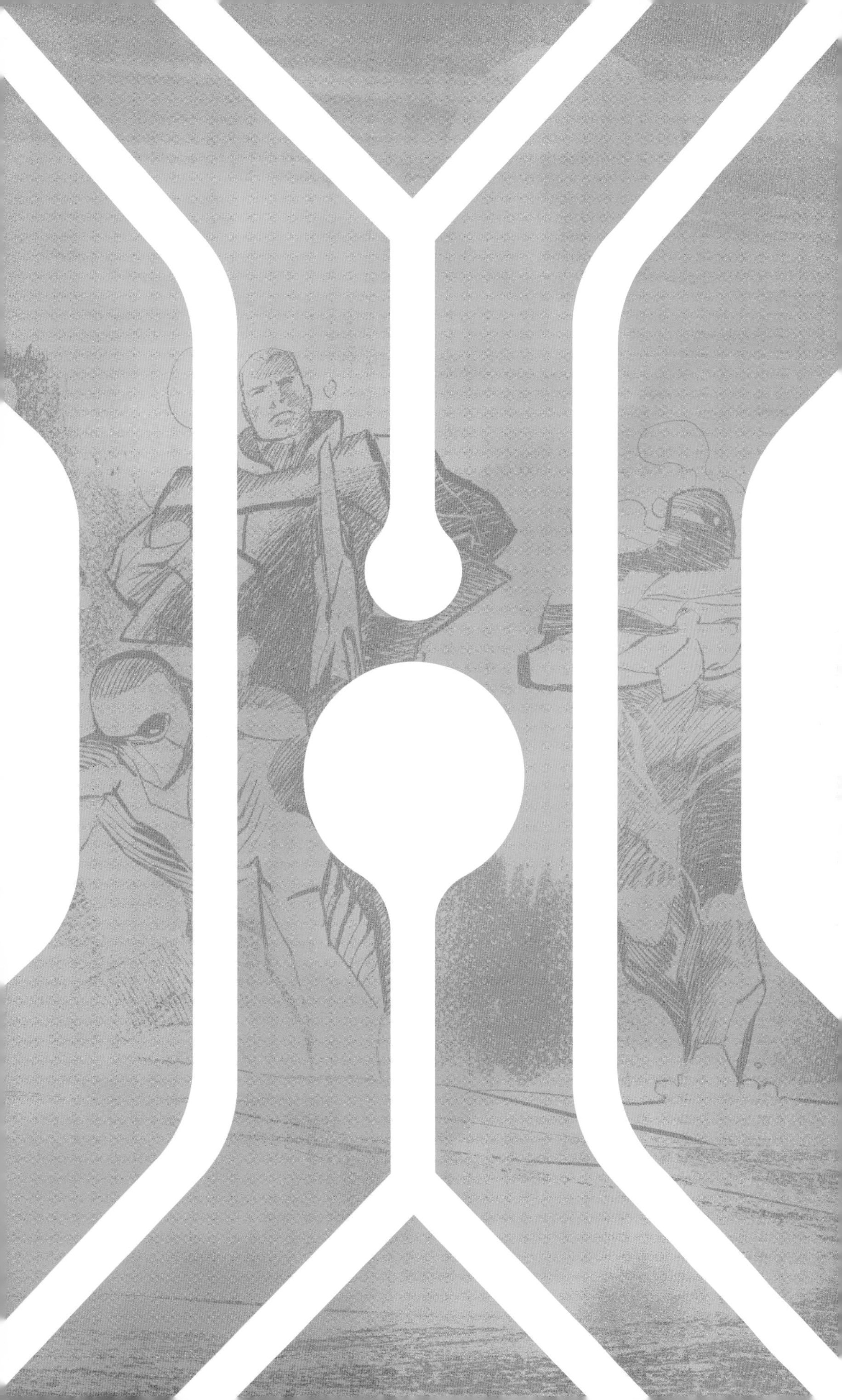

COVER GALLERY

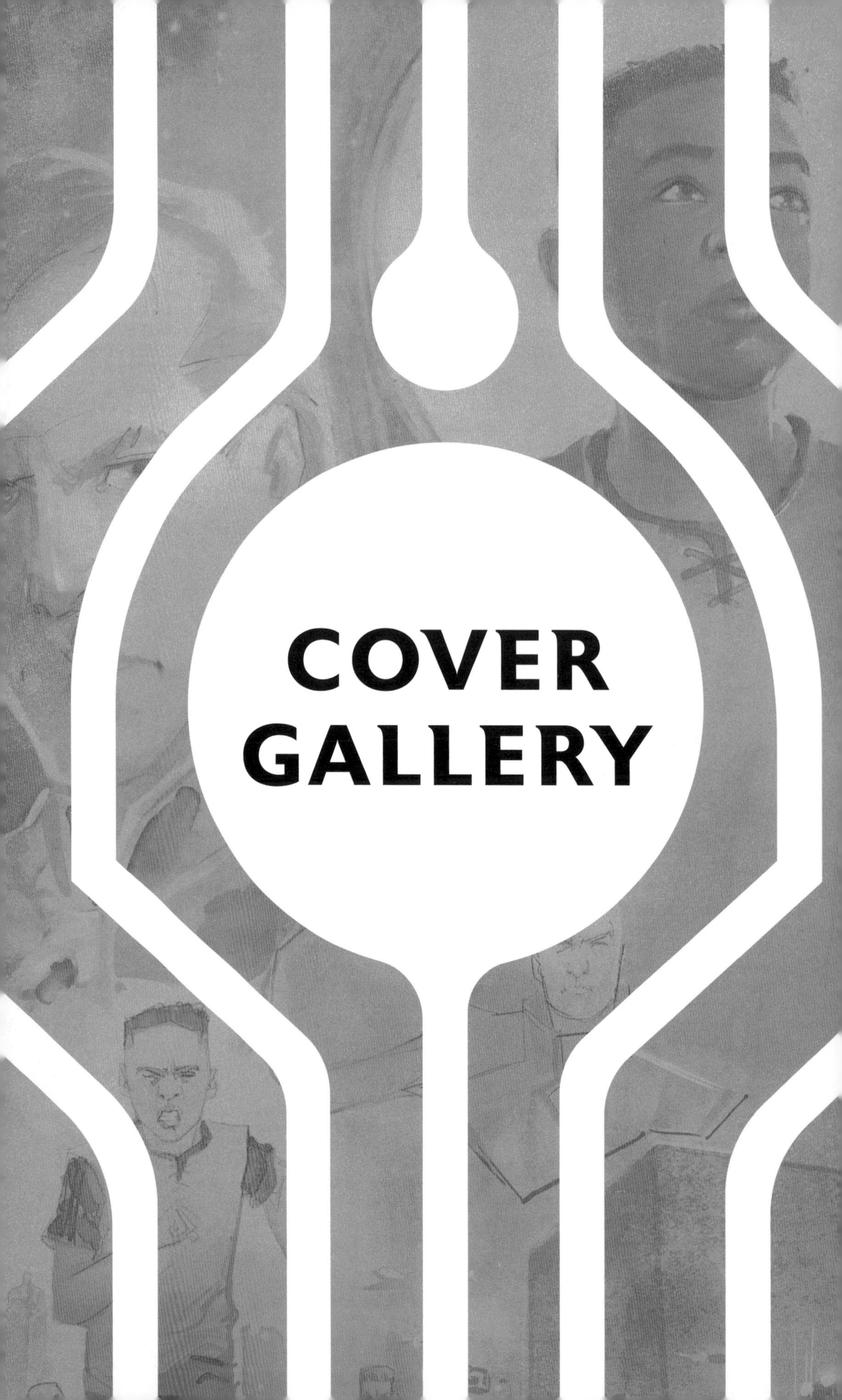

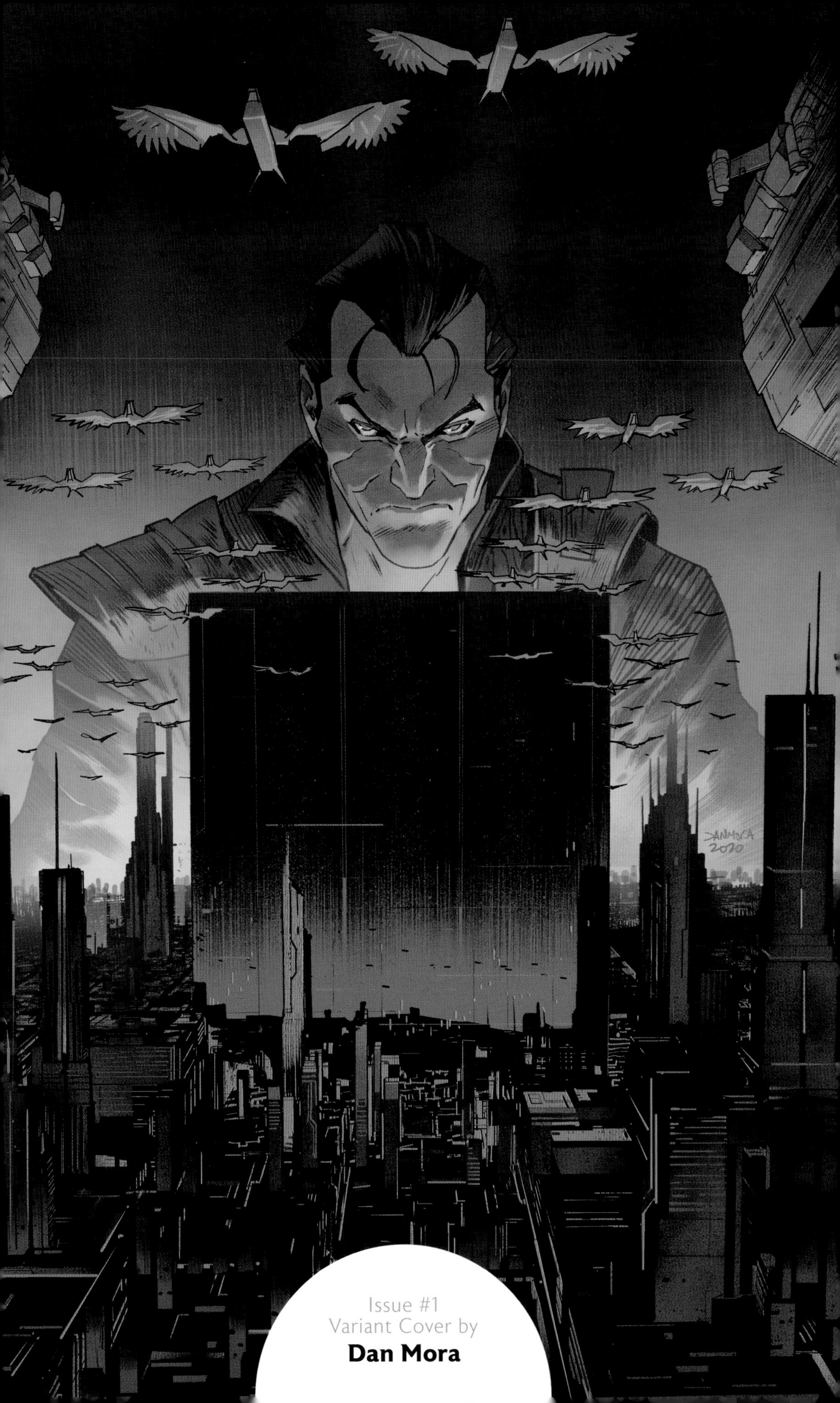
DANMORA
2020

Issue #1
Variant Cover by
Dan Mora

Issue #1
Variant Cover by
Miguel Mercado

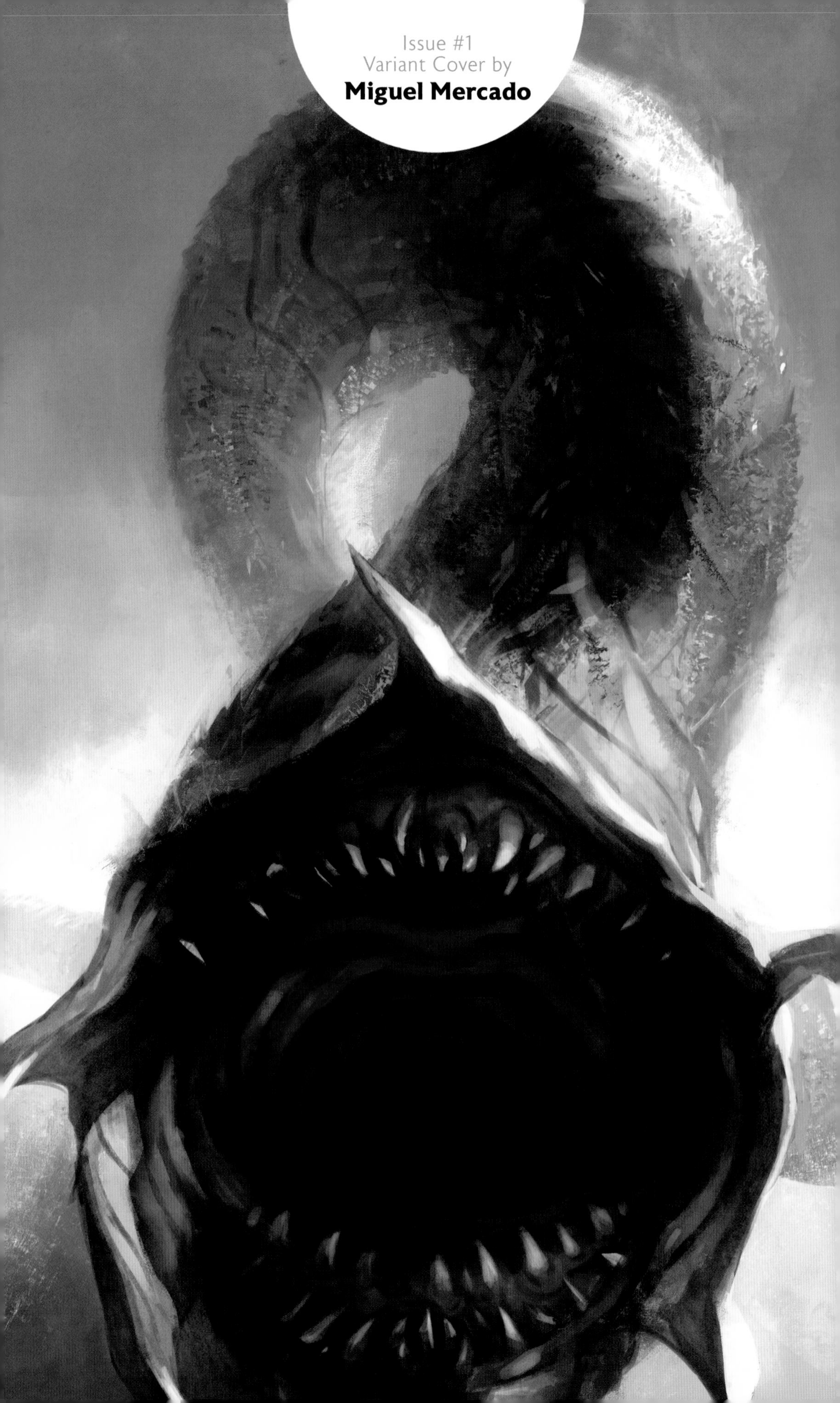

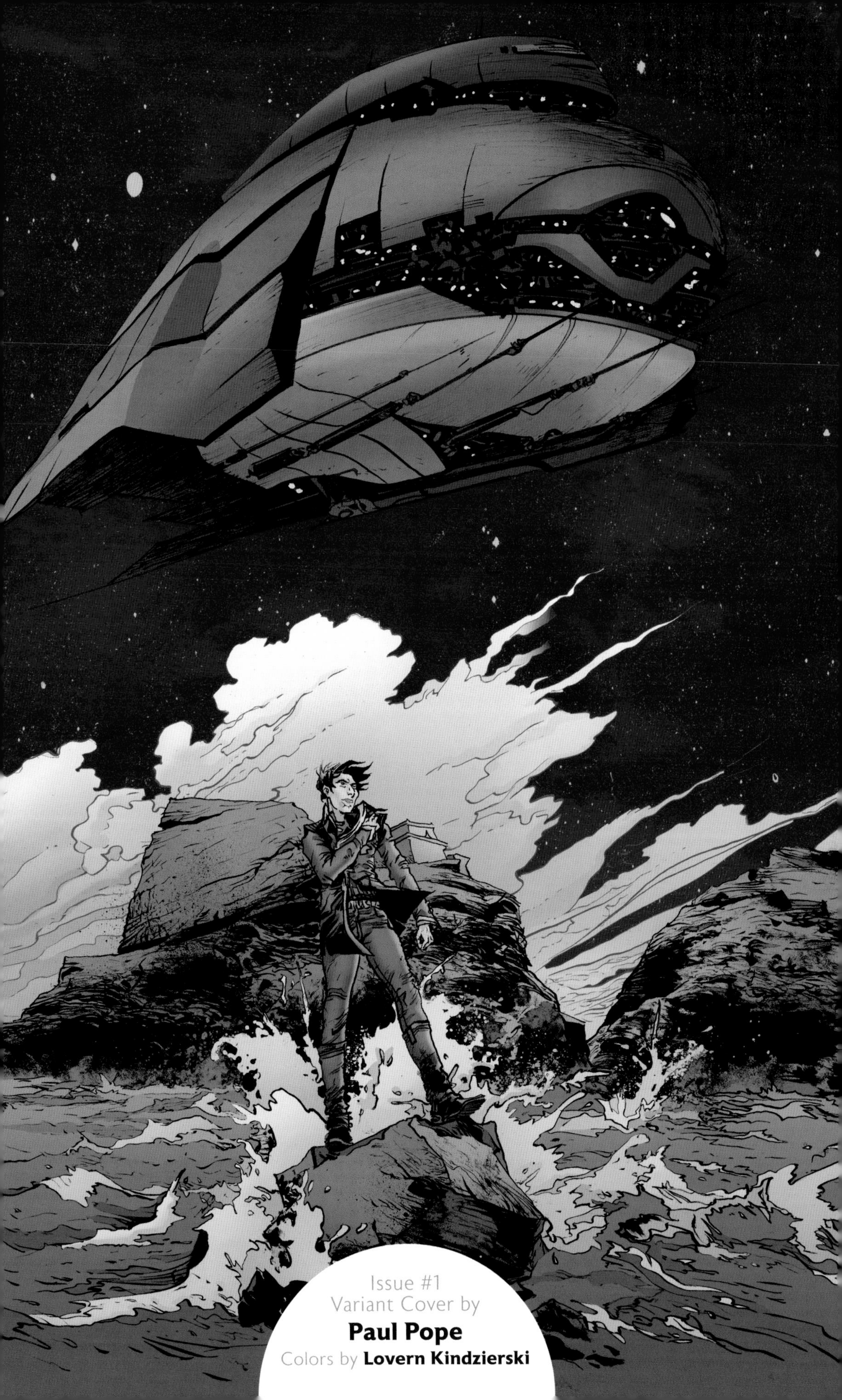

Issue #1
Variant Cover by
Paul Pope
Colors by **Lovern Kindzierski**

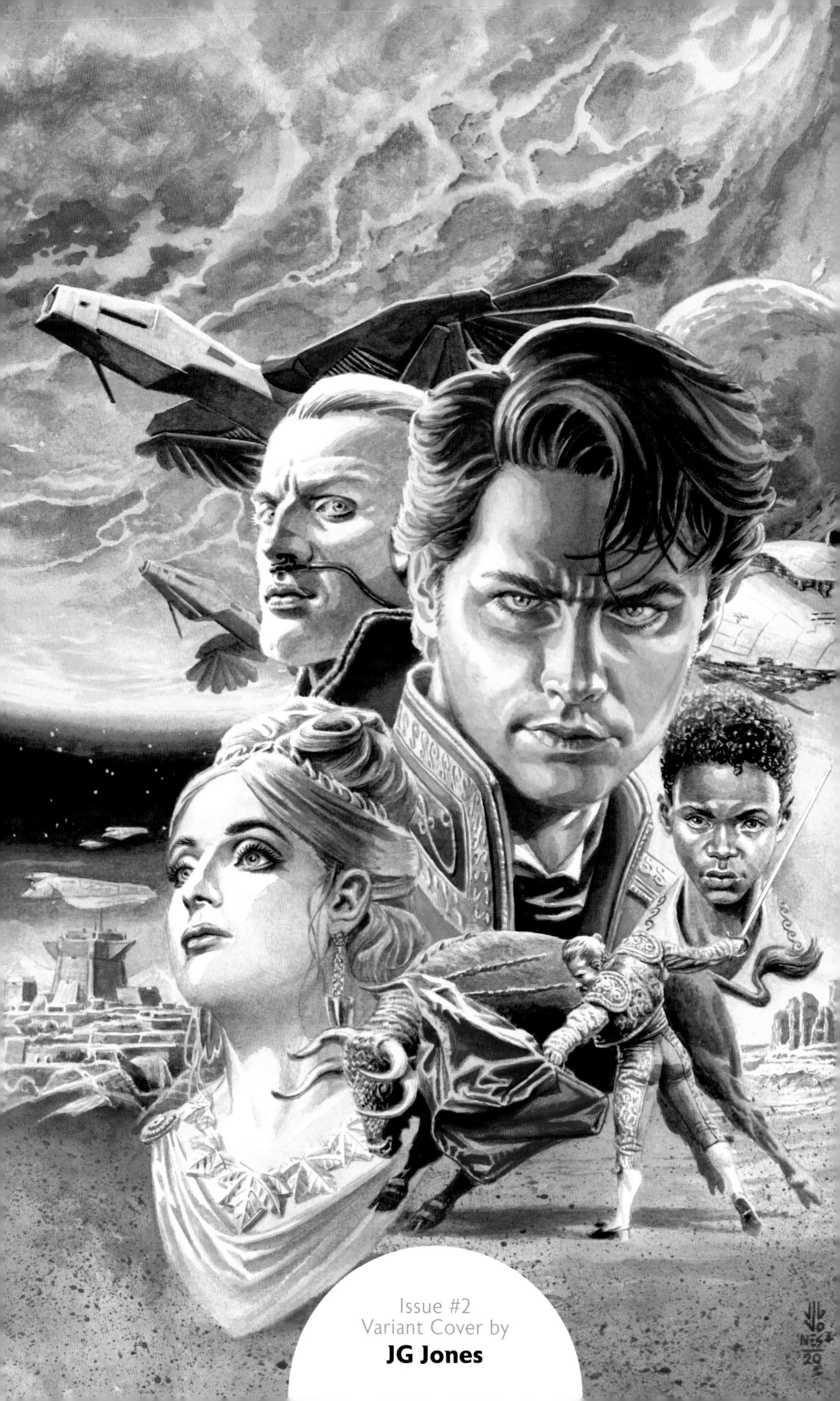

Issue #2
Variant Cover by
JG Jones

Issue #3
Variant Cover by
Rod Reis

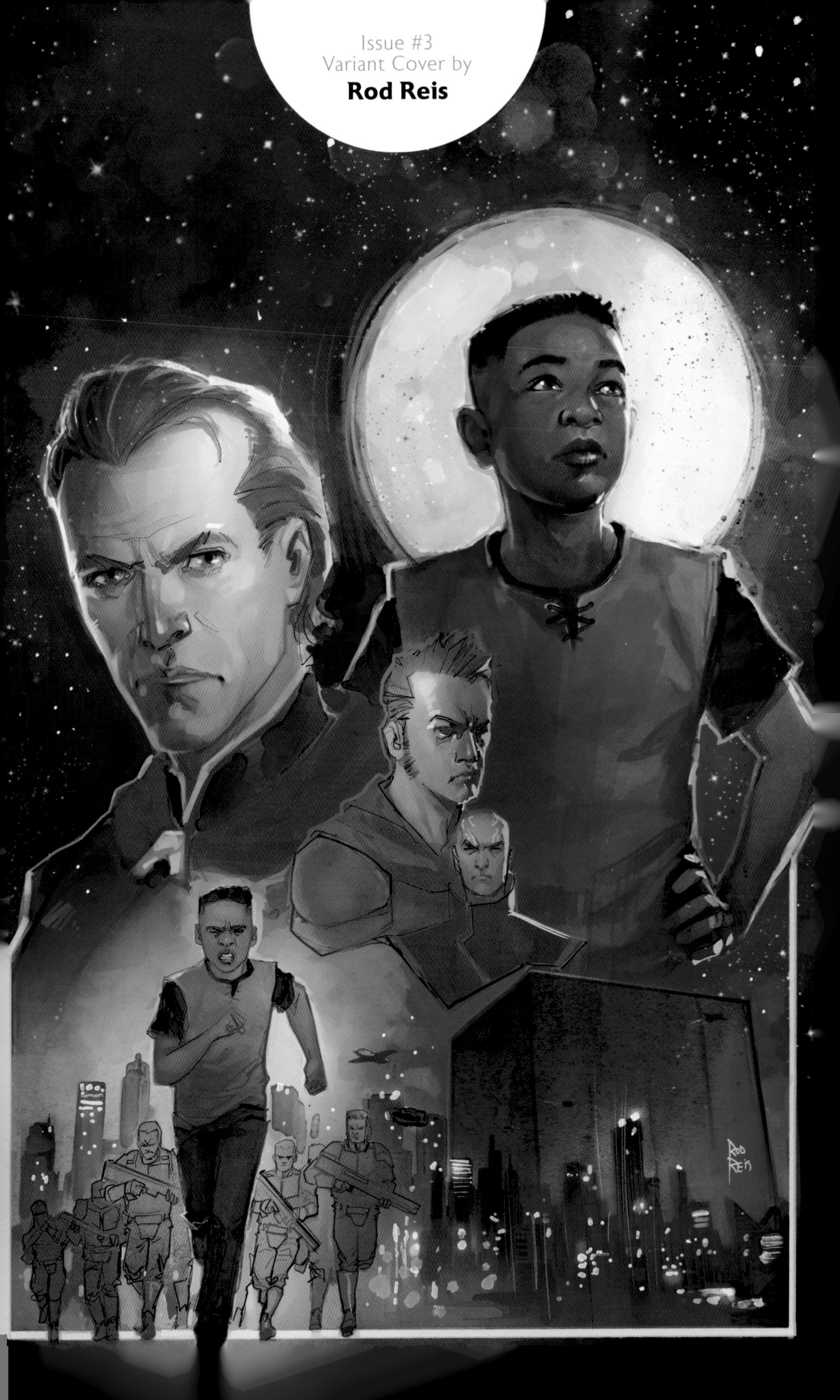
ROD REIS

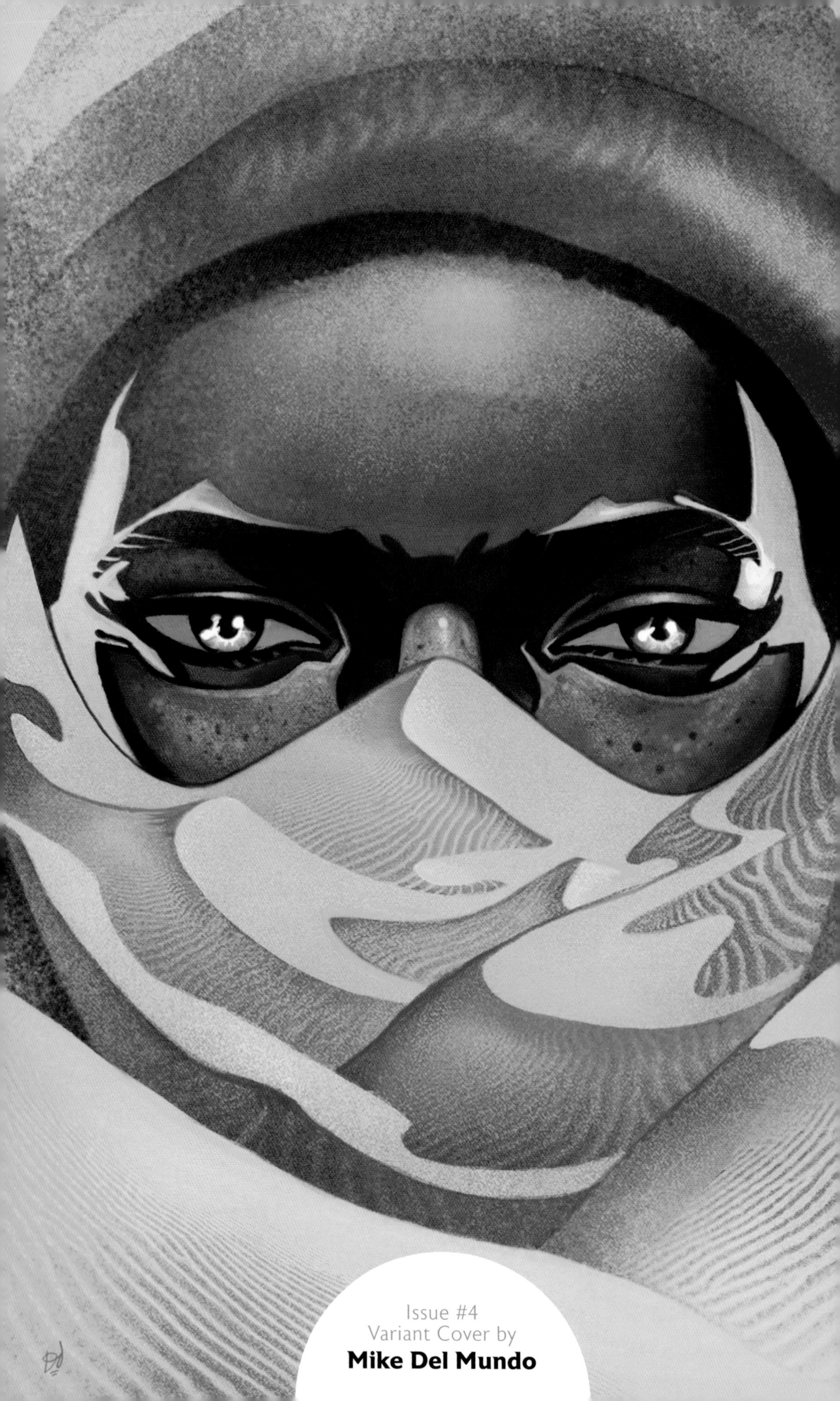

Issue #4
Variant Cover by
Mike Del Mundo

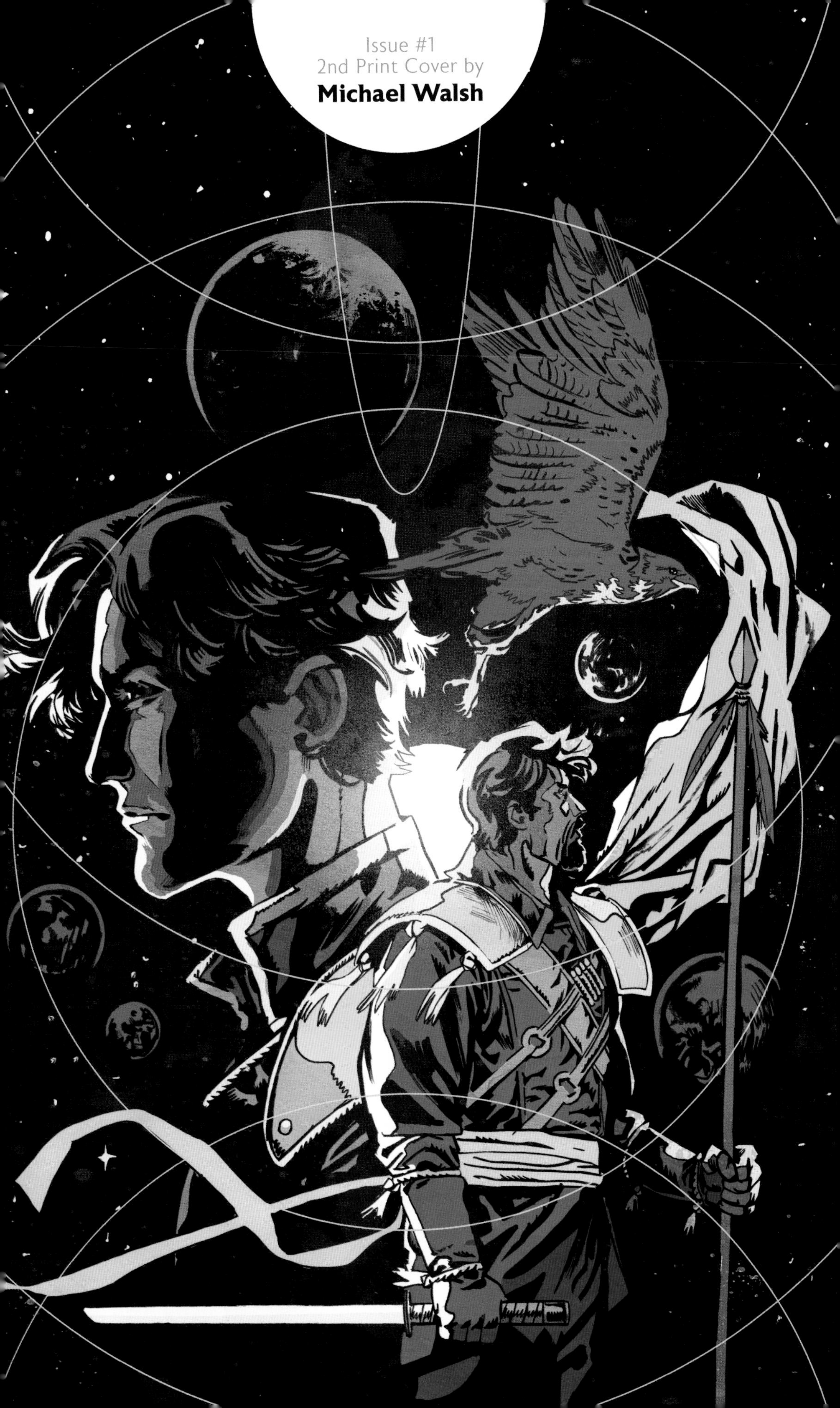

Issue #1
2nd Print Cover by
Michael Walsh

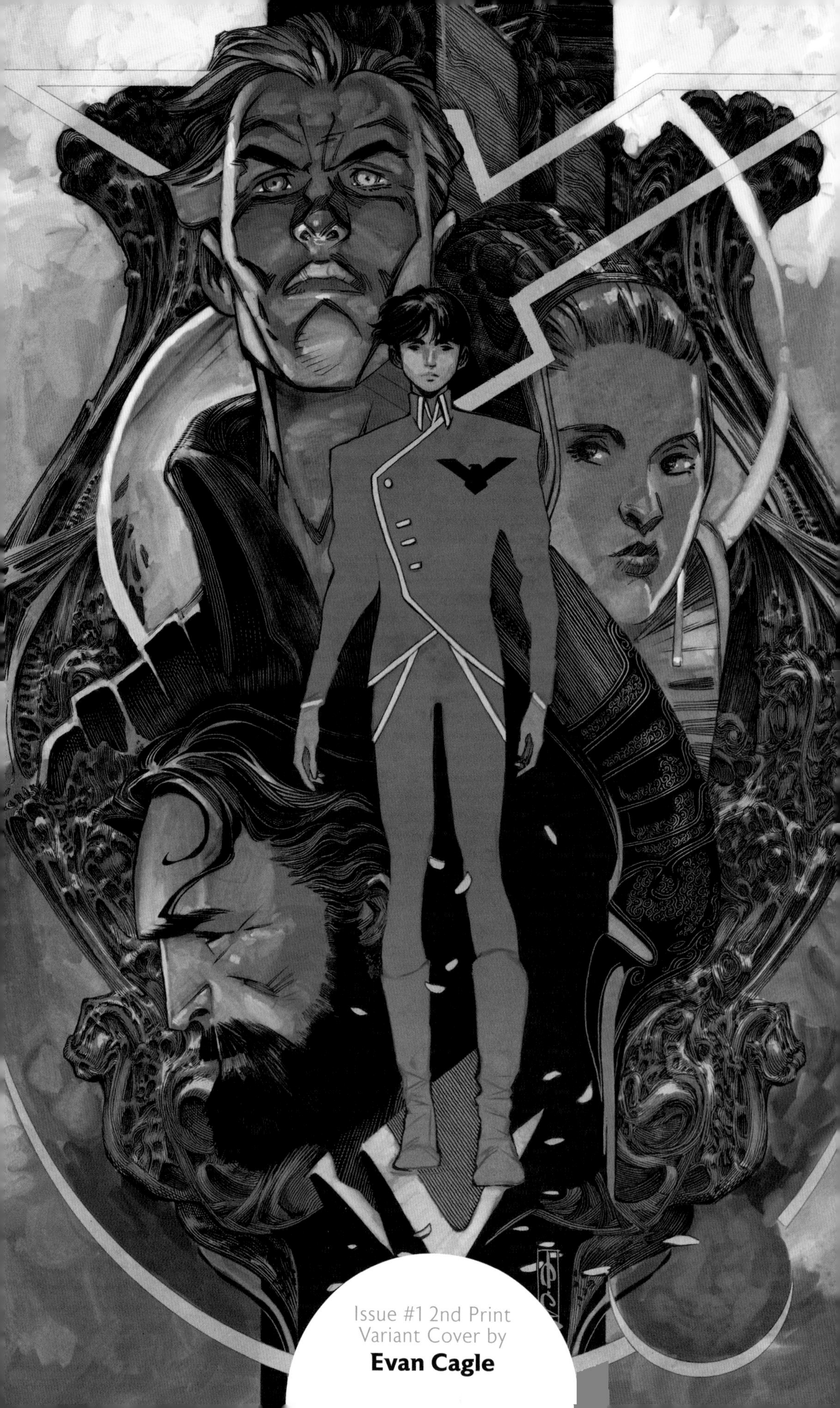

Issue #1 2nd Print
Variant Cover by
Evan Cagle

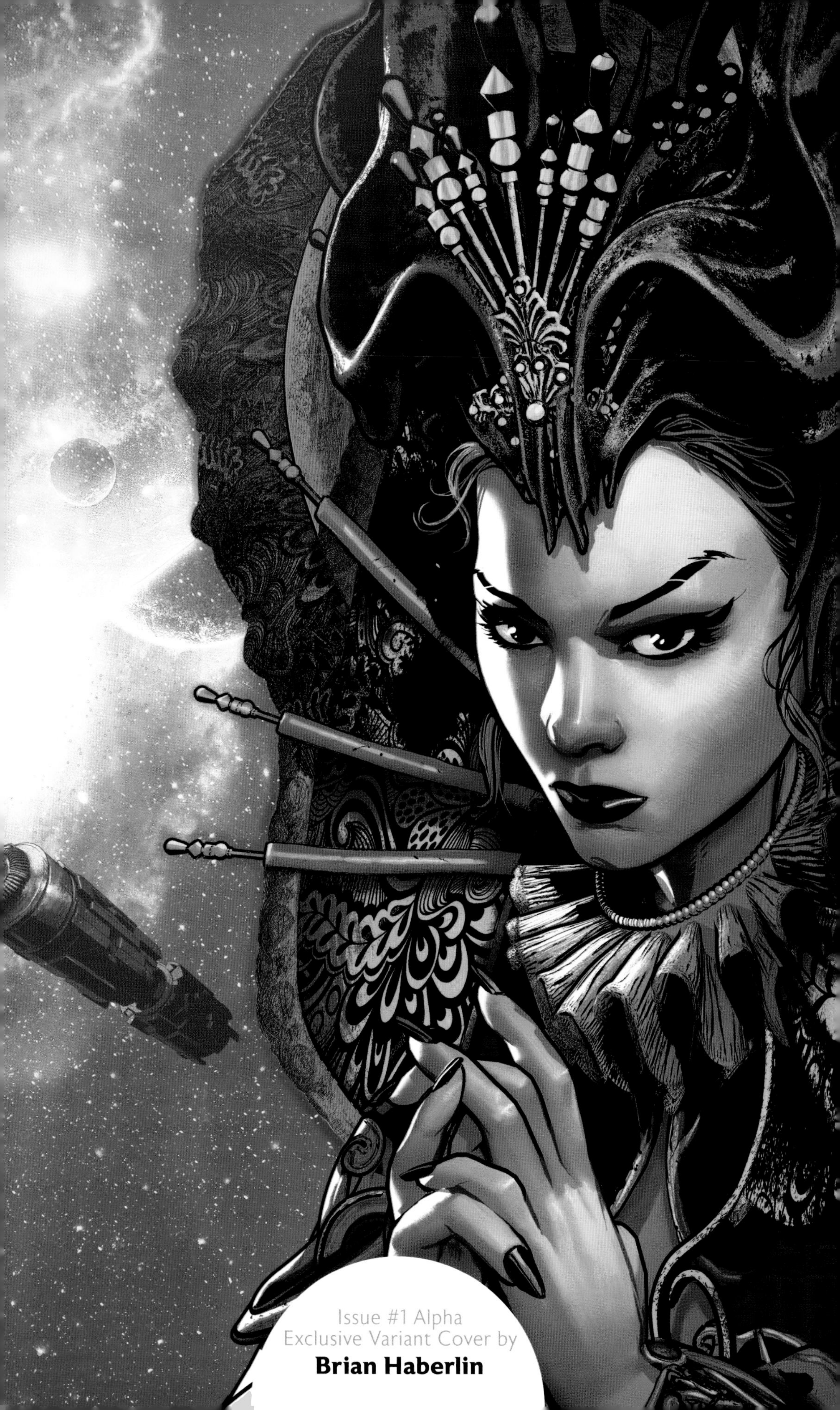

Issue #1 Alpha
Exclusive Variant Cover by
Brian Haberlin

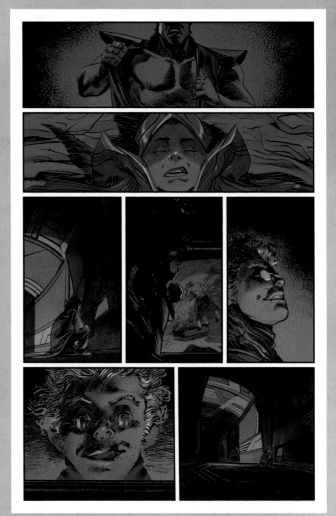

SCRIPT TO PAGE: **ISSUE 4, PAGE 7**

PANEL 1: Angry but finally surrendering, the Baron peels off his shirt to reveal his muscular body beneath.
BARON: Witch!

PANEL 2: Mohiam's head on the pillow, her eyes closed.
MOHIAM: I do my duty. Just think of all the hidden melange stockpiles you will now be able to keep secret from Emperor Elrood…

Panel 3: Outside, behind the bedroom wall, we see a simpering Piter de Vries, the Baron's twisted Mentat. He looks close to a high-tech peephole, a small glowing rectangular screen mounted on the stones of the wall. It's a dim hiding place, only one glowglobe in the background.
PITER: Ahhh, my poor Baron!

Panel 4: Closer in, we can see part of the peephole screen with Piter's face nearby. Details are blurry, but there are two figures grappling on the bed. Not too explicit.

Panel 5: Piter leans back, fascinated.
PITER: I have spied on many of your outrageous escapades, Baron, but not like this…

Panel 6: Extreme closeup of Piter, lascivious.
PITER: Ahh, if only I had set up recording devices…

Panel 7: Piter presses his face back against the peephole.

ISSUE 4, PAGE 12

PANEL 1: The back of the groundcar is open and Ommun is throwing out boxes of rocks, containers of debris. Stilgar is slumped in the front seat. Kynes comes running, in alarm.

        PARDOT: Those are my specimens! It took me weeks to collect them all!

        OMMUN: The desert is full of rocks. You can get more. We will take the Harkonnen bodies.

PANEL 2: While Kynes watches, confused, Turok and Ommun dump another Harkonnen body into the back of the groundcar. Several bodies are already there.

        PARDOT: But…why? To hide the evidence? The desert will do that all by itself.

        OMMUN: One does not WASTE so much water, Imperial man.

Panel 3: The groundcar rumbles off, kicking up sand. Ommun is driving, Stilgar slumped in the passenger seat. Kynes and Turok are left behind. Kynes stares in disbelief as his groundcar drives off.

        TUROK: We will make our own way. Ommun will be swift, getting medical care for Stilgar.

Panel 4: Alone in the desert now, Kynes and Turok two-shot.

        PARDOT: What is your name? Since we are stranded here together.

        TUROK: Is there a point to exchanging names?

        PARDOT: Well, I did just save your lives.

Panel 5: Turok closeup. Realization crosses his face.

        TUROK: Ah, the WATER BOND.

Panel 6: Turok trudges off, heading across the sand toward a nearby ridge of rock in the direction the groundcar headed.

        TUROK: Follow me, or you will die. We must make it to those rocks. We will be safe in the SIETCH.

Panel 7: Kynes hurries after him. Turok looks over his shoulder impatiently.

        PARDOT: What's a sietch?

        TUROK: You have much to learn.

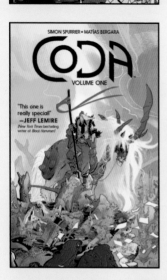